YOU'LL
NEVER
FIND
US

YOU'LL
NEVER
FIND
US

A Memoir

by
JEANNE BAKER GUY

Published 2021
Printed in the United States of America
Print ISBN: 978-1-64742-155-7
E-ISBN: 978-1-64742-156-4
Library of Congress Control Number: 2021904169

For information, address:
She Writes Press
1569 Solano Ave #546
Berkeley, CA 94707

She Writes Press is a division of SparkPoint Studio, LLC.

Book design by Stacey Aaronson

"What is truer than truth? The story."

—*Jewish Saying*

This is the story
of how my children were stolen from me
and how I stole them back.

TABLE OF CONTENTS

Two interwoven story lines, each told chronologically

YOU'LL
NEVER
FIND
US

ONE

Day 0

July 26, 1977, Indianapolis, IN

They weren't back.

On that July evening, a gentle breeze offset Indiana's summer heat. Inhaling the scent of fresh linen fabric softener, I carted dried clothes from the ground level laundry room to our second-floor apartment, emptied the basket onto the bed, and checked my watch again. It was a good hour past the time my ex-husband, a man of German precision, had agreed to return Ty and Megan, the only blessings of an ill-fated marriage. Though I had wanted my six-year-old son and three-year-old daughter to have a grand four days at a Missouri theme park with their father, I hated letting them out of my sight.

I hoped they hadn't had car trouble. Klaus, who had sold his prized Mercedes months earlier, said he'd gotten a used BMW repaired before the long weekend trip with the kids—but then, he'd said a lot of things.

After folding the clothes, I paced, listening. At first, all I heard were occasional shouts from the complex's nearby volleyball court, where Haywood, my husband of six weeks, was playing a post-sunset game with his brother, Bill. Unlike my fairytale-gone-awry ten-year marriage to Klaus, my new life held the promise of long-awaited happiness. Haywood's six-foot-four goliath stature brought love, warmth, and laughter into our lives; Megan and Ty had gravitated to him immediately, as had I, when our paths unexpectedly crossed soon after my thirtieth birthday. For them it was as if they'd found a new kid to play with, albeit a twenty-seven-year-old tall one, and we all seemed to breathe a little easier in our new family setting. The tumultuous years with Klaus had resurrected insecurities that had undermined me since childhood. Haywood's pillar-like strength provided a sense of stability when I most needed it. It was as if it had set me free from the guilt of the divorce and the constant angst of *how did it all go so terribly wrong?* in my first marriage.

I tried focusing on the fun the brothers must be having down on the court, my thoughts soon superseded by concerns about Klaus's lateness. I'd let my guard down five days earlier when, after months of hateful post-divorce arguments, Klaus suddenly offered a truce and apologized for his angry actions and disturbing behavior over my remarriage. He said a new job was on the horizon, and he wanted to celebrate by taking the kids to Six Flags for a long weekend.

Once again ignoring the subconscious voice of caution, I suppressed any doubts of sincerity and took his words at face value. A peacemaker my entire life—sometimes fear-based, sometimes for love's sake—I wanted them to be true. Blithely hoping for peace, I chose to trust Klaus. Because of the late hour, however, painful recollections of his arm-twisting divorce demands, including the unreasonable split custody, began flashing like a neon no-trust-zone sign in my head.

Finally, I heard a car pull into the parking lot and peered out the back-bedroom window, expecting the BMW. Instead, a longtime family friend appeared, Episcopal priest Reverend John Roof. Though unusual for Big John to stop by unannounced, his presence always brought joy since his robust humor matched his portly appearance. Closing the car door, John looked up and saw me watching from the window.

I waved. He didn't.

Head lowered, he walked toward our apartment building. I

opened the front door and stood on the second-floor landing, ready with a greeting. John climbed the exterior stairs, one labored step after another. Reaching the landing, instead of offering a hug, John pulled at the clerical collar tight around his thick neck. His normally jovial face was ashen.

"John?"

He didn't speak. Confused, I stared wide-eyed as he reached into his jacket vest pocket and produced a sealed white envelope. My breath caught in my throat at the sight of my name written in Klaus's unmistakable German script.

John's voice cracked as he said, "Klaus asked me to deliver this to you. I—." He handed me the envelope and stood motionless.

I opened the letter and scanned the single page of small, rigid handwriting.

"... *The children and I are on our way to Germany for good.* ... *We are in a place where you'll never find us.*"

My knees buckled. John caught me, breaking my fall as the letter dropped to my feet. With my face pressed against my knees, a wail rose from the back of my throat and the world went dark for a moment. In the darkness, I struggled to erase what was happening, but the nightmare remained. I could not will them back.

My children were gone.

t w o

Wrong Fairytale, Wrong Man

1950s–1960s

How had it all gone so terribly wrong?

Klaus had seemed the ideal fit for my dream: older, worldly, handsome—complete with that engaging accent. What a catch. I grew up believing in the 1950s fairytale, though little did I know my mother wasn't living the dream. Nonetheless, she wanted it for me and taught me to be a good girl, loving, kind—and smart. The indirect message: go to college, get an education, and get a good man. I would find happiness. She would live vicariously through me, consciously or not.

How did my ideas about men get formed? I knew nothing about my parents' relationship or marriage, only that their wedding picture reflected a most handsome couple, like two puzzle pieces that fit. I came to believe, since the 1950s era promoted sweetness and good grades yet downplayed a woman's strengths, it must take a man to make her complete. A girl's potential and desire to be strong, competent, to handle what life had in store for her, got little press. The unspoken lesson: a man was the most important thing in a woman's life. The unspoken goal: be a pleaser. With that as my focus, my vision became and remained clouded when it involved men.

I don't fault my mother for the omission, but clearly preparation for Relationships 101 was missing from my life, as I bet it was missing from hers. I loved my mom. She named me Jeanne after a friend of hers, but always called me Jeannie. She was my companion, my idol, but, sadly, probably defined herself as John Baker's wife rather than Mary Jane Baker. I mimicked her loving ways because serving and pleasing others should always come first. Despite being a smart girl, what other people thought of me carried more weight than what I thought of myself.

Many young women of the time bought into the patriarchal culture and focused on those two college goals: grow intellectually, *and* find the husband of your dreams. I was not a pearl-necklaced June Cleaver of the 1950s, nor was I a participant in the current decade's feminist turbulence. Born the second year of the Baby Boom, I straddled the cultures of the '50s and the '70s, determined my decisions would be my own, yet on a much deeper level still wanted—and needed—to be taken care of; I didn't trust myself.

I wanted the dream, the whole fairytale, and Klaus appeared to possess what I lacked: confidence. Like a character in a play, I had learned my role, learned my lines. My script called for deferring to men for confirmation of my worth. I thought this man, this older, presumably wiser and more worldly man, would complete me, as if I were a puzzle piece without intrinsic value, like my mom. That misperception was the misstep.

That's why it all went so terribly wrong.

THREE

Day 0 Continued

July 26, 1977, Indianapolis, IN

In the momentary darkness, I thought I heard Haywood's voice calling my name from the volleyball court. "Jeannie? *Jeannie!*"

Still crumpled at Big John's feet, I blinked and looked up into his stricken face, then snatched Klaus's letter from the second-floor landing where the Episcopal priest had broken my fall. I grabbed the metal railing for support and propelled myself down the stairs, shouting for Haywood who ran from the volleyball court with his brother Bill close behind.

Haywood and I had known each other such a short time before marrying. When we'd met in April just months after my divorce, I was smitten, as was he. I needed what this Hoosier anchor offered: strength and kindness. Four weeks into the relationship he proposed, I accepted, and our wedding followed in June. On the night of July 26, the six-week mark of the marriage, our future collided with my past, as if we were the target of a meteor.

"What's wrong? What happened?" my new husband asked.

"They're gone. Ty and Megan. Klaus took them. They've gone to Germany." I couldn't catch my breath. "He . . . sent John with a letter."

Towering over me, Haywood pressed me close and pried the letter from my clenched fist. "It's okay. It's okay. Let me see it."

His jaw tightened as he skimmed the contents.

Jeannie, the children and I are on our way to Germany for good. . . . My brother and I made all the arrangements . . . he will not disclose our location. . . . In reference to the condo, I gave Big John my power of attorney and I respect and hope that through this action you maintain his friendship—he cares for you. Again, we are in Germany, happy and together, and in a place where you'll never find us. . . .

Since your family had completely ignored me since you dumped me, I took the liberty and informed your father, mother and sister of my action. So, keep your theatrics and dramatizations to your current circle of friends for they don't know you yet. . . .

"Son of a bitch," Haywood whispered, before handing Bill the letter and helping me up the stairs into the apartment. While Haywood settled me onto the soft living room sofa, John went into the kitchen and brought me a glass of water. I looked up into his troubled face as I grasped the glass with a shaky hand.

"John," Haywood said, nodding toward the letter Bill held. "Have you seen this? How did this happen?" Bill gave John the letter.

"Oh my God," John said after reviewing it. Grabbing a pocketed handkerchief, John sank into the large chair across from me and mopped his brow, his forty-year-old face as white as his priestly collar. "This can't be. Klaus has been spending time out at our place a lot over the last two months. Midge and I tried reasoning with him, repeatedly, explaining that there was life after your divorce. He had been so distraught and angry about your getting remarried."

John wiped his brow again. "We thought Klaus was being interviewed for a job outside of Indianapolis and would need to move, at least that's what he said, and even brought some of his furniture out to our place to store it until he could get the condo sold and get settled in a new place. He and the kids spent this past weekend with us and . . ."

Haywood exchanged a confused glance with me and interrupted him. "They were at your place?"

"Yeah, and we actually thought he was doing much better. Last night, after packing the car to leave, he handed me power of attorney papers and said he needed to finalize the job north of here and would I handle the condominium sale in his absence. I said okay, and that's when he gave me that sealed envelope, asked me to wait twenty-four hours, then deliver it to Jeannie."

John looked directly at me and dabbed his eyes. Choking back tears, he said, "I cautioned him, whatever he did, not to do anything that would bring you harm or grief. I thought he was just buying some time to get settled wherever the job was, and then he'd be in touch. I've made a horrible mistake."

John's pain was palpable. Klaus had led John to believe the trip was about a job and he and the kids would be back soon, that the twenty-four-hour delay requested was time for him to confirm the job without me interfering. I could imagine the dilemma Big John faced. Perhaps a priest was obligated by canon law to follow the request, since Klaus had taken John into his confidence. John was well aware of the unorthodox split custody arrangement. I could imagine Klaus asking John for one last favor—that he wanted to keep Ty and Megan with him a few extra days and thought I'd take that news better from John.

"Oh, John, he used you," I cried. "Don't you see? He planned the whole thing."

I collapsed back onto the sofa cushions. John moved from the chair and offered a box of tissues, before the angry vortex in my head took control. *I was so stupid to have believed Klaus!*

Haywood took charge and contacted the Indianapolis police and the Marion County Sheriff's Department, then phoned family members—my mom, my sister Joanne, and my dad in Florida, my brother Jim in Birmingham, and Haywood's mom and dad who lived in town—and found that none had heard from Klaus or knew what had happened. As Haywood repeated the story over and over, my pain increased.

A police officer appeared, and Deputy Bronner, a young man from the sheriff's department came, and dutifully took reports. Haywood sat close with an arm around me as I recounted the details.

"On Thursday, my ex-husband, Klaus, told me he wanted to celebrate his new job by taking both kids for a long weekend to Six Flags—you know, the St. Louis amusement park."

"Wait," John interrupted. "He told you what? So, you didn't know he was out at our place?"

"I told you, John. He duped us all."

I explained our unorthodox split custody arrangement: on weekdays Klaus was custodial parent for our six-year-old son, Ty, and I had custody of three-year-old Megan. By decree, the children shared the same babysitter and were always together on the weekends, which Klaus and I alternated. I was strong-armed into the arrangement, without which he would not have agreed to the divorce finalized six months before.

"Klaus needed my permission to extend his weekend. He said he'd have Megan back Tuesday by 7:00 p.m. I consented and, considering the four-hour trip from Indianapolis to St. Louis, even offered my car rather than trust his unreliable vehicle."

I took a shuddery breath before finishing the story. "He turned down my offer. With a job finally on the horizon, he'd supposedly gotten the recently purchased old BMW sedan repaired. Friday evening, Klaus and Ty picked up Megan, planning an early start Saturday." My hand trembled as I set my glass of water on the coffee table in front of me. "I know now they never went."

Haywood showed the officers the letter, explained what Klaus had actually done, and introduced the officers to John. When John finished telling them what he knew, they noted the comments on their reports and stood as if to leave.

"We'll assign a case number and contact you with that information, ma'am," Deputy Bronner said. "There's little else we can do at the moment. I'm sorry."

The police officer echoed apologies.

"Can't you issue an arrest warrant or something?" Haywood asked.

The officers looked at each other and shook their heads. Since the children were with their father, there was no basis for issuing any warrants. Klaus had broken no law, Bronner explained, so they would consider this a domestic dispute.

Stunned, I reached for the letter on the coffee table, unable to reconcile the officers' words with the kidnapping proof I held in my hand. *How could there not be a law?*

After another round of apologies and empty condolences, they left.

Haywood called Dennis, my divorce attorney, who was not encouraging. Dennis knew the FBI would not step into a civil matter, and state warrants naming a parent as kidnapper under these circumstances were unheard of in 1977 in many states, including Indiana.

After Haywood replaced the phone's receiver in its cradle, he looked at me, his brother, then John. A long silence followed, interrupted by the doorbell.

Slumped on the couch, staring at the growing pile of tissues at my side, I heard Haywood talking in the background and heard John murmur a farewell with a promise to keep in touch. Nothing registered though until Karen, my best friend, sat down gently at my side and said, "Oh, God. I'm so sorry. I can't believe he really did it."

Though Klaus had lied about contacting my family members, he had called Karen late that afternoon and said, "You should get to Indianapolis because your friend will need you. I've taken the kids and we're in Canada. We board a ship for Germany tomorrow." Then he hung up. Not knowing what I knew at that point, she left work immediately. After a quick pack, she threw the bag in her car and made the three-hour trek from northern Indiana without stopping. I'd run out of tears. I'd also run out of words, so, leaning against my dearest confidante of seventeen years, I said nothing. Karen put an arm through mine and pulled me close, saying, "Oh, Jeannie. What are we going to do?"

Karen's question left me speechless. Klaus, intending to have the last word as was customary, left me no choice. I would have to find them and get them back. But how? How? No one was issuing any warrants. Even if they did, what use would they be since my ex-husband and my children were in Germany? Maybe we could somehow find him, reason with him, and get him to bring them back. Anything. I would do anything. My head was spinning with wild thoughts. I could give him full custody. Or maybe I should divorce Haywood and go back to Klaus. Suffocating with fear, I could see no other options.

Eventually, I made myself stand and stretch. I went into the kitchen to make a cup of tea. As the water started boiling, so did the grief.

You'll never find us.

I leaned against the wall, and wetness began trickling down between my legs. My wails rang through the apartment as I collapsed onto the cold tile of the kitchen floor.

He took them.

Haywood and Karen came running. They got me on my feet and cleaned me up.

"Jeannie, swallow this," Karen said. She dropped a mild tranquilizer on my tongue, followed by a sip of water before having me sit on the couch again. Within fifteen minutes, calm filled my body. When I stood, my legs wobbled. Haywood caught me as I lurched forward, scooped me into his arms, and carried me into the bedroom where Karen placed a blanket over me and turned out the lights.

four

College

1965, Bloomington, IN

"Who's that guy over there?" I asked my roommate as she negotiated a wedge of pecan pie onto her tray.

"Who? Oh, that's Nick, my boyfriend's roommate." Trudy scanned the large dining hall for an empty table. "His real name is Klaus," she said. "He's German. Very German."

We found a spot by a window overlooking the fall campus. "So why 'Nick?'" I asked.

"I guess Joe thought 'Nick' sounded more American—like Nicholas. Klaus didn't object, so the name stuck."

"How well does Joe know him? Did they room together last year?" I pressed, staring at the clean cut, square-jawed handsome face across the way.

Trudy took a bite of her pie. "No, I don't know where he roomed last year. This is only Nick's second year on campus, but he's a senior like Joe. Nick seems nice enough, though pretty much sticks to himself. He's already served four years in the Air Force, so he's several years older than Joe. I'm guessing maybe late twenties."

As a fledgling freshman, "late twenties" sounded as intriguing as his nationality. *German. Very German.* How exciting. It must mean he's very smart, very deep, and very worldly. My eyes followed Handsome Mystery Man exiting the building with his hands in his pockets. Mystery Man had a sway to his step, almost cocky, yet appealing. He walked as if he knew where he was going.

The next day at lunch, Joe introduced Nick as the two of them joined Trudy and me at a dining hall table. I smiled and attempted conversation. "Trudy says your name is really Klaus. So, what do I call you—Nick or Klaus?"

"Either works," he said, and continued eating. The reply might have sounded abrupt if not for that accent. And brevity aside, his good table manners were worth noting. My mother would approve. *Check.*

He may be short on words, I thought, *but look at him.* I had seen men like him only in the movies, and a movie was already playing in my head. He was my Richard Burton—medium height, stocky, and ruggedly good looking, with a hint of arrogance. With my slender five-foot-eight frame and long dark hair, I could be his Elizabeth Taylor. We would make beautiful children.

When I boldly suggested we study together later that evening, he brushed me off—not an anticipated reaction based on my earlier interactions with high school boys. I was, after all, on the homecoming court. Klaus's snub threw me. I guess my Hoosier-ness held no appeal for someone so sophisticated. Trudy caught the exchange and saved me from embarrassment. "Let's go, Jeannie. Errands await."

Sitting alone that night in the study lounge, I looked up from my book to find him standing there. My stomach tightened. All I could do was blink.

"May I join you?" *I loved the German accent.* "I was passing through and saw you," he added quickly, shifting his sharp blue eyes into the distance, only to lock them on mine a second later.

I couldn't read him. Had he sought me out? He sat down and politely asked a few questions about my book. As I whispered a response, his lips gave way to a smile while his gaze remained steadfast. My cheeks warmed and after a few minutes together in the hushed study area, the attraction became as obvious as his accent. He suggested we go for a walk, took my books, and led me outside.

I was the one now short on words; he appeared more relaxed, any guarded behavior gone. We ambled through campus and headed into town. Out of the corner of my eye, I saw him smiling, and I shivered, reacting to his presence as much as the cool evening air. Eventually, combing his fingers through his close-cropped brown hair, he leaned close and asked, "Are you cold? How about we stop at that little coffee house over there?"

"I'd love a cup of coffee," I replied. He offered me an arm, and we crossed the street. After opening the door for me, he found a secluded table, waited until we had ordered, and after a bit of an awkward silence, began sharing his story.

By eighteen, he was eager to see the world. To my ears, his childhood couldn't have been easy. Born in 1938 in a small West German town, only a few years after Adolph Hitler became Germany's Chancellor, he and his family suffered through World War II. He was six when his father died in a coal mining accident as the war continued. His mother, two months pregnant with the last of eight at the time of her husband's death, somehow held the family together.

In 1956, with Eisenhower in the White House and German immigration rising, Klaus, the only one of the eight siblings to say goodbye to their West German home, entered the United States via Canada on a permanent visa which required registering with the Selective Service. As a legal permanent resident, registration was mandatory since he entered the US before the age of twenty-six. He later applied for citizenship, causing forfeiture of German citizenship, and within a few years received the predicted draft notice from the Army. Enlisting in the Air Force instead, he used the opportunity to take college classes.

I momentarily thought about how different our backgrounds were relative to the draft and family history. The only uniformed male in my world was my maternal grandfather, who served in WWI. My dad never enlisted; I have no recollection why. My brother, eight years my senior, and brother-in-law, thirteen years older, received draft notices, followed by rejections, one for hernias, one for flat feet. I adopted a narrow mindset about the military, choosing peace over war, even while growing up in an Eisenhower-era family. I had no context for Klaus's involvement but thought him brave for joining the Air Force.

"They stationed me at the Kokomo base, just a couple hours from here. When my tour of duty ended, I still needed several credits toward my business degree. So, I—how do you say?—used my smarts and decided finishing here at IU's Bloomington campus made good sense."

His voice was strong and confident, exuding worldly experience. I had lived in Indiana my entire life and chosen Indiana University— not exactly a risk-taker. Even in high school, risk-taking wasn't my forte. The biggest risk I took was in late middle school when I got mixed up with the wrong crowd. Impressionable and wanting to fit in, I put my parents through hell with a questionable choice of friends. It wasn't until I met Karen, who would become my best friend, that hooligans lost their appeal. Ever the nice girl in high school, I walked the middle road—the one where you don't become part of the popular girl clique or join the cheerleading squad.

Having not sided with any one particular group, I ventured into the world of theatre and music—my two loves, and with Karen's support and encouragement, I made several friends. My unexpected popularity secured me a place on the homecoming court my senior year.

It was a moment of bliss. On homecoming night, under the stadium lights, I was one of five senior girls seated on the backs of open convertibles driven around the football field. In the spotlight at last, wearing a fitted, strapless-bodice gown with the crisp night air cooling my bare arms, I felt momentarily self-assured.

Our attendants escorted us from our cars and stood facing the stadium crowd as we held our bouquets, nervously awaiting the entrance of the senior class president. With a drum roll, Alex, tuxedoed and with crown in hand, stood several feet behind the line of contenders. Increasing the suspense, Alex walked the length of the homecoming court several times, pausing behind each girl, only to back away and move down the line. Finally, he crowned the winner. Mary Anne—the cheerleader.

The band played. The crowd cheered. I pasted a smile on my face.

Being runner-up sucked.

Once I arrived on Indiana University's 1965 campus, homecoming popularity seemed pretty silly and my education to date pretty narrow. My high school graduating class, like the entire school, had been all-white and all-American in every sense. Lew Wallace High remained segregated until 1966, integrating only after the Civil Rights Act of 1964 passed, prohibiting racial discrimination in employment and education. I believed in Martin Luther King Jr.'s advocacy of civil disobedience and non-violent resistance; I was a peacemaker and didn't agree with segregation. However, like a fish unaware of the water it lives in, I didn't recognize the white-privileged culture I lived in. Growing up with the absence of color in my small all-white world, I didn't realize how limited my understanding was of the social justice implications, because whiteness was the norm. Blind to the white-culture hierarchy, I naively thought passage of the new laws would rectify any inequalities.

Even as middle-class WASPs, we had had a maid. Mom loosely ran the household with the help of Elizabeth, our Black maid whom I adored. A five-foot-tall timid woman with a welcoming smile and a noticeable lazy eye, Elizabeth arrived at the back door weekly, fetched the glass bottles left on the steps by the milkman, and entered the house to clean and do the ironing. A linoleum-clad portion of our concrete floor basement was home to the washer, dryer, and ironing production, which is also where she and I would spend time chatting and giggling. She'd sometimes let me spray the clothes with water before she took a hot iron to them. The clean scent of the starch she applied to Dad's shirts helped cover the musty dankness of the basement.

Other than the interactions with Elizabeth, my Midwest world remained WASP-white. Black people did not mix with whites and lived in a confined singular section of town, though they made up about 40% of Gary's population.

High school hadn't offered the diversity in race, culture, and nationality I found so exciting my first year at IU—and for sure there had been no charming European men. At eighteen, meeting twenty-seven-year-old Klaus was for me part of a bigger, more expansive picture of what life could be. It felt like the right time to reinvent myself. In my naivete, I didn't possess the background nor the experience to realize what the effect Klaus's Hitler-era youth indoctrination could have on a relationship. I knew as little about cultural differences as I did racial ones, and the thought of dating this older, sophisticated man was the most adventurous idea I'd ever mustered.

I leaned both elbows on the table, listening intently, my fingers interlaced under my chin. I studied him, noting how impeccably handsome this man was in his crisp, white long-sleeved shirt. At the base of his left cuff, the face of a gold watch rested on the inside of his wrist rather than the top. How curious. Part of the European unique appeal. I took a breath, inhaling the magic of his company, and moved my folded hands in front of my lips, hoping for a sophisticated look. Praying the please-let-me-appear-calm prayer of an eighteen-year-old, I could feel every inch of my thighs pressing into the chair to steady myself.

He reached across the table, cupped my hands with his, and pulled them toward him. "I've never been comfortable enough to talk about myself. It's hard for me to let people know me. I was so nervous when I met you at lunch, I didn't know what to do. This is new for me." He paused. "But being with you feels good."

I was speechless. He let go of my hands as if the action might have been too forward.

I sipped my coffee, unsure of what to do, while he drank a cup of tea. *He brought me here, a coffeehouse, and doesn't even drink the stuff.* Afraid of losing the moment—and my nerve—I smiled and reached for his hands.

I was hooked.

FIVE

Day 1

July 27, 1977, Indianapolis, IN

I heard Haywood and Karen's hushed voices coming from the living room. My body felt heavy, its position unaltered with my cheek pressed into the pillow. The air conditioner whirred to life, blowing cool air across my clammy face and sticky lids.

As I awoke more fully, I heard another voice, one in my head: *he stole your children.*

I blinked in slow motion, rubbed my forehead, and dragged my tranquilized body from the bed.

Karen, unloading the dishwasher when I shuffled into the kitchen, stopped to give me a long hug.

"God, I'm glad you're here," I said, easing into the nearest dining room chair.

We'd become friends as teenagers growing up in the Midwest on the south side of Gary, Indiana, the white Anglo-Saxon protestant end of town. Though chatty, I'd been a compliant child during elementary school. I floundered through junior high, however, increasing my parents' stress by running with an undesirable crowd in the eighth grade. How I longed for approval, popularity, inclusion, all the while scared to the bone. I wanted to have shoes like Barbara, clothes like Patti, and a laugh like Linda's. Though invited to the parties where alcohol flowed, I didn't drink; I wasn't one of them. I remember my confusion at one party where, to act like I was having a good time, I let some chunky guy named Bucky give me my first French kiss, filling my mouth with his fat tongue. It practically gagged me. But I didn't stop him. I acquiesced. I deferred.

My mom and dad did not look kindly on my choice of friends and scheduled sessions with a psychologist, along with an ultimatum: either find new friends or find myself at boarding school. As I sat in Dr. Robert Ross's office week after week, handsomely framed degrees covering the dark paneled walls impressed and intimidated me. Based on those extensive credentials I felt I had no right to question his authority and, at fourteen, rather than put stock in the arrogant, self-aggrandizing, patronizing undertone I sensed, I instead revered "Dr. Bob," his preferred moniker. What saved me though wasn't his professional counseling. Dr. Bob had a daughter my age—Karen, and she was the answer to everybody's prayers. I dodged boarding school, Dr. Bob became almost like a second father, and Karen and I became best friends.

When I was with her, I knew kindness; I could feel her strength, calmness, and insight. When I was with the good doctor, I knew my place. However conflicted I felt about him, he was a doting father to Karen and by extension to me.

Karen and I made quite a pair. By my freshman year of high school, I had morphed into a pretty girl. I retired the badly permed hair from junior high and lost several unwanted pounds. Next to my five-eight frame, olive skin, and long dark hair, Karen was maybe five-foot-four, eye-catching with shoulder-length blond curls, crystal blue eyes, and soft features. Knowing my love for music and theatre, she convinced me I should join the drama and choral departments—her favorites. It was an easy sell.

Karen and I became inseparable. On November 22, 1963, the day someone assassinated President John F. Kennedy, we sought each other out amidst the ensuing chaos that engulfed the school hallways. She was the friend I needed as we suffered the shock, unable to comprehend a tragedy unlike any other experienced.

JFK. My mother and I had both fallen in love with him, even though our household had supported Eisenhower the previous decade. Young, handsome, well-spoken, and smart, a man we could believe in, Kennedy personified hope for the future. Perhaps the bigger draw for me involved the subconscious pull of the fairytale—Camelot through and through.

Once we found each other after the news broke, Karen and I didn't even speak—we left the hysteria of the crowded halls and found a quiet side spot on the steps of the massive open staircase that connected the high school's second and third floors. Dazed, we sat together and wept until the final bell rang.

And here we were, sitting together again, this time at my small dining room table, dazed, unable to comprehend the current moment's tragedy. "I thought I heard Haywood. Where is he?" I asked.

She poured me a cup of coffee and offered some cream. "Gone to run an errand. Won't be gone long. How are you feeling?"

"Groggy, stupid, angry, scared. All the above." My lip trembled as I choked up.

She reached across the table and put her soft hand on mine. "We'll figure this out, Jeannie. I called my father while you were sleeping, and he'd like to talk, as soon as you feel up to it."

Feel up to it? I didn't know when I'd feel like doing anything, especially having a conversation with her father, Dr. Bob—he who had been my counselor when I was a teenager, later a marriage therapist for my mom, and the one who had disapproved of my divorce.

A minister and a psychologist, he'd also been the unofficial mediator, an instrumental negotiator, during the early stages of the divorce. Klaus had seemed to respect Dr. Bob and accept his counsel.

I swallowed a few sips of coffee and made the call.

"Jeannie, I think, all things considered, it would be best if you worked through me to get the kids back. Klaus obviously feels as if you forced his hand with this new marriage of yours."

I could almost see Dr. Bob, leaning his solid frame back in his leather chair, flanked by an impressive wall of bookcases that dominated his office. He always sounded so sure of himself, always so reasonable. "I understand Klaus, and I understand the male psyche. Let me handle this for you, Jeannie."

I stared at my half-empty cup. Karen, sitting across the table from me, offered more, but I declined. "Bob, I just want my children back," I sighed. "What should we do?" I took a slow sip.

He told me, if Klaus would agree to return, I should give Klaus custody of the kids. Full custody. Both of them.

"What?" I sputtered. "How can you say that? He kidnapped them! He's taken them out of the country, for God's sake! Klaus should be jailed, not rewarded with custody."

"Jeannie, he's their father. You don't want to see him behind bars." Dr. Bob's voice was calm and clear. "You want this unfortunate situation worked out in a way that's best for everyone concerned. I'm your best hope, probably your only hope, for reaching that solution."

For a moment, I wondered whether I should call my attorney, because a gut part of me wanted Klaus sent away. Revenge, however, would only fuel the fire of Klaus's wrath, which terrified me. I'd already made a huge mistake by stupidly thinking the split custody arrangement, a fear-based agreement, would ensure an amicable future. Now, I felt like a traitor to my children, the ones I loved the most. I was so confused. I just wanted my children back with me, safe and sound, whatever the cost to me.

The police insisted Klaus hadn't committed a crime. If they couldn't arrest him, I didn't know how I'd get the children back, despite the custody order. My head still foggy, I couldn't come up with where to start, who to turn to, what to do, and I felt the convoluted legal system had turned its back on me. *Who was I to think I could find them? And here was a man willing to help me. I should listen.*

Dr. Bob, arrogance aside, understood Klaus and seemed confident in his ability to handle things, if I did exactly as directed. What else could I do?

I clutched the edge of the table and took a long shaky breath, wanting so badly to be smart enough to handle this, but my insecurities surfaced and took hold.

"All right, Dr. Bob. All right," I said. "Whatever it takes. Just get me my kids."

My voice quivered as I thought of the last glimpse I'd had of Ty and Megan, smiling, excited, waving goodbye through the car windows as Klaus pulled out of the parking lot only five days earlier. Megan, having just turned three and buckled into her car seat, with her tousled dark blond locks and that impish grin, blew me an exaggerated kiss. Ty, almost seven and slim-faced with his baby fat long gone, waved with both hands, making silly faces which I replicated as they rounded the corner.

Had I told them I loved them?

WEDDINGHOFEN (WEST GERMANY)
  JEANNIE GIVES YOU TOTAL CUSTODY CALL DR. BOB SUNDAY
  JULY 31 MIDNIGHT INDIANA TIME
  LOVE KAREN

"*Love, Karen?*" I said, when she handed me a copy of the telegram she'd sent per her father's instructions, to Klaus's brother, Fredi in Germany.

"I know," she said, with a little grimace. "It felt strange writing that on the form, but I wrote what Dad had said. Do you think I should have left out the 'love'?"

Seventeen years she and I had been friends. She knew my entire marriage story and had lived through all the chapters. Though love was not what she felt for Klaus, she deferred to her father, as she had so often done in the past.

I could only shake my head and say, "I don't know, Karen. For the moment, I guess we'll do as your father says."

The world had gone upside down and backwards. If some twisted idea of love had made Klaus steal the children, maybe Karen's "love" could convince Klaus he had won and that bringing Ty and Megan back was in his favor.

I sat on the couch, staring into space while my friend bustled around the apartment. She answered endless phone calls and took messages from family members, the babysitter, and my office. I'd only had the energy to return the call from my boss, Dave, at Indiana Bell Telephone Company. After I'd explained my absence from work, he said, "Please keep me posted, and don't worry about things here." Attempting a lighter note, Dave added, "Without diminishing your role as one of our best staff associates, we can manage. I mean it; you take all the time you need."

But my perception of time had changed. Without my kids, there was too much of it as the day stretched out before me—and too little, as the tranquilizer fog started lifting and I considered all the details that would require serious attention if Klaus accepted my offer and brought the children back home. I soon realized Dr. Bob's telegram did not include the contingency we had discussed on the phone: Klaus's maintaining Indiana residency unless otherwise agreed.

I sat down at the dining room table again, still in my bathrobe, and began scribbling lists on a legal pad and imagined what giving Klaus full custody of Ty and Megan would involve. I would want unlimited visitation; where would they live? The "new job" was obviously a lie—how would he support himself? Would I be responsible for child support payments?

Haywood and I were just establishing ourselves as a couple and as a family. We were also financially strapped. He worked as a truck driver, hauling steel, and I was a telephone company staff associate writing training material for service reps, a junior rung on the corporate ladder. Taking on this madness with Klaus—financially and emotionally—was not part of the plan. And I knew Haywood would not approve of Dr. Bob's strong-arm tactics, nor the unthinkable custody change. That wasn't Haywood's modus operandi.

When you have kids with a person though, that person is part of your life and your children's lives, for better or for worse. Right now was definitely worse.

I swallowed hard and reread the letter in its entirety.

Jeannie, the children and I are on our way to Germany for good. Ty and I decided two months ago that such a move would be the best for both children. It would mean togetherness as brother and sister, one place to live with someone who is willing to sacrifice a portion of his life. My brother and I made all the arrangements by ourselves without help from any of my friends and he will <u>not</u> disclose our location. If you feel like communicating with me or the children, address the letter to my brother. In reference to the condo, I gave Big John my power of attorney and I respect and hope that through this action you maintain his friendship —he cares for you. Again, we are in Germany, happy and together, and in a place where you'll never find us, nor will you be able to threaten me with court action again. By the way, don't worry about my monetary debts to you, they will be paid off in time that much I promise you.

Since your family had completely ignored me since you dumped me, I took the liberty and informed your father, mother, and sister of my action. So, keep your theatrics and dramatizations to your current circle of friends for they don't know you yet. Karen and Dr. Bob also received a note and I hope that either one of them contacted you by now.

Good-by Jeannie, take care of yourself and don't worry
about the children for you know they are in good hands.
   Klaus

He would have me believe that Ty, our six-year-old, had something to do with this decision? And one of his brothers helped make the arrangements? Which of the five? The children were in good hands? Seeking order out of insanity, I jotted down a dozen issues. Klaus obviously needed some sort of counseling, though I doubted he'd agree, and I wondered how we would settle future differences on raising the children. Recent memories of Klaus's blatant manipulation of them made me queasy. One night after Klaus had learned I was dating Haywood, I went to pick Megan up from Klaus's condo to take her home and she pulled away from me. She announced, "Daddy cry if I go. I can't leave Daddy alone." The babysitter also confirmed the troublesome influence. Klaus told Megan Haywood wasn't her friend. "Klaus is filling that little head with such mean garbage," the sitter had said.

Klaus had them in his physical possession completely now, had control over what they were to think. At three and almost seven, they didn't stand a chance; the damage was being done. The odds of me affecting any of it, even something as simple as babysitting arrangements, were not good now that I had offered full custody through that stupid telegram.

What had I done?

Not trusting my judgment, I had deferred. Again. To a man.

The yellow legal pad caught the tears that rolled down my nose. I watched the words I'd scrawled smear and dissolve and realized exactly what I had done. Klaus was arrogant, rigid, and manipulative, and I'd walked myself right into this mess by falling in love with him in the first place.

s i x

Love Story

1965, Bloomington, IN

During my freshman year at IU, it was no wonder that Klaus, or Nicky as I sometimes called him, thrived on my attention.

He admitted never having dated before. His father's untimely death in the coal mining accident challenged the large family left behind: seven children and a pregnant wife. Growing up fatherless in their West German village had left little time for fun or romance. Even so, whenever we were together, Klaus exercised old-world manners—holding open a door, or offering a chair. He planned all our campus concert outings since we shared a love of classical music and made sure we became regulars at the foreign film series at the local arts theatre. During performances he would attentively whisper, "You are so beautiful," and I'd feel as if nothing else mattered. I thrived on his attention as much as he thrived on mine. He willingly gave me the attention my dad, busy with work, golf, or his music combo, didn't.

Klaus phoned my dorm room each night after we studied together, completing the evening with, "Just wanted to say goodnight," words that echoed in my head as I fell asleep.

Watching from the stands, I couldn't take my eyes off him at soccer games. He was one of IU's stars during those early soccer years when the coach was working hard at gaining the program varsity status. Fit and trim, Klaus effortlessly controlled the ball while moving up and down the field. Occasionally I'd see him scan the stadium and, once finding my face, delight in impressing me.

After one exceptional game where he scored the winning goal, we headed to nearby Lake Lemon for a celebratory picnic. For such Saturday excursions we often packed a picnic basket filled with an assortment of fresh fruit and mouth-watering German foods: blutwurst, leberwurst, nose-bursting limburger cheese, *butterkäse*, stout rye bread, and Black Forest ham.

Sitting on the blanket he spread on the sunlit grass, we munched on blutwurst and cheese, hearty bread, and fresh fruit. As I reached for more cheese, I noticed a textbook packed below the food. "Nicky, you brought your book? I'm impressed."

"The Air Force was, what's the expression . . . no picnic?" He flashed a smile, proud of the pun. "But thanks to them, the more I study, the sooner I'll have my degree. And, one other good thing happened. I found out all commanding officers weren't stupid idiots. I actually met a good one."

"What made him better than the others?" I asked.

"He was *Cherman!*" He laughed, revealing perfect teeth through a now-familiar broad smile, and I laughed as well.

The attention he showered on me made me oblivious to the impact of his background, his upbringing as part of an assumed gifted race, an Aryan-filtered attitude and ideology. All went unnoticed, or at least unquestioned. I accepted his comments as worldliness and wisdom.

We both leaned back on our hands and talked about the future, bright as the cloudless sky. With military service over and a business degree almost complete, a comfortable life in his adopted country was within reach. Eventually, once he'd found a good job and the right woman, he said he wanted to have kids.

As I bit into an apple, I studied this remarkable man's profile. With every hour I spent with him, the list of perfections grew: nonsmoker, not a big drinker, and wanted a family. *Check. Check. Check.* I was sure he was The One.

After our picnic, as Klaus walked me to my dorm, an arm securely around my waist, it struck me: I hadn't been voted Homecoming Queen of my high school senior class, but Klaus had chosen me and crowned me with his attention. For him, I would never be runner-up.

Christmas break came all too soon. We were reluctantly heading in different directions; family awaited me in Gary, while Klaus packed for Kokomo—a two-hour trip honoring a commitment to visit his former favored German commanding officer. As I was closing my suitcase and getting ready to leave, he showed up at my room for a goodbye hug.

"I bought you something. Since we won't be together over the holidays, I want you to have this and think of me."

I opened the gift-wrapped package, a record album of German Christmas carols. I slipped it on the turntable and delighted in the Vienna Boys Choir singing, "O Tannenbaum."

Suddenly the three-week break seemed like an impossibly long separation. I cried, kissed him, and buried my face in his neck, wetting a nicely starched shirt collar with tears. After he carried my luggage downstairs and walked me to my car, we kissed one last time. I could see him in my rearview mirror, watching me as I drove off. *Life with a man like this couldn't be anything but good.* I thought about only one thing, only one person, the entire three-hour trip home.

My entire family got together over the holidays as we always did: Mom, Dad, Joanne and husband Mark, brother Jim, Paulette, their two little girls and two-month-old son. I talked my mom's ear off over the break, providing heady details about the "man of my dreams" and his many talents and accomplishments. Even Dad seemed pleased with his youngest daughter's news. Nicky and I talked as often as we could, mindful not to abuse my parents' phone bill.

Sitting in the living room, warmed by the fireplace, the family and I watched as the snowfall magically changed Gary into a storybook scene. Our Christmas tree completed the moment, fully adorned with large multicolored lights, ornaments gathered over the years, and tinsel galore, standing proudly in front of the picture window. My good-natured brother saw fit to tease me about the ever-present smile on my face, saying the glow competed with the sparkling tree. "Uh oh, our little sister's in love," Jim winked at Joanne. "Any guesses as to how many more times she'll force us to listen to 'O Tannenbaum'?"

Two months later, after attending a late-night film at the arts theatre in downtown Bloomington, Klaus and I drove back through the wintry evening and pulled into the dorm's parking lot. Klaus shut the engine off. All was quiet. I looked into those blue eyes and confessed, "Nicky, I'm falling in love with you."

He shot out of the car, ran around to the passenger side and yanked the door open. Breathless, he scooped me up and carried me across the fresh snow to the safety of the dry sidewalk before saying, "Would you repeat that?" and kissed me, hard.

SEVEN

Day 8

July 29, 1977, Indianapolis, IN

Settled on the living room sofa, I welcomed the afternoon breeze cooling my face as the air flowed through the opened patio doors of the apartment. I had pen and paper on my lap, ready for taking notes, though my mind had already wandered, like it had been doing repeatedly over the past three days. Rev. Verner's voice on the other end of the line almost startled me when he spoke.

"I'm sorry. I can't do a reading for you," he said, his voice quiet and noncommittal.

I paused until I could calmly reply. "What do you mean?"

His answer felt a long time coming. "I simply have no information for you."

"Why not?" I said, this time my distress obvious, as fear grew in the pit of my stomach.

Contacting him hadn't been my idea—I doubted a psychic would be any help. We'd already made what felt like nonstop calls over the last three days. Phone calls were, for all intents and purposes, our only source of information: we had contacted numerous authorities—the police, the sheriff's department, state officials, and multiple calls to my attorney who was investigating our legal options; we notified family members and friends; we asked for help from business associates. The results were not encouraging. It didn't appear 1977 laws were in our favor. A couple of work friends insisted Rev. Verner, a well-known Indianapolis clairvoyant, could give me a lead, or at least some sense of where Klaus and the children might be. When Verner refused conversation, I was more devastated than I thought possible.

I wasn't sure what I'd expected from him. An address and phone number would have been nice. Failing that, I'd at least hoped for some assurance they were okay, wherever they were. Hanging up the phone, I tried accepting the outcome of the brief conversation: he didn't have any information.

In the back of my mind, I couldn't get past the idea that Rev. Verner knew something. What would a psychic be reluctant to divulge, so reluctant that he'd turn away a paying customer?

My imagination was again running wild.

Stop it, Jeannie, I told myself. Although Klaus had many flaws, harming the kids or knowingly endangering them seemed unthinkable.

But there are so many kinds of danger.

Stop right now. Don't even think about it.

Back at the dining room table, I flipped through the pages of my legal pad. When I reached the list that ended with "Consult psychic?" I crossed through that idea with a heavy black line. After I stared at the pad for a minute, I ripped the page out entirely and rewrote the damn thing, minus that entry. My list of options grew shorter each day.

Shorter, and more expensive.

Dennis, my attorney, whose fifty-dollar-an-hour bills were already adding up, had suggested potential courses of action. If we "pulled out the big guns" we could ask the district attorney's office to "search and destroy." They would somehow magically locate Klaus, even if he'd taken refuge outside the United States. I noted the suggestion, as Dennis seemed particularly taken with it. This would be the most proactive route, with an initial price tag of $5,000, which would cover my lawyer's fees to deal with the district attorney, obliterating three months of my salary. However, given what little I knew, that plan wasn't credible. We were one of how many hundreds of thousands of cases? Unconfirmed US reports ranged from 60,000 upwards of 100,000 annual parental kidnappings. How could I believe I'd receive some sort of priority when even the local police couldn't do anything? I didn't buy it.

Haywood and I could push the DA's issuance of a kidnapping warrant, which would allow apprehension by any Indiana officer of the law. Filing official Missing Person Reports on the children would broaden the search to include the continental United States, though I didn't know if that meant a caseworker could actively search and work within a network of all forty-eight states, or if the plan was nothing more than a be-on-the-lookout-for approach. That held little promise considering the multitude of US cases, and with Indiana's re-examination of parental kidnapping laws in its infancy in 1977, things were in an overall state of flux.

Hiring a private detective held some appeal. As well-meaning as the police were, they seemed resigned there wasn't much they could do about missing children who were with their father, even though Klaus had clearly stolen them. Since the police were unable to follow through initiating a case, I would have to hire a private investigator or become one myself.

Rubbing my forehead, I stared at the cluttered table. On the top of a growing pile of papers I caught sight of the July 4, 1977 *National Observer* an Indiana Bell VP had taken the time to deliver. The senior executives had all been great and offered whatever assistance they could. The front-page headline caught his attention: *Parents Who Kidnap Their Own Children: Denied Legal Custody, 25,000 Parents A Year Regain Their Kids By Snatching.*

Written by journalist Sarah Bird of Austin, Texas, the story was horrific, and made it painfully obvious how easy kidnapping a child was. The non-offending parent has little recourse and, in order to *retrieve* a missing child, resorts to snatching the child back. Bird notes, "Firm statistics on this troubling phenomenon, born of sky-rocketing divorce and laissez-faire legislation, are hard to come by, since it is not a criminal offense. Although no records are kept, one legal journal estimates that 25,000 children are snatched annually."

Snatching? Some parents retrieved their kids by kidnapping them back? *How great that'd be*, I thought. I wouldn't have to sit and wait for phone calls or telegrams, wouldn't need to hang on the words of clairvoyants and attorneys. I could be my own detective, my own police force.

Good grief. What was I thinking? The idea was overwhelming. I was a mom. I worked for the phone company. I was smart and well organized but I was no gumshoe. Tracking Klaus across the US, perhaps across the Atlantic, searching a country whose language I didn't speak well even after two years of college study would be insanely impossible.

Then I pictured six-year-old Ty, so serious and sensitive, tucked away somewhere in Germany where he didn't speak the language and knew no one except Klaus. Megan would have trouble as well, though she had a more easygoing personality, and Klaus had always doted on her. She was so young. She would learn . . .

"Jeannie—are you okay?"

Haywood's voice jolted me out of my trance. I hadn't heard the apartment door open, nor his keys dropping on the counter, or even my name called out from the living room. Not until my new husband stood over me, stroking my hair, did I realize he was home from work. The worried look on his face revealed his concern, a far cry from the carefree way he presented himself when we first met.

Regardless, he smiled and said, "You look tired, babe." I sighed, relieved by his soothing presence and grateful he was home.

He led me to the sofa and held me close. I stared into his handsome face before closing my eyes. I drifted off, reminiscing in my mind about meeting his brother, Bill, and the circumstances that brought Haywood and me together earlier in the year, not realizing it would change my life.

"Hi, Bill. Just checking in, making sure our new artist-in-residence has everything an artist needs," I said.

"Jeannie—hi!" There stood my thirty-something charge. It was the end of March, a couple months after my divorce. The phone company had contracted with local artist Bill Ware for the creation of a large mural for the lobby and multiple paintings for our new eighteen-story building. "Even with this March weather we're having, I love the view from my studio. I can't wait to bring my wife and kids up to see it."

"That's why we put you on the seventeenth floor," I laughed, walking over to his makeshift worktable positioned in front of the floor-to-ceiling windows, which provided an unobstructed view of Indianapolis's downtown circle. "Not too shabby for a floor that's under construction."

"Works for me. It's given me plenty of room to spread out and not have any worries about doing damage to anybody's office," his sense of humor evident. "Thanks for taking care of me this last month. I know it's not exactly part of your job description."

"The General Commercial Manager's Executive Assistant does whatever is needed," I said. Overseeing his work and getting to know this talented guy provided an entertaining distraction from my post-divorce life.

After finishing high school, Bill attended Baylor University to enter pre-med. But Bill and blood didn't mix; you couldn't even talk about bodily functions without activating his gag reflex. His artistic talents prevailed, and he left medical school, following his own heart instead of operating on someone else's.

I shared some of my personal story, giving him the Reader's Digest version of my marriage and divorce.

"So, Jeannie," he said with a smile, "One of these days you really should meet my brother, Haywood. Based on what you've told me, you could use a little fun. If nothing else, he'd make good company for you."

"Thanks, but no. Maybe later. I'm not looking for any company right now. I'm just coming up for air, if you know what I mean. Even though my former husband and I remained separated for over a year, you've got to remember it's only been about two months since the actual divorce," I said.

"Haywood's situation is pretty much the same as yours—that's one reason I keep bringing it up. My brother's marriage didn't last long, maybe a little over a year. And get this: while Haywood was out of town working, his wife cleared out the contents of their duplex and filed for divorce. I never did like her. Sure am glad they didn't have any kids. Our sister said it was like they were kids themselves, just playing house."

"Not right now, Bill," I said. "Really." I had a lot on my mind. The brief peace with Klaus had deteriorated and my level of exhaustion seeped into my response.

Later that week, Bill called me from IBT's first floor lobby. The mural boards had arrived—cracked. Exasperated by the reported art project glitch, I took the elevator to the mezzanine, which overlooked the lobby, so I could view the situation from above.

I could see Bill talking with a man wearing old blue jeans and a ratty cream-colored sweatshirt. Tall and buff, with his short sleeves revealing muscular arms, Mr. Blue Jeans resembled the famous Mr. Schwarzenegger. Bill and Mr. Blue Jeans spotted me as I rode the escalator down to the main floor and headed their way.

"Jeannie, this is my baby brother, Haywood."

"Baby brother?" I laughed. His hand span alone must have been ten inches. "I'm sorry, I assumed you were the delivery man. I was ready to chew you out for bringing damaged goods." Eyeing the perfectly intact boards, I said, "Hmm. There's nothing wrong with them, is there?" and noted a smile on Baby Brother's face as he flipped brown shoulder-length hair out of his dark blue eyes.

"Well, actually I *am* the delivery man," he said. "Just doing Bill here a favor. I drive a truck so I offered to pick up the mural boards and drop them off—not drop them. I don't deliver damaged goods, ma'am."

Before handing me an invoice, he circled the date. It took me a minute before recognizing the whole thing as a clever April Fools' joke.

Haywood's genuine smile and hearty laugh made an impression, and Bill took it all in. After Haywood and Bill tried blaming each other for the practical joke, Bill suggested the least they could do was buy my lunch. I took Haywood up the escalator to the second floor waiting area and found us a comfortable sofa while Bill excused himself to clean up. With an easygoing nature and sense of humor, Haywood had no trouble making conversation.

"I've never known anyone named Haywood," I confessed, interrupting him.

"They named me after an uncle, a really great guy."

"So, what do your friends call you?" I asked.

"Haywood," he said, followed by a belly laugh.

"Okay. Haywood. Works for me." I nodded. *Straightforward; I like that.*

Bill showed up a few minutes later only to let us know he must bow out, feigning a scheduling conflict. "You guys have fun," and headed back upstairs with a wave over his shoulder.

I'd been had twice in a matter of minutes by this duo, both with good intentions.

We walked to a popular nearby deli, where I—in heels and corpo-

rate suit—stood at one of several counter-height tables and enjoyed a
hot roast beef Stromboli amidst the din of lunch-hour patrons' noisy
conversations. Haywood towered over me, his height augmented by
steel-toed work boots, apparently at ease with himself and the world.
My shoulders relaxed, and I felt myself smiling, enjoying his
playfulness. I liked him. Bill had been right about Baby Brother:
Haywood was good company.

After our second lunch date a week later, I called my friend Dotti,
eager to share my "new man" news. I admired her. Dotti, only three
years older than I, had been my trainer when I joined Ma Bell in
1969 as a service representative. With a street-smart sense of self, she
didn't hesitate to caution me in true Dotti-fashion. "I'm happy for
you, Jeannie! But try to pace yourself, girl. Considering you're just
coming off the marriage-go-round from hell, I don't recommend
jumping on the rebound wagon. Been there. Done that. Those blind
rebounds are usually more like suicide with Novocaine—we don't
feel a thing."

"Oh, Dotti, come on," I laughed. "This is different. This guy is
genuine. He's fun, he's cute, and his whole demeanor practically shouts
how much he loves life. He's got gusto—the exact opposite of Klaus.
You know what I really like about him? Not just how he treats me, but
the way he treats people in general. Just wait till you meet him."

I had already tried the fairytale dream: married an older man, a
college graduate—and the results proved there wasn't anything magical
about that formula. With Haywood, I thought life could be simpler;
he was refreshingly bright and blue collar with no collegiate airs.

"I've got to be honest with you, Jeannie," Dotti said. "I think it's
too soon, but I'll keep my fingers crossed, okay? You keep me posted."

On April 15, Haywood arrived for our first dinner date. Megan
was with Klaus for the weekend, so I got dressed for the evening and

finished putting on my lipstick. My bedroom window overlooked the parking lot below, and when I spotted my date, I giggled like a teenager. Exiting a white TR7 sports car like an expanding accordion, he flashed me a smile and climbed the exterior stairs to my apartment. I answered the door before he could finish knocking, grabbed a wrap, and the two of us headed for the car. We cruised down to a small town an hour south of Indianapolis and checked on his beloved surrogate grandmother before going to dinner.

Nashville, adjacent to Brown County State Park, known for its fall foliage, was a quaint artists' colony, winter population 600. When autumn rolled around with an influx of tourists and vacationers, that number jumped to 6,000 or more a day. The eye-popping fall colors of the state park, lots of country shops, art everywhere, and the famous Brown County fried biscuits drew sizeable crowds.

This would be my introduction to Grandma Lee, an old friend of Haywood's mother, and part of Nashville's ambiance. Haywood waved a hello as the TR7 crunched over the pebbled driveway of her once-white cottage near the center of town. Sitting in an old rocker on her modest front porch, she waved back and, as we stepped onto the porch, put out a long, slim cigarette in a large glass ashtray. I would discover the white smock dress complete with a colorful apron was her signature look, as were the tortoiseshell hair-combs that kept her long, fine white locks atop her head. A genuine character. This was a woman I could see myself spending more porch time with.

After a good hour-long visit with her, Haywood and I headed for dinner. When we pulled into the parking lot of Noble Roman's Pizza Parlor, he said, "I know it doesn't look like much, but the pizza here is out of this world. You're gonna love it."

Pizza? Not what I'd been expecting, yet somehow exactly what seemed right: pizza, beer, Nashville's atmosphere, and Haywood. I felt alive and relaxed. Throughout dinner he talked—my God, he could talk—and I laughed. *So, this is what life could be like.*

Haywood was the youngest of three children born into a blue-collar family. His alcoholic father—a painter by trade—was a self-educated man, his brilliance dulled by the booze. I found out Haywood's Camel-smoking mom had managed the Indy 500 racetrack coffee shop for over twenty years. I'd met brother Bill, and now was curious about the remaining family members, which included an older sister, Helen, who married at sixteen to get away from home.

"But I was Mom's favorite," Haywood added and winked. Why was I not surprised?

We talked about our first marriages, my difficult ten years with Klaus, and Haywood confirmed what Bill had already told me about his—he married the beautiful daughter of a union man he admired, based more on that admiration than love for her. Knowing the marriage had lasted little more than a year, I confessed Bill had given me some background. "I bet he did," Haywood laughed. "Bill's not the only one who's glad the divorce will be final by June."

After dinner, we drove home with Leo Sayer's "When I Need You" playing on the radio, stopping at a small park a few miles from his rented shotgun-style duplex in an older part of town. Haywood cut the engine, and we enjoyed the quiet, at first looking out our windows, then at each other. Ever so slowly, he leaned forward and kissed me softly on the lips. The quiet continued and neither of us spoke. He started the car and, once we were on the road again, simply took and held my hand, completing the moment and creating a sense of comfort and safety for me. All was right with the world.

"I think I have some wine here somewhere," he grinned once we were inside his house. He rummaged around in the refrigerator and poured the last of a bottle of red into a mason jar.

"You're not having any?" I asked, leaning against the doorway between the kitchen and the living room.

"I don't drink the stuff. One of the guys I play softball with brought that wine over yesterday. I'm just glad there was enough left so I could offer you some," he confessed. "If I drink anything, it's a beer now and then, like back at the pizza place."

We moved into the low-lit living room. Leaning my back against the stairway wall, I sipped, and he stared. "I want to kiss you again." I didn't stop him. His massive arms enveloped me as I heard, "Please stay. Stay the night." Placing his hands on my hips, he turned me and guided me up the enclosed staircase to the second floor. I stopped midway, my heart pounding, and announced, "I'll stay tonight, but it's nothing more than that."

Haywood whispered into the back of my neck, "Then don't stay, because I already want you with me every night." He pressed his head between my shoulder blades, sighed, and waited.

I paused, reached for his hand, and slowly led us up to his bedroom.

Such were the memories of our meeting and falling in love three months earlier. Now, curled up next to him asleep on the sofa, looking at his furrowed brow brought me back to the moment and the current circumstances, and the realization that this good man had gotten a lot more than he'd signed up for with me. After three days of limbo, I needed to offer him an out.

I nudged him awake and said I wanted to review our options. "Haywood, if I told Klaus I'd, you know, go back, I'm pretty sure he'd return with the kids. I love you, but maybe we should split up. Maybe it's just not in the cards for us to be together."

He stretched, yawned, and smiled. In a firm voice he said, "Jeannie, that is not an option. I'm not letting you go, and we're not letting Klaus get away with this. Listen to me. We will find them and bring them back, whatever it takes. You got that? No more stupid talk about us going our separate ways."

I nodded with relief as he hugged me.

"Now, tell me, did you get in touch with that psychic guy? Did he give you any useful information?"

"No. Nothing."

Haywood poured me a glass of wine, then helped himself to a Pepsi. "Well, you tried. So, what next?"

I exhaled and looked at my list. "I think we should sell my Ford, and cash in my Indiana Bell stocks. It's not much—probably around $2,000—but that'll help pay the attorney's bills."

"Okay, let's start with that. I can help unload the Ford. I've got a buddy who's in the business."

Sipping my wine, I couldn't help feeling that finding a man like Haywood, with such fearless strength and optimism, was a stroke of luck I didn't deserve. I'd already messed things up so badly the first time around when I should have seen the signs. Or, perhaps, I had fallen in love with a love story.

eight

Sorority vs. GDI

1966, Bloomington, IN

Coat and purse in hand, I exited down the stairs to the large lobby of the Kappa House. Klaus had moved to Indianapolis after graduating in the spring of 1966, and I returned to IU and joined the Kappa Kappa Gamma sorority in the fall, my second year on the Bloomington campus. Klaus had arrived for our date that night: dinner and a movie. There he stood in the foyer with my sorority "mom" Marilyn, complaining loudly about the fifty-five-mile trip from his Indy studio apartment.

"Idiot frat boy, probably drunk or just stupid," he said.

I grimaced, then hurried toward my date, who greeted me with an award-winning smile.

"What were you saying?" I whispered.

"What do you mean? I was just telling her I almost got run off the road by some guy."

"You called that guy an idiot frat boy. So, does that make me an idiot? If frat boys are idiots, are sorority girls idiots, too?" My face felt hot with embarrassment. This was a side of his personality I had seen many times and repeatedly ignored. Klaus often displayed disdain for those not like him, making remarks about non-whites or, in this case, those who he didn't feel were his equal.

"No, of course I'm not talking about you. Hey, what's the big deal?"

Marilyn, still within earshot, said, "Jeannie, let's talk for a minute.

Would you excuse us, Klaus?" Marilyn caught my elbow and walked me back up the stairs, closing the door once we were in her room.

Marilyn, a senior and designated mentor, continued, "First, you know that I want you to be happy, don't you?"

When I nodded, she heaved a sigh and said, "But, Jeannie, Klaus's arrogance, his jaw-dropping propensity for needing to put somebody down, is hard to take. Just when I think I get a glimpse of a nice guy, some derogatory remark falls out of his mouth and I'm thrown for a loop again."

Klaus had disliked my joining a sorority and moving into the Kappa House my sophomore year and let everyone know it. A proud GDI—God Damned Independent—on campus the previous year, he often said, "Frat boys are idiots who can't take care of themselves."

I wanted to believe his words reflected the maturity of a twenty-seven-year-old, of his self-assured and unpretentious nature. His age seemed an understandable factor regarding impatience with the fraternity scene.

It was hard explaining that. Marilyn had never seen how sweet and thoughtful Klaus could be, or how romantic.

"Jeannie?" She was waiting for my response.

I knew she had observed behavior and heard insults that were cringe-worthy. Socially Klaus displayed an arrogance only mildly veiled as humor. "Too bad there aren't more Germans around here. Things would be done right, rather than half-assed," he'd said frequently, followed by a laugh. And we'd had more than a few fights because of his impatience with me, some embarrassingly when other people were around. He could be downright obnoxious at a restaurant. I wanted Marilyn's approval, so I downplayed it.

"Marilyn, I appreciate your concern. I know Klaus seems abrasive sometimes. You know his life hasn't been an especially easy one. He's worked so hard to even get here and get an education. I know you see him as demanding, even rude, but he's so . . ."

My voice trailed off as I searched for the right words. Just then, I heard my name called from downstairs. Klaus provided impatience on queue.

"Look, Marilyn, I'll talk with him. I'm sure I can make him understand how he comes across. I think he'll listen to me and, you know, change, learn to go a little easier on people."

Although she didn't reply, her face clearly showed how unlikely she considered that change. "Go on," she said, "we'll talk some more later."

As Klaus and I walked out the front door and down the steps of the Kappa House, I said, "Klaus, that entire scene *was* a big deal."

"Oh, come on. I'm sorry." And beneath a layer of baffled irritation was a brief I'm sorry kind of look. We walked toward the car with silence between us until he said, "Hey, I got two tickets for that concert tonight."

I lifted my head for the first time and really looked at him. "I thought the concert was sold out."

"I have my ways." A smiled crossed his lips. "No stupid movie for you tonight. And I almost forgot—I brought you something." He hurried ahead, opened the car door, and with a flourish, presented me with a single red rose with a spray of baby's breath, wrapped in a sheet of white tissue paper.

I melted. "Oh, Klaus. Thank you."

As I settled into the seat, I felt a tiny stab as one of the rose's thorns pierced my index finger. I said nothing. It wasn't a serious injury. I convinced myself it was like our relationship and the issues we had. They weren't big deals, were they? We always made up and inched our way forward. Yes, admittedly Klaus could be harsh, but he also knew how to make me feel like a queen.

In the driver's seat, he smiled at me as the car started with a momentary roar. I smiled back and quickly brushed away the drop of blood, because queens didn't worry about little wounds like that.

NINE

Day 9

Nine days had passed since the kidnapping. Nine long days filled with calls: numerous calls to and from Dennis, my attorney, him checking on us and us wanting to know if the various authorities—any of the authorities—were willing or able to help; calls from family members and friends wanting to know what they could do, especially Mother, who had reached out to her attorney trying to work things from her end. She called whether or not there was news. With all the activity during those days, with all the what-ifs, it seemed all we were doing was waiting. Waiting on authorities, waiting on the attorney. Waiting.

Each time the phone rang, my body reacted with a start. After a flash of hope, followed by a stab of nameless dread, I picked up the receiver as if I were grasping a sleeping cobra and said, "Hello?" I glanced at the kitchen clock: 1:30 p.m. I was relieved the caller couldn't see my afternoon pajama-attire. I wished Karen were still there fielding calls as she had done for the first few days after Klaus absconded with the kids.

"Jeannie, I have news this time. I have a telegram from Fredi."

Mom's voice was steady, with a don't-get-too-excited sort of tone. She had called Dr. Bob at his Walkerton, Indiana lake house, and after talking with him, decided she couldn't count on or wait for his direction. As Ty and Megan's grandmother, she wasn't waiting for anyone's approval. She'd sent Fredi a telegram.

IMPERATIVE YOU ANSWER – SICK AT HEART ABOUT KLAUS
AND MY GRANDCHILDREN – HAVE YOU HEARD OF OR KNOW
OF THEIR WHEREABOUTS? USE NITE LETTER TO ANSWER –
DEEPLY TROUBLED – MARY JANE BAKER

Fredi. Klaus's oldest brother, the one with whom I'd felt the closest connection, responded, breaking his silence.

My heart began pounding, but I offered an equally calm reply, even as I steadied myself by abruptly sitting on the couch. "Okay, Mom. What does it say?"

"'KLAUS ANNOUNCED TRIP VIA CANADA TODAY – NOT ARRIVED – AM UPSET – WILL SEND MESSAGE.' It's signed Alfred Manthey." The good news is it's dated August third, mere days after I wrote. A quick response, honey."

Klaus announced trip today? Not arrived. Am upset? It made no sense. Klaus's letter to me indicated he and his brother had made all the arrangements, and we should communicate through correspondence with the brother. So why did Fredi sound surprised and upset? Fredi liked me, and he'd seemed kind, like a man you could count on, a solid man who would be straight.

My chest tightened as I pondered the words. Nine days after Klaus had stolen my children, living with the pain of missing them was harder than anything I'd ever done or ever imagined doing. "Doing" wasn't the right word though; I wasn't actually "doing" anything except waiting. I walked through days like a sleepwalker, probably because sleep was so elusive.

Haywood tried comforting me when he wasn't attempting distraction tactics. When he occasionally succeeded, both comfort and distraction felt like disloyalty to my kids, who were God only knew where, alone with a father who, for all his talk of love and self-sacrifice, had upended them from the only life they'd ever known.

"Jeannie, are you there?"

"Yes, Mom, I'm here. I'm thinking," I said. "You know, Fredi might be covering up for Klaus, but I can't believe that. I think Fredi really doesn't know."

"It's possible," she said. "Maybe Klaus realizes Fredi's loyalty might be divided. Could be Klaus is keeping his location secret from Fredi, perhaps getting settled somewhere before taking anyone into his confidence."

"Or maybe they never left Canada." My voice quavered. It was hard thinking about Ty and Megan stuck somewhere in a different country, different surroundings, without their toys, their clothes. Without me. But that was better than reading every newspaper I could lay my hands on, looking for any report of a sinking passenger ship crossing the Atlantic.

There was a lot of cold, empty ocean between Canada and Germany. Megan hated cold water; she would squeal and cling to me, even at Dr. Bob and Lois's lake house. I'd wrap my arms around her and say, "It's okay, sweetheart," and she would look at me, so trusting, so sure I'd keep her safe.

A sob escaped me. "Mom, I—"

"I know, sweetheart," she murmured. Then a touch of steel came into her voice. "We're finding them and bringing them back, you know, even if we have to go get them ourselves."

My mother. Made of steel *and* filled with love. I can't ever remember her *not* caring for me. One childhood memory after another surfaced: letting me be her little sidekick at the neighborhood ladies' coffee klatches, teaching the four-year-old me how you use bobby pins to curl your hair, and snuggling with me in the front seat of the car cruising toward Chinatown with Dad and their friends. She'd always been there for me, radiating love, grace, and humor, ready with the undivided attention that was so hard for either of us to get from my father.

I remembered a long-ago summer day on vacation at Michigan's

Corey Lake, when Dad squinted at her over dinner and asked, "Did you change your hair?"

She sat there, cool as the flip side of a pillow, and said, "Yes. I wanted something a little different."

She'd never have admitted to Dad that her impromptu bangs resulted from leaning in too close over her cigarette lighter while fishing from her rowboat in a hidden cove on the lake.

My father pretended he didn't know that she sometimes smoked; she pretended not to know about Dad's dalliances here and there. And their arrangement had worked—until it didn't.

Now, my mother, a divorcee since 1972 and living in a Florida condo, had aimed her full laser-focused attention at getting her grandbabies back. Assuming Klaus would need passports for the kids before taking them to Germany, Mom contacted a local Florida lawyer who informed her that although we couldn't revoke the children's passports, applying for new ones was a possibility. She'd called me a few days before with an announcement: child stealing was now a felony in Florida and maybe it might be worth checking Indiana's laws for any revisions; involving the court at this point might make sense.

None of this would do any good though until we figured out where Klaus and the children were.

Another sob rose in my throat. "Mom, from what I understand, Indiana's laws are in a state of flux. And anyway, I should have seen this coming. I completely failed at protecting my kids. Maybe they're better off without me."

"Don't say that." She sounded adamant. "Don't you even think that! The children belong with you. And as far as I'm concerned, Klaus by all actions has given up any claim to call himself a loving father. We'll get them back—just the way I got you back when you disappeared."

That memory made me smile and mentally pay tribute to the

strong and loving stock I came from. She'd lost me for all of thirty minutes one morning when I, a brave four-year-old, without telling her, gallivanted off with a five-year-old girlfriend headed for school. Even when Mom arrived at the school at the behest of the kindergarten teacher, she planted kisses all over my face with great relief, and listened intently to my exciting tales about school as we walked home hand in hand. Only then did she caution me to check with her first before leaving the house unannounced again.

"Jeannie," Mom's voice on the phone sounded so close, as if she were down the street rather than a thousand miles away in Florida, "when you're a mother, or a grandmother, you do whatever is necessary to get your children back and keep them safe. You do whatever it takes."

I felt a little better.

"In fact, I'm contacting Sylvia about this," she said.

Sylvia. My mother's department store co-worker and longtime friend . . . and another psychic. I'd met her briefly on a visit a year or two before. Her hair was a mystery because she always wore wigs—and a bit too much lipstick. She was probably fifty-something yet looked older, as if she'd been through too many packs of cigarettes, too many martinis. Sylvia loved the bar scene and the boyfriends.

"Mom, I like Sylvia. I just don't know how much I trust her abilities, what with her being an alcoholic and all."

"I know, honey. I felt the same way at first before she made a believer out of me. She has a real gift, Jeannie. She cares and worries about the people she helps. I would imagine her gift is a two-edged sword, and she may not cope well under the weight of the cases she deals with. Regardless, because of the accuracy of her visions, the Broward County Sheriff's Department consults with her. They've called her several times to—well, she's helped them . . . find people."

From the way her voice trailed off, I could only imagine what condition those people had been in when the officers found them.

And after the failed outcome of my first contact with a psychic within days after the kidnapping, I wasn't excited about trying another one. However, Sylvia, bless her psychic heart, had helped Mom finally leave my straying father, so I felt an obligation to reach out. Besides, it behooved me not to overlook any possibility of help.

"Okay, Mom," I said. "Whatever you think."

I felt so torn. While I wanted to discount any clairvoyant's predictions, alcohol-induced or otherwise, especially after the dead-end disturbing contact with Indianapolis's popular Rev. Verner, I also desperately wanted someone to help. *Please, God, let that person be Sylvia.*

ten

And They Wed

1966–1967, Gary, IN, and West Germany

A lone with my father in the family's comfortable living room, Klaus said, "John, may I speak with you?" It was December 24, 1966.

If memory serves me right, snow covered the ground that night and painted a more favorable picture of Gary, Indiana, than the usual one with the ground covered in a thin layer of gray soot emanating from the town's north-end steel mills. A tall Christmas tree with colored lights, ageless ornaments, and silver tinsel graced our modest home's large living room window. The logs crackled behind the fireplace screen. I could just imagine the scene with my father as described by Klaus after the fact: Klaus, formal, respectful, ardent. My father, taking a seat in his favorite living room recliner, waiting.

"I wanted to thank you for your nice response to my letter asking for your daughter's hand in marriage. It meant a lot to me. So, Christmas Eve is here, and well, I'd like to propose to Jeannie tonight after dinner." Klaus took a deep breath. "So, sir, if you've changed your mind, now's the time to tell me," and enjoyed a laugh with his future father-in-law.

Dad was as hooked as I was.

Over the past year, we had shared holidays with Mom and Dad at our family home in Gary, Indiana's steel mill capital. The well-mannered Klaus I had fallen in love with charmed my parents as well. He helped Mom around the house, changing light bulbs or repairing the loose hinge on the back door, always with a smile.

While the men conferred, Mom and I moved around the kitchen, putting away the groceries Klaus had carried from the car. Though we didn't talk about it while we prepared dinner, we both had some idea of the living room conversation taking place.

As I watched Mom wedge the Christmas turkey onto the crowded lower shelf of the fridge, awaiting its late evening placement into the family's famous turkey roaster, I pondered her marriage to my dad, wondering what it was like. I cannot recall a single time Mom and Dad fought or even had cross words. No alcohol issues. Yet with his insurance work schedule, music gigs, and golf games, which I assumed was most every family's routine, how could he have been there for Mom? Did she feel loved and cared for? I wouldn't have known because she never complained. Growing up, I had wanted attention from Dad that wasn't mine to have until my late teens when we enjoyed those music gigs together. Mom rarely went. Was my marriage to be like theirs?

How did my dad prepare me for life with men? He didn't. Did any father of that era? I dated some real losers during high school and, though I noted my father's disapproving looks, when I'd hit my early rebellious teens, I didn't care. I suppose it was the "get attention any way you can" mentality at that point. He didn't like dealing with such issues—not even the time I'd been out with a ne'er-do-well boy and my whereabouts were unknown. When I arrived home way past curfew, an angry dad greeted me in the living room, raised his arm to backhand me and said, "I ought to . . ." but he didn't. Corporal punishment wasn't his thing, even when frustrated.

Turkey safely stowed, Mom closed the fridge door and faced me. Our eyes met for a long moment, woman to woman. She smiled. I could see her sole focus was now on me; her baby was getting married.

I'd noticed how she glowed while watching Klaus and me, believing that this Older Man would take care of me and make me happy. Her perceived and unspoken feelings of disappointment in my father seemed assuaged by my chance at happiness with Klaus.

I wondered how my mother, voted the prettiest girl in her class, had felt when she met my dad—voted most handsome boy in his class—back in 1933, four years into the Great Depression. Dad, almost five years her senior, swept her off her feet as the story goes. Did the excitement and charm of an older man play into their courtship and ultimate 1935 marriage when she was a mere nineteen? By the time I came along in 1947 as the unexpected third and last, Dad, not wanting another child, chose work (and fun) over me: an insurance agency vice president during the week and a self-taught piano-playing leader of a jazz combo on the weekends. As I was to find out later, the need and affection for other women rivaled his love of music. Dad passed on that love of music to me, for which I was grateful. His penchant for other women, however, did not elicit gratitude from my mother. During my childhood, she never spoke about my father's transgressions and unfaithfulness. They would remain a secret until after I left home and met and married Klaus.

Klaus had shared some of my dad's thoughts and advice from their recent engagement correspondence, which, in hindsight, signaled serious issues in my parents' marriage. Dad wrote, "I've so many things to offer in the hope you two can find true happiness together. Certain basic elements must exist: love, kindness, understanding, and the ability of maintaining honesty and communication with one another. The need, too, of finding interests which lend to mutual compatibility so you share your living with each other. Unfortunately, our present standards usually require so much of the man's time seeking a comfortable living that he is soon engulfed within himself. The wife is often wrapped up in the many problems of maintaining the household and can easily find her time so occupied that the team is somewhat pulling towards a goal, but also losing the close ties."

Dad's advice revealed an inherent sadness. Though it would be years before Mom shared information about Dad's transgressions, she and Dad seemed to have lost their "close ties" and had grown apart, resulting in his seeking relationships outside the marriage.

What Dad referenced in his letter would not happen to us, I thought. Klaus was not like my father, in all the right ways, and we could fix anything needing change. We wouldn't grow apart. I'd be a good wife, a helpful wife, and besides, his tenderness and maturity outweighed any misconstrued arrogance and gruffness.

The Christmas tree provided the perfect backdrop for a starry night Christmas Eve marriage proposal. Down on one knee, Klaus proposed admirably according to old world custom. After my "yes" he slipped the ArtCarved diamond ring on my finger and proudly kissed me, though apparently uncomfortable with my parents watching. Happy jitters, I was sure. He knew he was marrying into a family of huggers. After the proposal and Christmas Eve celebration, Dad said, "Nick, you're a smart, stable, self-confident guy. I like that, and I'm glad you two have found each other." He smiled at me and added, "Honey, I'm so happy for both of you."

Klaus, holding me close, reached over, shook my Dad's hand, and said, "Me, too, sir."

In the summer of 1967, at the age of twenty, I became his bride. The local paper's wedding announcement reflected the times: the picture identified me as Mrs. Klaus Manthey, followed by a write-up about him. I was the daughter of "Mr. and Mrs. John H. Baker," with only one reference to my given name, and no reference to my mother by hers. I skimmed the text, missing the patriarchal overtones, for all I really noticed was the photo of the oh-so-lovely gown.

Caught up in the excitement, Nicky and I had found little to disagree about during the actual planning. We were both from Protestant backgrounds and, although not a churchgoer, he agreed we should hold the wedding at my family's church. Our choices for matron of honor and best man: my sister, Joanne, and Klaus's commanding officer, Bob Kugelman. Joanne's husband Mark and our brother Jim were also members of the wedding party, making it a family affair. Karen, now inextricably woven into the fabric of my life, was chief bridesmaid and helped with all the details, lightening our planning load.

Ours was a traditional wedding and the kind many girls in the 1960s dreamed of—elegant gown with a lengthy train, large sanctuary, dramatically long aisle, with a full dinner reception for several hundred people. Ladies wore gloves and hats during the ceremony, regardless of July's heat. My sorority sisters were there *en masse* as loving well-wishers, fingers crossed.

Laughing, Klaus and I brushed rice off each other in the backseat of our bright red Pontiac Catalina as Jim drove us to my parents' house after the reception. Tin cans tied on the bumper rattled as we kissed and counted money all the way home, cash gifted mostly from friends on the dancefloor who were part of Gary's large Polish population. Polish immigrants began settling in the Chicago area in the mid-1800s and spread southward into Indiana, including Gary when newly built in the early 1900s. Poles had a tradition, unknown to my family, of buying dances with the bride at the reception, so I had danced until my feet ached. We had a wedding night reservation at a five-star Chicago hotel followed by a flight to Frankfurt, West Germany the next day, and the unexpected $1500 would definitely enhance our European honeymoon.

My big brother, by then twenty-eight and married for seven years with three kids, stole the last dance. "Are you happy, Sis?"

Jim's words caught me off guard. Or maybe it was the wistful look on my brother's face, a look that said he knew something I didn't.

"I am, Jim, though my feet might disagree," I laughed.

"Nick seems like a good guy. You love him?"

When I nodded assurance, Jim said, "Well, good. Then I'm happy for you."

I could tell there was more. Jim waited until the music stopped and spoke carefully. "Just remember you can always count on your big brother. I'll always be there for you, okay?" Jim hugged me, escorted me across the dancefloor to Klaus, and shook his hand. "You're a lucky man, Nick. Take care of my little sister, you hear?"

Klaus chuckled as he put an arm around my waist and kissed my hand. "No worries, Jim. She's mine now and I know what I have."

I peered over Klaus's shoulder, as he neatly signed the guest register as "Mr. and Mrs. Klaus Manthey." He beamed, and I blushed as the front desk agent who handed him the room key said, "Congratulations, Mr. and Mrs. Manthey. Have a good evening."

Klaus took my hand, and we shared a soft chuckle as we took the elevator to our twelfth-floor suite. With the door locked behind us, the noise and activity of the day fell away as two virgins stood holding hands, silently studying the glittering skyline of Chicago outside the expansive floor-to-ceiling windows.

I giddily took over the bathroom, closing the door, changing from my street clothes into an ivory peignoir, smoothing my hair and brushing my teeth before taking one last mirror check and re-entering the bridal suite.

Klaus stared at me speechless while stumbling toward the bathroom. I muffled a giggle as I heard him moving around, running water, clearing his throat.

The strap of my nightgown slipped off my shoulder as I situated myself against the bed's pillows, waiting, until my husband, clad in white boxer shorts, opened the bathroom door and walked with anticipation to where I lay.

Holding champagne glasses, we laughed and toasted each other several times, hoping to relax. The chilled bubbly worked its magic. Klaus wiped a tear from his eye, kissed me gently, and said, "I love you, Jeannie. I want this to be perfect for you. You've made me the happiest man on the planet."

Smiling, I let myself go and we kissed passionately. I was married and ready for bliss.

"Jeannie, we're late. What takes you so long?" Klaus said, irritated yet again.

"Fixing my hair and nails and doing my makeup takes time," I pouted. "You don't give me enough lead time. I want to look nice for you tonight at the nightclub."

Good sex notwithstanding, seventy-two hours after our transatlantic flight, I found the honeymoon bliss intermittent at best, while simultaneously awestruck by the beauty of the family's West German homeland. The tiny village of Altenbögge-Bönen presented a world so different from my Midwest landscape. I did my best to make Klaus proud as he presented me to a family he hadn't seen in five years, but as the group relaxed and laughed with each other, he seemed increasingly tense and short-fused with me.

I'd been nervous about meeting the widowed matriarch, the seven grown siblings, and their families. Although stereotypically Northern German in their lack of open affection, their sincere smiles and good nature put me at ease. On the night after our arrival, Fredi, oldest of the eight, held a celebration for us at their home. Klaus acted as interpreter, speaking German, then translating for my benefit. I would respond, and he'd reverse translate. When they'd tell a joke or a funny story, they'd all laugh, then grow quiet while Klaus shared the moment with me in English. When I laughed, they'd all laugh again. Klaus was talking so fast he became confused and spoke German to me and English to them.

The more wine we drank, the funnier things became. At the end of the evening, sister Ulla surprised me with a hug as she left and said, "*Gut gemacht, Bruder!*" (well done)

In my heady state, I thought the joy of the moment would continue forever.

It was the wine.

Early one overcast day, when I asked if we could spend some time touring France, Klaus had scoffed at the idea, ultimately relenting and agreeing we could lunch there. "The French are dirty, self-centered, and obnoxious," my tactful husband said. Several hours later we arrived at a little French border town, the name of which I couldn't pronounce, had coq au vin, which he pronounced over-salted, and returned to *Mutti's* house the same afternoon while Klaus continued denouncing the French, their food, and their weather.

"Hey, why don't we go nightclubbing tonight?" he suggested later, sounding more upbeat.

I jumped at the idea. I could wear the little black cocktail dress I'd bought in anticipation of a night on the town. After the disastrous French excursion, spending the evening at a German nightclub sounded like a brilliant plan.

However, taking as long as I did to primp, redo my hair, and change clothes was like adding more salt to the French lunch. "Well, don't you want me to look nice?" I repeated.

"This is getting ridiculous, Jeannie. You look fine." Klaus was pacing the little bedroom again and spoke without even looking at me. Finished at last and happy with how my new little dress fit, I slipped on my heels and picked up my purse, ready for a magical evening.

We drove to a club less than an hour outside the village. The building looked a little shabby on the outside; perhaps that was un-derstandable—the inside should be important, not the exterior lit by the fading daylight when we arrived. Inside, my eyes momentarily had trouble adjusting to the smoke-filled darkness. As we sat down at a small table, I noted the stage centered in the dimly lit room and squinted. Was that a bed? Puzzled, I looked at Klaus, who was intent on studying the menu and didn't see my questioning gaze.

I didn't know what to say, or expect. He ordered a bottle of wine, unusual for him. Pretending everything was fine, I sipped my first glass and was glad when the food arrived. We were halfway through our schnitzel and *rotkohl* (German red cabbage), when the show began.

A lone woman emerged from the darkness stage left and sat on the edge of the bed. A quartet of jazz musicians in a nearby corner played as she unbuttoned her feathered vintage robe and kicked off her matching feathered mules.

By the time she dropped the outer garment and slowly wriggled out of a sheer silk nightgown, I'd pushed my plate aside and instead gulped the wine my new husband poured. As I sat wide-eyed, embar-rassed and uncomfortable, I thought *this is a sex show, not a night-club routine.*

The thirty-something performer—the stripper—had noticeable bleached-blonde hair and an even more noticeable red birthmark on the inside of her left thigh. At a loss, I drained each glass Klaus filled for me. Usually not a heavy drinker, on this night he was different. I watched him watch the performance with those blue eyes glued to the stage. More wine. *Why was I brought here? We're on our honey-moon. Who is this guy? A guy who had never dated and was a virgin decides a live sex show is the perfect entertainment venue for his new bride?*

He sat staring, speaking only when ordering a second bottle of wine as the woman onstage draped her pink panties over the wooden bedpost. His gaze never left the stage other than when refilling my glass. I didn't speak; I just kept drinking what he poured for me and inhaled the smoky air.

When we finally left the club, the night air hit me. No sooner had we had reached the parking lot before I began retching and vomiting. By the time we got home, room-spins had taken hold.

I refused his offer to unzip me. Shutting myself in the bathroom, I struggled out of the new cocktail dress on my own and kicked the sweet thing to the cold tile. I staggered back to the bedroom, curled up on my side of the bed, as close to the edge as I could without falling off, and slid into a woozy sleep.

The next day was a nauseated blur.

"Can I get you anything?" Klaus said, coming into the bedroom to check on me mid-morning.

"No. Well, maybe some coffee," I said, too miserable to deal with the night before.

"I'm sorry you feel bad." He sat down on the bed and handed me a cup of let's-call-a-truce, adding softly, "I know you're upset with me. We'll do better from here, okay?"

He wrapped both arms around me. Another opportunity to make up and inch our way forward. I relented. "Okay," I said. "Okay."

Maybe married life would smooth things out once we got Stateside. I could hope.

ELEVEN

Day 21

August 16, 1977
Indianapolis and Nashville, IN

S itting at my desk at Indiana Bell, unable to concentrate, my head filled with memories of my son.

I rocked, feeling the sway of the rocking chair as I sat holding my four-year-old son chest-to-chest, Ty's jammy-footed legs draped down each side of mine so he could sleep. It was dark, long past midnight, and the doctor's office wouldn't open until morning. Until we got the penicillin that would clear an unrelenting ear infection, sitting upright was the only thing that calmed and eased his body. Lying flat caused Ty to cry in excruciating pain. And his pain was mine, so I rocked and held my child close.

We would sit like this until the sun came up.

He moaned and shifted, saying, "Mommy . . ." We nestled closer as tears rolled down my cheeks.

"Mommy . . ."

"Jeannie. Jeannie?"

I blinked and looked up. Afternoon sunlight flooded my office. Somewhere, a phone was ringing. Neil, a nice-old-guy and Nashville, Indiana native with whom I carpooled to Indianapolis, was standing awkwardly by my desk. Neil cleared his throat as he nervously jangled his pocketed car keys and said, "Your boss called me, thought it might be best if I took you home early. He said, uh, you weren't feeling well today."

I touched my dampened cheeks and closed my eyes to the blinding August sunlight, with one lone thought in my head: my children were gone. Gone for twenty-one days, an unimaginable blackout of five hundred and four hours. "Not feeling well" was an understatement. Like Ty's ear pain, the search was excruciating. Each idea, each attempt to find them proved futile—one dead-end after another. My attorney kept pushing the district attorney for warrants with no results. Three weeks, and with all we'd tried, Ty and Megan's whereabouts remained a mystery. The odds were against me.

Dazed, I stood obediently and gathered my things. Neil escorted me down the elevator, helped me into the car and closed the door. My head rested against the passenger-side window as we drove over city streets, onto the state highway, then an hour south to Brown County's Nashville where our "new" home was. The Indianapolis apartment had become unbearable. Standing night after night in the doorway of the kids' empty room and staring at their abandoned toys had just been too hard. Within a few weeks after the kidnapping, Haywood and I packed our belongings and moved into the semi-historic rental house in Nashville where our wedding took place. Regardless of the circumstances, Grandma Lee, Haywood's surrogate grandmother, delighted in having us as her next-door neighbors.

Neil dropped me off, and once inside, I kicked off my shoes and curled up in a ball on the sofa, numb and rocking. The memory of rocking my son wouldn't go away. I silently swayed alone, thinking about and missing my boy. If he needed me now, I could offer no comfort, and there was certainly none for me. With knees pulled under my chin, I rocked until the room grew dark and Haywood came home.

"Hey, honey," he snuggled close. "You won't believe what I just heard on the news on my way home. Elvis died. This will devastate my sister. She was such a fan. Hard to believe the king of rock 'n' roll is gone." When I didn't respond, he said, "Honey? Did you hear me?"

"No. Sorry. What did you say?"

Noting my beyond-oblivion stare, Haywood saved the news for later. Instead, he kissed my forehead and whispered, "I said I missed you. How was your day?"

I relayed the information about my boss calling Neil and Neil retrieving me early. "I just couldn't keep it together." My voice trembled. "I think about the kids when I should focus on updating the office manuals. And then, I go over and over things in my mind, wondering what else we could do. With all we've done, all the calls, all that the attorney is trying, nothing is moving us any closer. I feel so helpless, so damn helpless. Haywood, what if we never find them?"

He handed me several tissues and pulled me close. Being wrapped in his arms somehow helped, as if his strong and fearless traits were transferrable. Haywood believed we would find Ty and Megan. When I had said maybe it was a mistake for us to get married and maybe I should go back with Klaus, Haywood scoffed. "The only mistake was you marrying Klaus."

When I married Klaus, I had been so sure.

twelve

Newlyweds

1968, Indianapolis, IN

S itting at our wobbly kitchen table, I looked at the list I'd written on neat little note cards. The first item, "dinner," was well under-way. A big chuck roast had already been cooking for ninety minutes. Our upstairs neighbor, married for nearly two years, had shown me her secret recipe. I'd watched her slather the beef with butter, garlic, salt, and pepper, then pour a cup of coffee over the whole thing before she foil-sealed and baked said roast at 300 degrees for several hours.

My trial run a week or two before had been a success. Klaus had taken that first bite cautiously, chewed, and looked at me with barely concealed surprise.

"*Lecker,*" he'd announced. For him to comment at all was note-worthy, much less offer such high praise by naming the meat delicious. "Very tender, almost like *Sauerbraten.*"

I had glowed. Cooking had never been a priority for my mother, so my meal prep training suffered. But she sure could bake: pies, cakes, cookies, though that skill will only get you so far. Klaus ate almost any-thing I made, although when I placed another plate of macaroni and cheese—the bright orange stuff that came from the little blue box—on the dinner table, his face always fell, and I suspected he was thinking of *Mutti.* Though I knew she had raised eight children on her own dur-ing a bleak post-war landscape of continuous shortages, I pictured her feeding her brood an endless succession of gourmet delights and rib-sticking entrees.

I also told myself she hadn't been a student at the time. Since I'd transferred to the IU Indianapolis campus, my days were a whirl of classes, chores, and cooking. Though our garden (aka basement) apartment was small, there was always something that needed to be swept, scrubbed, or peeled. There was always an exam approaching, a paper due, groceries to buy, or Klaus's unironed shirts calling me.

Klaus periodically helped, but job duties at Western Electric as a systems analyst were demanding. Arriving home, he loosened his tie, neatly closeted his dress shoes, and settled into an easy chair with a deep grunt and obvious frustration. The boss hadn't elicited the foul mood. The fault lay, according to Klaus, with several coworkers who seemed especially difficult, and Klaus had to make up for their incompetence. Though I winced at his derogatory descriptive language, I imagined he'd had limited interaction with people from different backgrounds. The American workplace was a multi-cultural environment. He would adjust, I'd think. And for the moment, I needed to be supportive; he was working his way up the ladder, after all.

The second item under "dinner" on my list was potatoes, now washed, peeled, and ready for boiling and mashing. I also had a large can of green beans on the counter, all set for warming.

"Dessert" was last on the list, and I was excited. I'd never made a strawberry pie before and it sounded wonderful, and so easy: fill a prepared pie crust with a mixture of strawberries, sugar, cornstarch, and water. I bought frozen pie shells as a timesaver rather than rolling out the dough.

Klaus, I imagined, would be pleased, and proud of me for trying something new with company coming. I had met Midge Roof in my lit class. After we had lunch together a few times, we'd become fast friends, so I'd invited her and her husband over for dinner. John Roof, an Episcopal priest, sounded like a wonderful man and I hoped he and Klaus would hit it off.

When Klaus and I had first met, I knew he had few male friends. Having another couple in our lives would help. Klaus was picky about who we associated with, which, I told myself, was understandable, given that work as a systems analyst required one to deal with different people all day long. I still cringed though when recalling our awkward dinner with Mr. and Mrs. Ming, who ran a local flower shop. Even knowing Klaus's negative feelings about cultural diversity, saying that evening had not gone well was an understatement. Tonight's dinner guests would turn the tide.

With dinner underway, I looked over the rest of my list. My German class midterm was on the horizon, and I had massive amounts of preparation hanging over my head. Clearly, none of that would be possible this evening. I'd catch up over the weekend, unless Klaus insisted on picking up more German classic movies at a local video rental store on Saturday.

Sighing, I rolled my shoulders up and down a few times, easing the tension. Sometimes, when I sat quietly like this, I missed life on Bloomington's campus. There were always so many interesting people to talk with, so much going on. Now, as a married woman living in Indianapolis, things were different, and as I hurried down IU's Indianapolis extension's hallowed halls, I could only glance at the local posters for sit-ins, love-ins, and protests against our escalating Vietnam involvement. I was usually running for a bus, or thinking about dinner responsibilities, and besides, I knew Klaus would nix attending anything like that, anyway.

While college had been wonderful, the whole point was to get smart, worldly—*and*, of course, find myself a husband. With my central marital mission accomplished, finishing my degree at the extension campus was just the icing on the cake.

I looked at the clock on the kitchen wall. Klaus, my handsome blue-eyed husband, would walk through the door anytime now. He'd smell dinner cooking and gather me in his arms, just like when we were dating. Maybe he'd whisper he wished we didn't have company coming and suggest that we take a little "pause" before they arrived at seven.

It was an intriguing idea, a fantasy though, one I doubted would happen given Klaus's dislike for displays of affection as a married couple. It baffled me. Wasn't a happy marriage based on such affection? A significant reason a girl married? Boys, based on Klaus's actions, were obligated to court and woo, and then their work was done. An emotionally withdrawn stand-in seemed to have replaced the attentive man I fell in love with. My family had always been openly affectionate; we were huggers. Just a cultural difference? Or was the honeymoon literally over, with married life lacking any passion? Maybe great cooking would inspire some affection.

The instructions I'd scribbled on an index card seemed incomplete though. Studying the recipe again, I pondered things for a minute and guessed my way through the timing dilemma. Maybe half an hour? At 350 degrees? I just didn't want to be fussing with the dessert when our guests arrived.

As I surveyed the pie, proud of how pretty it was with the bright red strawberries piled high—and not even baked yet—Klaus walked in the door. "Hmm. The roast smells good," he said, and gave me a peck on the cheek before heading to the bedroom to change. So much for the gathering-me-in-his-arms scenario. I sighed. However, making him happy remained important and, after an ideal dinner, I was sure there was still hope for a late evening rendezvous.

Midge and John made the evening easy with upbeat conversation and the good reverend's great sense of humor. Klaus was actually enjoying himself until dessert, which proved inedible. Who knew the pie was not meant to be baked? Our company acted like it was no big deal, saying they were beyond full. After they left, Klaus railed, "I thought you had a recipe, for God's sake. It was a simple pie. Experimenting on company made us look bad, you know. Why would you do that?"

I had so much to learn. I wondered how Elizabeth Taylor and Richard Burton were getting along. Had I confused the big screen with real life? My decisions seemed to rely on outward appearances: my parents' supposedly happy marriage; Klaus's supposed worldliness and maturity. There was so much I hadn't considered. The differences in our attitudes, worldviews, and upbringing were becoming increasingly apparent.

THIRTEEN

Day 26

August 21, 1977, Nashville, IN

I stared out the open kitchen window at the field behind our country house and felt the comforting Brown County fresh air on my skin. Sunday, August 21, my sister's forty-first birthday. I wished I were in Florida celebrating with her and Mom, though any celebration right now felt wrong. I wished my mom and my sister weren't so far away. Talking long distance was expensive. At least, on this Sunday afternoon, Nashville, Indiana afforded me the peace and quiet of provincial living.

Maybe too much quiet; thoughts about the mess I'd made of my life filled my head.

If Mom and Joanne were close by, they wouldn't allow me to spend so much time with my neurotic thoughts, going over the ordeal, wondering what I could have done differently, wondering if this was all my fault. I'd been so lost in the dream when I married Klaus. I had made so many mistakes. *If only* became my afternoon mantra—if only Klaus and I had talked through our differences, if only I hadn't been so starry-eyed, if only I had sought counseling early on, if only I'd been stronger, been smarter, been a better wife. Over the nine-year marriage, I had become so removed from my husband that what I had sought was happiness elsewhere. If we had been happy, if we had at least talked, maybe . . . I don't know. I just wished things had been different.

I sighed and finished reading Saturday's mail—a cheery letter

from Joanne and a note from a dear friend who had sent prayers saying, "It is wisdom I seek now trying to pen you a note; you, precious
and undeserving of such injustice."

Was I undeserving of such injustice? I wasn't always sure.

Picking up my mug of coffee from the kitchen counter and the
recent July/August issue of *Woman's World* magazine another friend
had given me, I traipsed through the old country house, settling in
the rocking chair awaiting me on the screened-in front porch.

Parents As Kidnappers by Alan D. Haas. I sipped and read.

"Nowhere in the U.S. is there a legal statute that makes it a crime
to kidnap one's own children. No local, state or federal agency exists
to enforce the legal custody or visitation rights of mothers and fathers. For divorced parents, it is always 'open season' on children.
There is a strong feeling in the judiciary that these are primarily domestic squabbles and should be looked upon as such," commented an
assistant United States attorney.

So, if Klaus had left the state with my car, that would be a crime.
Since he took the children, the law considered it merely a "domestic
squabble." The current legal climate fostered "court—or forum—
shopping" as well. Parents with physical possession of a child could
choose the court they felt would hear their case and more likely provide a favorable judgment. Those parents had a legal incentive to
abduct their children.

I cringed as I read, "The absconding parent almost always
crosses state lines, frequently assumes a new identity, and renders
the victimized parent legally without recourse since the courts are
unwilling to intervene. . . . The latter must either conduct a long
search or hire private detectives at great cost, frequently to no avail.
Tugged back and forth in a child-custody battle, such children frequently suffer serious psychic and emotional scars, victimized by
the escalating bitterness of the parents. Clearly no one comes out
ahead in such cases."

In the three-and-a-half weeks since the kidnapping, I had experienced the hands-off attitude of the local police, sheriff's department, state police, FBI, and the courts. From the night we realized Klaus had abducted the children, the reactions of the local police officer and young deputy from the sheriff's office foreshadowed what lay ahead. Since the children were with their father, there was no basis for issuing any warrants. As the deputy had explained, Klaus had broken no law.

In the ensuing days, Dennis, my attorney, had broken the bad news to us that the FBI would not step into a civil matter, and state warrants naming a parent as kidnapper under these circumstances were all but unheard of in 1977's Indiana legal climate.

That attitude also meant not only would I have to search for and find the children myself, I could also plan on spending a small fortune. The 1934 Lindbergh Law was of no help because its definition of kidnapping specifically excluded the parents of children, and a federal bill to amend that law was gathering dust in the House of Representatives. Although ten states had adopted the Uniform Child Custody Act of 1968, Indiana was not one of them, and the law became effective only upon adoption by state legislatures. Haas also pointed out the Uniform Child Custody Act only prevents a parent from seeking custody in a state which had adopted the Act; it does little to discourage child snatching.

Too bad Indiana wasn't following California's lead, where they had not only adopted the Uniform Child Custody Act, they had passed the toughest anti-child-snatching legislation, a law that made it a felony, with a max of four years imprisonment, to hold or hide a child in that state in violation of a custody order. They didn't make it a crime to kidnap one's own child, but they were headed in the right direction. Unfortunately, it didn't affect my situation.

If state and federal laws were still so arbitrary, so skewed, and favored the abductor, I could only imagine what I'd find on the international front. We were, after all, dealing with ". . . international wrongful removal and retention of children." Yet as far as I could tell, a 1961 international treaty on the books from the Hague's Protection of Minors Convention regarding child abduction lacked any enforcement provisions. A German court, once Klaus took up "habitual residence" there, could grant him custody of the children and allow him permanent residence. Even though this was an "interpretation loophole" and not the intent of the treaty, no one had fixed it.

That the US Passport Office was ". . . willing to help, albeit unofficially, to prevent a child who has been 'stolen' from *leaving* the country," was of no consequence in my situation. My children were already gone.

The *Woman's World* article closed with, "One of the most promising new developments in divorce procedures where couples recognize the folly of treating children like property or possessions is an arrangement calling for joint custody."

When I read that, a sharp and bitter laugh escaped from deep within me. Did the author really believe a forward-thinking custody arrangement would prevent abductions?

Joint custody, which was a relatively new 1970s idea, meant the parents shared the authority to make child-raising decisions, and should have a prepared plan for conflicts. Joint *physical* custody, also called shared parenting, split the burden of the entire child-rearing obligation; the couple decided how much time the children would spend with each parent.

Our *split* custody agreement, rare at the time, had gone above and beyond that. We didn't just split responsibilities; we split the children. Klaus became the legal custodial parent for Ty, and I became Megan's. Our divorce agreement stated that the children were to always share the same babysitter and be together on the weekends which we alternated; neither of us could change those circumstances without a modification by the court.

And yet, regardless of the explicit terms of our legal agreement, here I was without my children. Custody arrangements, unique or otherwise, didn't stop him. Custody arrangements work if, and only if, both parents recognize the folly of treating their children like property or possessions. I thought I had done the right thing, the fair thing. Instead, my passive agreement had damaged my children's young lives, and broken this mother's heart.

I shut my eyes and kept rocking.

fourteen

Porn

1969, Indianapolis, IN

With graduation looming, my German class ended early one sunny day. Facing an unexpectedly free afternoon, tackling some overdue spring cleaning seemed like a good idea. I started with our bedroom, unearthing a large cardboard box stashed behind Klaus's shoes at the back of the closet. Because its weight precluded lifting it onto the bed, I maneuvered the container onto the bedroom floor and opened the flaps.

The box was full of books. Odd, I thought, that Klaus had closeted them when our living room book cases had empty shelf space. The contents were all paperbacks, all pocket-sized, with lurid, splashy-colored covers. I kneeled and looked closer. *Campus Sex Club. Naughtipuss.*

The images on the covers were mostly women, although shadowy male figures often lurked in the backgrounds. I stared at one after another, sifting through the box and feeling dirty.

The Lust Game.

Sucking air, I shook my head in disbelief and disgust. Nonetheless, I couldn't resist opening a book and reading a few paragraphs, then flipping forward and reading a few more titillating bits and pieces. My body betrayed me. Confusion—and embarrassment at my body's heated reaction to the book's contents—fueled my growing anger.

His *Playboy* magazine subscription was one thing, but a box of porn, after just two years of marriage? Clearly, I was not enough for him, although I had certainly tried. I wondered if there was something wrong with me. Closing the book, I studied the buxom blonde on the cover, wondering if that was what Klaus actually wanted and was thinking about when he and I . . . I sucked in another troubled breath.

A book titled *Shame Slave* hit the bedroom wall before I knew I was throwing it. Then, book by book, I scattered the rest all over the floor and left the room as I heard the front door open.

Klaus walked in, already removing his tie, said hi, and headed for the bedroom to change clothes. Heaving an audible sigh, he backtracked into the living room, where I sat expressionless on the sofa.

"Jeannie, what were you doing?"

"German class got out early today. I thought I'd do some spring cleaning." It surprised me at how calm my voice sounded.

"Those are *my* books."

"Obviously."

His eyes darted around the room while his brain apparently searched for a plausible explanation. After a few minutes of silence, he sat down at the other end of the couch, head bowed, and silently looked at the floor.

In the same low and deliberate tone, I said, "You know, Klaus, I'm sure there's some good reason why you need those books, and why they are hidden away in our closet. I just can't come up with anything at the moment. Apparently, neither can you."

His mouth opened. Before he could utter that first word of defense, I cut him off.

The screaming shook our garden apartment, maybe the entire building. I couldn't stop yelling. "You bastard, you goddamn bastard! Why am I not enough for you? All I've ever asked for is some affection, some signs of love—and this is what I get. How could you?"

When he attempted to respond, I screamed louder.

Finally, Klaus ran into the bedroom and dove, still fully clothed, under the covers. I followed, unrelenting. When I had worn myself out shrieking, I stormed out of the apartment, walking the streets until I came across a coffee shop, where I sat alone and sipped, replaying all of it. Had I over-reacted? I hadn't listened to any explanations, and there might have been one. He might have purchased them before we got married. I could have found a saner way to address the situation. Was it even about me? There was so much I didn't understand about him and so many conflicting thoughts in my head I couldn't sort through them.

He was asleep when I returned, clutching the far side of the bed just as I'd done on that awful night of our honeymoon. Tired, confused and still hurt, I kicked off my shoes and, without waking him, crawled into bed.

It was forty-eight hours before we spoke. An apology cracked opened the conversation door.

"I'll get rid of the books, Jeannie. I didn't know how to tell you about them. They're just books. Stupid, I guess, but as a young guy I thought it was a manly pastime. Honestly, it has nothing to do with you or our marriage."

With that, I apologized for screaming. After a safe moment of silence, my husband sidled up to me and wrapped both arms around my neck. "I love you, Jeannie. We'll do better from here, okay?"

He loved me—and wasn't that what mattered? Being so young when his father died, how could Klaus have even developed a picture of a happy marriage? I thought about all his other attributes: he took our finances seriously, paid the bills, and loved me the best he could.

Maybe this blowup happened for a reason. It even shed a little light on the honeymoon's strip show fiasco. As we trashed the sleazy paperbacks one by one into the apartment's alley dumpster, I decided this was a turning point and things would change. Maybe Klaus would learn that affection, not pornography, was foundational to a loving marriage.

And maybe I could work on my overreacting.

FIFTEEN

Day 30 & 31

August 25–26, 1977, Nashville, IN

Letters from Klaus began trickling in over a three-week period, all postmarked from Germany. By day 30, John Roof and my father each forwarded a letter. Three more had yet to arrive.

The letters in my possession became part of the growing pile of documents overtaking the kitchen table. Each evening, I sat with coffee or wine as needed, poring over every word, searching for clues, details, for something I had missed.

Klaus wrote they were happy and loved their new German homeland life. What happened to Canada, I wondered? He said Ty was attending an American school, and they were all well. The letter John and Midge received, dated August 18, indicated Klaus had gotten a systems analyst job with an American company, working thirty hours a week, yet had somehow traveled with the children to Spain, Sweden, and Belgium.

I pushed the letter aside, stood, and stretched my back. Clearly, this would be a "wine" evening. I pulled a glass from the nearest cabinet and filled it with merlot. Hovering over the table, I sipped and studied the letter again. *Spain. Sweden. Belgium?* Remembering how little free time I'd had as a single mom, I wasn't sure what about his new life was believable.

In the letter he told John and Midge, "My sister and sister-in-law, who live next to each other, will take care of the children." The only sister and sister-in-law who lived close by one another lived in

Hamm, three hours from Frankfurt, the city where he told Fredi he was living.

I had met all of Klaus's siblings on our honeymoon—the two sisters and the five brothers—and other than Fredi, our contact since had been minimal. If he had convinced them I was an unfit mother and a terrible wife, they very well might rally round their mistreated brother and poor children. I couldn't be sure they'd respond if I attempted contact, or be helpful if they did.

When the phone rang, I tried not to jump—or hope—which was always a challenge. I heard Haywood answer from the living room phone. "Hi, Joanne. How's Florida?" he said. "Sure, she's here. Let me have her get on the kitchen extension."

Joanne explained Mom had called her because a letter from Klaus had arrived. *Letter number three.* Joanne had headed over there immediately. "I'm at Mom's condo now. Can you handle me reading the letter over the phone?" Joanne asked. "I'm telling you, Sis, Mom's a wreck after seeing it. She can't stop crying."

Though postmarked August 18, she told me the letter appeared written prior to the kidnapping.

Dear Mom!

Thank you very much for your birthday card in June, I was glad to hear from you since I last saw you in February. Things are just going superb here, my plans for the future for my children and myself are now in full swing after months of detailed planning and lots of soul searching, a means that your daughter is not familiar with. I do not intend to be judge and jury in the decision that I have made but my instinct as a father whose main and only concern is the well-being of the children. I have decided that no judge can tell me what to do with my children nor will any one of my children be raised by some non-related creep.

Since my respect for you is very sincere—let's face it, you were my mother—I consider it my duty and obligation to inform you personally of my intentions, whether they are right or wrong. I hope that I do not get emotionally carried away but we did have our good times together, times that left a lasting impression on my life and I also know that we had some bad times which somehow were suppressed by all the good times we had. Looking at the present time span we could label it a bad time for me because I cannot forget the last twelve years of my life and the uncalled for interruption (idiotic). If you detect a tone of cynicism in me then you are right because I still don't and never will admit that our marital problems were sufficient to dissolve a family. Truthfully I am still searching for the real reason but no luck. The only major item could have been the abortion in 1975, or possibly her job? I just don't know. What does off-set my thinking was her complete refusal for counseling, her unwillingness to salvage and save a family that did have its normal ups and downs but yet was more stable than 85% of all the other marriages in this country, and her unwillingness to make sacrifices for her children, for let's face it, we put these little buggers in this world and it is our duty and responsibility to assure them a proper life.

Well, Mom, that brings me to the main reason of this letter. I have taken upon myself the responsibility of giving Megan and Ty a life in which they can live together as real brother and sister, I have decided in addition to the above reasons to take both children back with me to Germany. I don't approve of them living apart, being used as puppets in a world that they have been forced to live in. Also Jeannie's repeated threat to take me to court has also influenced my decision for I cannot live in such an environment of constant fear of losing my children. I should mention at this point that

I had given Jeannie a choice: give me the children with unlimited visitation rights for Jeannie and I would stay in Indianapolis or else. So as you can see, depending on her decision, she is aware of my move.

Arriving at my decision has kept me awake many, many nights, the pros and cons were thoroughly weighted against one another and the question that prolonged my departure was two-fold. First, was I willing to sacrifice the next 15 years for the well-being of my children and secondly, how would I explain in the years to come to my children why their mother did not come with us. If you put yourself in my position you can see the importance of these questions. Well, the decision has been made, I am willing to do it, I am willing to sacrifice and provide to my children a life of security, health, love, enjoyment, and all the things they deserve, and all I want in return is an occasional hug or kiss and a "Daddy, I love you!"

Mom, I promise you right now that I will take care of both of them and that in years to come I will never say something bad about Jeannie towards the children but at the present time I could not do it. I know she loves the children (?) but she wasn't and still isn't willing to make sacrifices for the children. Her temporary marriage is enough proof, for all she cares about is Jeannie and only Jeannie. You know as well as I do that children can sense this and Ty is living proof. Sure he likes her, he even calls her his weekend mother who never fulfills her promises she makes to him, regardless how little or unimportant they are.

Sorry, I am getting off the track. The future plans have been worked out in detail with my brother. I am flying out of Toronto, Canada on 7-28 leaving my car and a few personal belongings with my uncle in Toronto. Since nobody in this country knows my uncle's name and address and that civil cases can't be enforced in a foreign country, I don't have to hide my destination. Now, should there be complications with the children in Germany in a year or so, then I will most likely move back to Canada. As I said before, legally neither country gives a damn about a custody agreement from the State of Indiana, and finding me is another story. I know Jeannie will have a fit about this and I know she will give a hell of a performance. She is good at that but I can't let my children continue to live like this. Painful will it be for her but painful was it for me when she dumped me and I know she'll find a book about positive thinking when separated from your children (it worked on her divorce). Yes, I am sarcastic again because she should have read a book on children and happy family life.

Well, Mom, I guess I could go on and on for a while. Too bad things didn't work out as expected but neither will her current status last long. Please don't condemn me for what I am about to do, give it some time, let the emotions settle down before you judge me. I hope that you know me well enough to realize that the children are foremost on my mind. The children will remember you the same way that I know you— good times, smiling faces with laughter and happiness, in such a way we wish to always remember you.

Love,

Klaus

And Mom, remember:

Far better is it to dare mighty things,

To win glorious triumphs,

Than to take rank with those poor spirits

Who neither enjoy much nor suffer much,

Because they live in the gray twilight

That knows not victory nor defeat.

When Joanne finished reading, a long silence followed. I looked up and saw Haywood standing in the living room with the receiver pressed against his ear, watching me, his expression a mixture of love, compassion, and anger.

Klaus believed his own story and was, in his mind, the long-suffering martyr; I was the selfish one, abandoning the loving family he alone had tried to preserve. And the outright lies were maddening for me to hear and undoubtedly gut-wrenching for my mom to read. My repeated threats to take him to court? Lies to justify his loving actions. In one revealing breath saying *"I have decided that no judge can tell me what to do with my children nor will any one of my children be raised by some non-related creep"* and in the next putting himself on a pedestal as the upstanding father who understood true sacrifice. I found the comment about his ultimatum—give him full custody and he'd stay in Indianapolis, or else—astounding, as if the ultimatum gave him permission to kidnap the kids. And his statement that, out of sincere respect for my mother, he felt an obligation to tell her he had taken her grandchildren to Germany, taken them out of her life, infuriated me.

I hated him, hated him with every painful breath I took.

The next night, my sister called back. I didn't know if I could handle another phone call. After she'd shared Klaus's letter the night before, I'd slept little and had dragged myself through another endless day at work in Indianapolis. Home again in Nashville, a messy house and a pile of bills—bills I wasn't sure we'd be able to pay—greeted me. When Haywood walked in, bubbling over with a new idea: he would quit his job, we'd get a loan, open a picture-framing shop, and just watch the money roll in, I replied so sharply that he did an about-face and left the house.

I felt out of control. The early August telegram from Fredi had been a thread that got us nowhere. More than a month after the kidnapping, we were no closer to knowing the children's whereabouts than on day one. As I slid into depression, Haywood had taken the brunt of my grief.

I knew he'd probably retreated next door and was sitting on the porch talking with Grandma Lee. The chain-smoking old lady, his mom's oldest friend and a big part of southern Indiana's ambiance, was a refuge on the days when I inadvertently took out my frustrations on him.

I propped the receiver on my shoulder, got a glass of water and stood at the kitchen table rolling my tired shoulders as my sister spoke rapid-fire into the phone. "Slow down, Joanne. I can't understand you," I said.

Joanne inhaled deeply on the other end of the line and started over. "Klaus and the kids are not in Germany. They're still in the States. They headed west, she thinks."

What? What was she saying? I shivered with a trace of excitement. Hope, who had become a stranger in recent weeks, stirred inside me, though abruptly settled next to my old friend Confusion. "What are you talking about, Joanne? *Who* thinks?"

"Sylvia," she said.

Sylvia. The alcoholic clairvoyant. Mom had contacted her several weeks before, but Sylvia hadn't come up with anything, at least nothing that made sense.

"Right," I said cautiously. "Just tell me what's going on. Did she get a vision or something?"

My sister tried toning down her excitement, but it bled into every word. "Here's what happened. Mom was still so upset last night about Klaus's letter that she asked me to contact Sylvia again, hoping she could pick up some new vibrations, or whatever you call them."

I thought about Klaus's letter and started simmering again, thinking about the lies and the pain he was causing my mom. I sat down at the table and pushed the pile of paperwork aside. "Go on. What happened next?"

"Okay. This is what Sylvia told me. 'Hold the letter for just a moment and then read it out loud.' So, I did as she said. She listened carefully and, after I finished, there was a pause. Then she said, 'Read me the part again about his plans to travel to Toronto and then to Germany.' After hearing it one more time, Sylvia said in a slow, definitive voice, 'They're not in Germany. They're not on their way to Germany. And they didn't go to Canada.'"

I tried sounding calmer than I felt. "She was sure about this, Joanne?"

"I asked that exact question. She was sure. She said they're traveling in a relatively small, dark maroon vehicle and they've had some car trouble. They're fine but it's slowed them down getting to their destination."

My mind was scrambling. Klaus's BMW was black, not maroon, though regardless of color it broke down often enough. He could have had it painted or could have traded it in, anticipating authorities might look for him. Car trouble. I imagined them stranded on a bleak desert highway, or in the pouring rain. I could hear Ty asking, "Are we there yet?" Ty got so bored on long drives, and this would be the longest one he'd ever taken. And Klaus, never wanting to stop when Ty needed a bathroom, would always say, "You should have taken care of that when we stopped for lunch."

And Megan. She often got carsick, unless I held or distracted her.

Wait. This wasn't real.

Probably not real. I wasn't ready to believe. Not yet.

"So, what was their destination?" I asked in a low voice and held my breath.

Joanne replied just as quietly, "Sylvia said, 'West. They headed west.' She repeated that they'd had car trouble and said you'd find them somewhere in the L.A. area."

I couldn't quite believe any of this. Still, something like relief flooded through me. "She said I'd find them."

"Yes," Joanne said. "But not right away."

One more question. "Joanne, was she sober?"

After a brief pause, my sister said, "I think so. Mostly."

I could tell she believed Mom's friend, partly because Joanne had history with her. Five years earlier, Sylvia had told Joanne's husband, Mark, his future would include a white house with a cupola and a couple of kids. Mark had scoffed at the idea, since their house included nothing resembling a dome, wasn't white, and they had only one adopted son. After twenty years of marriage, however, Mark and Joanne divorced. Soon after, he remarried and moved into a white house with a cupola with the new wife and her son from a previous marriage. Sylvia, alcoholic or not, had proven herself accurate once again.

It was distressing enough thinking of Klaus and the kids possibly hunkered down in Toronto, or hiding out with a willing family member in Germany; somehow, throwing even the long shot of California into the mix was beyond overwhelming. In a city as big as Los Angeles, a man—and a couple of scared kids—could get lost. Where would I even begin?

Remembering I wasn't alone in this search, I knew I had to try.

Haywood, as I'd guessed, was sitting on the cozy front porch of our neighbor's cottage, drinking a Pepsi and soaking up the last rays of the August sun. I called hello as I walked across her pebbled driveway. The beloved Grandma Lee, dressed in her white smock and colorful apron, amply filled the old rocker. Her signature tortoiseshell combs decorated a bun of white hair atop her head. She returned a gravelly hello and drew deeply on a Virginia Slim Menthol Light, rivaled in length only by her fingernails, before offering me a cup of tea.

I shook my head, mouthed Haywood a private apology, and said I'd had a phone call.

"Any news?" Haywood's face brightened, indicative of his appealing, ever-hopeful nature, so ready for the solution he was sure waited just around the corner. Whenever I despaired, he wrapped me in those muscular arms and said that everything would be okay with such confidence I could hardly doubt it.

"Sylvia thinks Klaus and the kids are somewhere out west, in the Los Angeles area. She did a reading over the phone, while Joanne was holding the letter Mom received from him," I told them.

There was a moment of silence before Grandma Lee took a long pull on her cigarette and blew a perfect smoke ring. I waited for Haywood's comments, hoping they'd fill the dusk with undying optimism, and involve some sort of plan—even an impractical one.

Finally, he said, "This is Sylvia, your mom's coworker—the lady who drinks?"

I nodded.

"The one who said Ford would be re-elected in a landslide?"

Ford. I'd forgotten about that. Joining him on the porch swing, I sank down, feeling my measured excitement drain away, like air escaping a leaky balloon.

Grandma Lee spoke. "No one bats a thousand all the time," she said as she stretched out her sandaled feet. "Not even people who have special gifts."

I looked at Haywood, a man so full of ideas, always so sure, believing that between the two of us, we could figure anything out. Now though, I saw a different picture: a dejected man with slumped shoulders and tired features. Here was a guy who drove an enormous truck all day and sometimes into the night, hauling steel all around Indiana. And when returning home—a home that should have radiated happiness with toys scattered across the floor, kids' laughter, and a smiling new wife—he found a crazy woman, on the phone running up more bills with the lawyer, reading articles on child stealing, or in the darkened living room, curled up fetus-like on the couch, nonverbal.

"Don't you think we could make a few calls? The police maybe?

Or a private detective . . ." My voice trailed off. I had no idea where to start.

Reaching for Haywood's hand, I sighed with relief as he reciprocated by draping an arm over my shoulder.

But when he spoke, the words belied the hug. "We call, uh, who? And we tell them what?"

I had no answer.

sixteen

Birthing Takes Time

1970, Cumberland, IN

I considered the view from one side, then the other, and backed up a step, studying myself in the mirror over the bedroom dresser. My burgeoning belly was straining the waistline of a dress that had been a size too large when I bought it. Klaus walked up behind me smiling and found wrapping his arms around my middle difficult.

"You think you'll make it another couple of months?" he teased.

"I think so," I said, relaxing into the embrace. "Days at work sure seem longer and longer, though."

I enjoyed beginning my 1970 career at Indiana Bell Telephone as a residential service representative. Along with an exceptional salary, the service rep role afforded women positions of authority, unusual for the 70s. With this newfound power and freedom, something had shifted inside me: my value as a person. The sought-after title of Mrs. Klaus Manthey no longer identified me. I was becoming Jeannie Manthey.

But a year after I started with Bell, and less than three years into the marriage, something else was shifting inside.

"Jeannie, you will be a beautiful mother," Klaus murmured, kissing my neck. We were experiencing a new sense of closeness; he wanted a son, and I was carrying his child. Although we hadn't planned the pregnancy, Klaus's delight was obvious, and he quickly bought a celebratory name-your-baby book. All at once I was the recipient of my husband's attention, even as I wondered what sort of father he would be.

As a graduation gift, my own father had generously forgiven the college loan he'd extended, and then offered help with the down payment on our new house outside of Indianapolis. We had gratefully accepted the money. The Indy basement apartment was feeling oppressive. Our larger, brighter new home was an enormous improvement, especially with the baby coming.

My mother once told me Dad hadn't shared in her enthusiasm when she became pregnant with me. Understandable, I suppose. My brother, Jim, and sister, Joanne, were seven and ten years old respectively at the time; perhaps Dad had thought two kids were enough. Although Mom never referenced his feelings when I was young, I'd always felt I spent a good part of my childhood unsuccessfully seeking his approval, which set the stage for a mixed bag of father-daughter emotions. When I turned seventeen, I would go along to some of his evening gigs, have dinner with him and the other musicians, then listen to his jazz combo. Mom didn't enjoy going and was often working at the department store, so I'd be his date. Those were good times, and I loved being introduced as John Baker's daughter.

Maybe being a grandfather would be a better calling, I thought, as I touched my big belly. Dad's recent heart attack might have provided a new appreciation for life in all its forms—even a crying baby.

Several reasons made Mom consider divorce earlier that year, and at first her resolve seemed unshaken by Dad's health scare. The thought of my parents getting a divorce was upsetting, but no more so than the thought of her answering phone calls from his girlfriend. I loved my dad; however, I'd cheered when Mom walked out and stayed with Joanne and her husband, who were living in Florida. The whole situation made me look at Klaus with renewed gratitude: though not as perfect a husband as I'd hoped, I couldn't imagine unfaithfulness as one of his faults.

As if he'd read my thoughts about Mom, Klaus said, "I almost forgot. Mary Jane phoned before you came home. She asked if you'd call her when you got a chance."

I disentangled myself from Klaus, suddenly feeling tired and swollen. And a mid-week phone call from Mom made me uneasy, so I dialed her number immediately.

As everyone did lately, she asked how I was doing and how much longer I planned on working.

"A few more weeks, Mom," I said. "Indiana Bell's mandatory maternity leave forces me out the corporate door at seven months. I'll stay until then."

"Are you sure?"

"I love my work," I reminded her, "and we need the money."

"Yes," she sighed. "The money."

I waited for her to tell me why she'd called and finally prompted her. "What's going on?"

"Jeannie, you know how much I love you," she said, "And you've got an idea of how complicated life can get."

"Yes, I guess I do," I said cautiously.

"I had a phone call last night," she said, "a long talk, with Dr. Bob."

She sounded tired, and somewhat defeated. A terrible suspicion rose within me, starting low and moving into my chest. I waited.

"He's been spending time with your father and says your dad is really devastated. Bob reminded me of the vows we took, and how every marriage goes through its rough times."

Oh, no. "Rough times? Mother, I—"

"Let me finish, Jeannie," she said, as if her decision depended on getting her words out without interruption. "Your father loves me, even if he doesn't always show it. He loves all of us, but he hasn't had the life he thought he would have. This heart attack has scared him. He realizes now how precious life is, how important it is to be with people who truly love him."

He cheated on you. Repeatedly. And when you left, he immedi-ately moved his girlfriend and her young son into the condo. My belly felt leaden, and pushed upward against my lungs, preventing the intake of air. I leaned against the kitchen counter and focused on breathing deeply and slowly.

"He's learned his lesson, honey," she said. "Dr. Bob says if I leave him now, at this low point in his life, he could die. I could never for-give myself if that happened."

Dr. Bob. The man always had something to say. This time, his influence did not sit well with me.

Hyperventilating and furious, I wasn't sure whether Mom was trying to convince me or herself that she was doing the right thing. I could tell my silence unnerved her. When she spoke again, her tone changed, and sounded almost pleading. "You've only been married a few years. Once you've been with a man for a long time, twenty, thirty years, things look different. Things are just. . . not simple."

"Mom, I don't know what to say. I just want you to be happy. This must be so hard for you."

I wanted things to be simple. When I left work in a few weeks, my plan was simple: become a beaming hausfrau. As we settled into our new Cumberland, Indiana, house with the German Shepherd puppy we'd bought, I wanted us happy while we waited for the baby —and even happier afterward. I wanted my mother, my baby's grandmother, to start a new chapter, too. Regardless of my love for Dad, the happiness in their marriage had vanished long ago. Whatever was missing, my father had looked elsewhere and staying together, even after thirty-five years, seemed senseless.

Klaus came into the kitchen and looked at me, concerned. He mouthed, "Is everything okay?"

No, I shook my head. Things were not okay.

SEVENTEEN

Day 42

September 6, 1977
Nashville and Indianapolis, IN

"How long do you think it will take them to get back with me?" Haywood stayed focused on the road. The morning traffic between Nashville and Indianapolis seemed unusually heavy. "I'm not sure, Babe. CBS is a big company. They probably have employees who deal with transcript requests. Hopefully, they'll rush it once they see why you want it."

A few days before, I had taken some liberties and accessed Klaus's phone bill on a break at work. Under the circumstances, I prayed for forgiveness for my actions rather than asking permission. Reviewing the calls, I had puzzled aloud over one placed on June 9, the day before Haywood and I got married. "CBS, Inc., New York?" I said within earshot of a coworker. When I explained the backstory and confessed my transgression, she about fell off her chair.

"Oh, my God. I know why he called them! Sometime in May I was watching *60 MINUTES,* and they did a story about parents kidnapping their children. I can't believe I didn't say anything. I totally forgot it had been on. I feel like such a dunce."

"Don't feel bad," I said. "I remember seeing that same broadcast and can't believe I didn't think to contact them after he took the kids. Klaus must have seen or been told about the show. Oh my God, is right. The perfect instruction manual." I could imagine the moment: Klaus, brooding over the prospect of my wedding to Haywood the next day, remembering the broadcast and, with one clever call, ordering the transcript. After the conversation with my coworker, I had contacted CBS and ordered my own copy. A long shot, perhaps, but maybe, just maybe, it might reveal an important trail of breadcrumbs.

Haywood hit a minor pothole, and my briefcase slipped off the seat. As I reached for the handle, the story on the car radio about Voyager-I briefly caught my attention. The spacecraft had begun an eighteen-month mission investigating the atmospheres, magnetospheres, satellites, and ring systems of Jupiter and Saturn. Focusing on world news was difficult, though. I had too much else on my mind. I dug into my briefcase, pulling out a letter Big John had copied and forwarded, and switched off the radio as I reread it.

Dear Klaus,

It appears the house has been sold, for $28,500. We decided to sell it at that price since this is the first and only legitimate offer made since your departure.

That means there will be less money in the proceeds to pay off your loan due on Oct. 17. The realtor figures there will be about $2,500 remaining following closing costs and pro-rated mortgage and maintenance. Jeannie gets $1,000 of that, leaving $1,500 for you. Now I need your thought on what to do about the loan. The realtor figures the closing will occur within two or three weeks, provided the buyer qualifies, and he assumes it will.

Jeannie is still hoping you'll have a change of mind and bring the children back to Indiana. She says she's willing to change the custody of the children so that you have both of them, as long as she has visiting rights. I know Dr. Bob wrote to you and I'm sure Jeannie has conveyed this to you through Fredi. In my opinion I believe this would be best for the children, as they have a right to see their mother and receive and give her love. As I appealed to you before you left, I again appeal to you that you consider not causing Jeannie more undue grief. It would seem that both of you would have a great portion of what you want and guarantee the children would have access to Jeannie's love.

Please give me your conclusions on both items which I have addressed in this letter at the earliest moment. Please give the kids our love. Tell me how they are doing as we all miss them very much.

Your friend,

John

BCC: Jeannie dear,

I hope he is open to the last two paragraphs. I'll let you know, if and when, he responds.

Love,

John

Big John was trying to help and playing another long shot. Secondarily through that help, I might actually get the $1,000 I was due from the condominium sale per the divorce agreement. And Haywood was trying, too. Good-natured, with that give-you-the-shirt-off-his-back attitude, he helped in every way possible. "How about I drive you to work today," he had offered that morning, even though it was his well-deserved day off.

As we headed toward Indianapolis, I was about to express my appreciation when Haywood slammed on the brakes. The car ahead of us had stopped without warning. "What the—?"

From the passenger seat, I could see what had stopped the flow of traffic, and I held my breath. A young mother was putting her child on the school bus. School had started.

I shook my head. "No," I moaned. "No."

Haywood looked over at me and saw the obvious written on my face. He reached out and cupped his hand over my fist resting on the seat. The tears came. My chest hurt and my eyes blurred.

I had no child to put on the bus.

eighteen

Birth

1970-1971, Cumberland and Indianapolis, IN

In late October, three long weeks past my due date, Klaus and I made the midnight run to the hospital and our son arrived. At last.

At first, nothing, absolutely nothing else mattered. We were so in love with this child that once home from the hospital we hardly put Ty down. Holding my new baby boy, I'd press my nose against one tiny cheek and inhale that intoxicating brand-new-baby smell. While I fixed dinner each evening, I peered into the family room and watched Klaus talk and coo softly to the bundle on his lap.

"Isn't he something?" Klaus said repeatedly over dinner.

He beamed, and I was happy. We were a family. This family, however, needed a second paycheck. Even though I knew finances were Klaus's top priority, it still surprised me when he offered no hausfrau objections and instead encouraged my return to work.

When Ty was ten months old, I made my way back to Indiana Bell, this time as the president's Customer Complaint Coordinator and supervisor of a steno pool. Though a proud mama, I found myself relieved I was part of the work world again; so much at home was weighing on me.

Even with the addition of our beautiful son, even seeing Klaus's obvious fatherhood joy, the happy family scenario had quickly faded. We were in our new Cumberland home outside of Indianapolis with a new baby. What could possibly be wrong?

At first, I suspected the culprit to be postpartum blues. After a few months, though, I knew better. Exhausted and sitting at the dining room table one night after preparing dinner, cleaning up the kitchen, getting Ty ready for bed and rocked to sleep, I longingly looked at Klaus as he watched the news in the adjoining family room. Instead of an invitation to join him on the couch, a litany of complaints, yet again, filled the air.

I made my way over to him, nudged Anci, our German Shepherd off the sofa, and sat close. "Klaus, can you keep it down a tad? I just got Ty to bed."

As if I didn't exist, he continued watching and reacting. "These guys are so stupid. They need to be put in their place. I could handle things so much better than these idiots."

Why doesn't he look at me? I wish he would notice me; ask how I'm feeling. Other than delighting in playing with Ty, nothing else and no one else, including me, seemed to make him happy. *Was I no longer the object of his affection as I had been when pregnant with his son?* I had to ask myself, *was I jealous? It didn't feel like jealousy.* His constant complaining about life in general—the news, the neighbors, his work, his colleagues, other cultures, women—continued to take its toll on me and on our relationship.

My head filled with a tiny bit of terror, but I asked the question anyhow. I carefully took his hand and said, "Klaus, what would you think about our getting some, you know, counseling, marriage counseling? I'm feeling like we're in a downward spiral here. You're so angry about so many things. I just think we could find somebody to help address what's not working and make things better."

Abruptly facing me, he pulled his hand out of mine and said, "What's wrong with you? We do not need help. You, maybe, but *we* don't." Mumbling, "Is there any dessert?" and heading for the kitchen, he tossed the remote on the coffee table, startling the dog who jumped out of his way.

I didn't answer. I went to bed, tired of his abusive comments and criticisms. We were at a crossroads. My naively wishing things were different did not make them so. I wasn't the object of his affection; I was an object. Attempts to even discuss our troubled marriage revealed the enormous schism, as if we were standing on opposite sides of the Grand Canyon.

We took a mini-vacation, a Florida-bound trip to visit my parents. They were in the throes of working things out after Dad's heart attack, but the air seemed a little heavy between them. Maybe that's why Mom picked up on my hidden angst so quickly. Sitting out by the Ft. Lauderdale pool just steps from their end-unit condo, Mom and I sunned and watched Klaus play with Ty in the water.

"Honey, are you and Nick okay? You seem so, I don't know, testy with each other," Mom asked.

"Remember when you called me last September and told me you were getting back together with Dad? Made no sense, Mom. Being unhappy is being unhappy, regardless of whether a person's been married for three years or thirty years."

She cocked her head, noting my sharp tone, and stared at me. Her intuitive question had caused a lightbulb moment for me. Something came over me—a wave of strength and courage, a new attitude. Attitude with a capital A.

"Mom, I'm just saying that, regardless of the time you've put into a relationship, if a marriage doesn't meet the needs of both parties, it's time to rethink the plan. I don't think we, meaning women, are here to be subservient, to be less than, to be miserable. I have a voice, I have needs. I matter, Mom. You matter. Being the sacrificial lamb because of someone else's choices just doesn't work for me."

I looked over at her and saw tears wetting her cheeks. "Oh, Mom. I'm sorry. I didn't mean to—"

She dabbed her eyes and reached over and held my hand. "It's okay, honey. I needed to hear that. It's hard waking up to the truth sometimes, isn't it?"

I loved being back at work. Working gave me something else to think about besides the devastating marital issues at home. What's more, my new role was challenging and supervising people came with a steep learning curve.

"Ma Bell changed the dress code," my previous coworker Nora said when I stopped by my former business office on a Monday morning, checking on my old service rep friends. "Pantsuits. We can wear pantsuits!" she said as she hugged me.

This new decision eliminated the existing and emphatic "skirts or dresses only" company policy. I liked the idea of getting on a more equal footing with my male counterparts—at least concerning attire. Salaries were another matter and awaited change, but being promoted into a more important role provided the new me with another layer of courage. New clothes, new position. New Jeannie.

The following Monday, Attitude and I walked into work dressed in a new polyester pantsuit. I strutted past my former boss, shooting him a look. Mr. Former Boss was a handsome suit-and-tie jock—and I was still simmering over his recent compliment regarding the way I handled an irate customer. "Hmm, a woman who is pretty *and* smart," he had remarked.

He was one of many men who enjoyed and touted their male privilege. It was like the time as the only woman on the elevator, I received no greeting from five male suits one morning. They talked amongst themselves while their cool glances spoke volumes. Being sized up as "just a woman" or worse, a babe, stung.

Pretty *and* smart? *Yeah. And one day I'm gonna have your job.*

My new boss, thank God, was one of the decent guys. "Jeannie, we promoted you into this role of the president's Customer Complain Coordinator because you were capable. You have a way with people and we know we can count on you."

Filling my closet with fashionable pantsuits, I set out to prove him right and make a name for myself. My salary helped defray expenses, but it became about more than the money. The job acknowledged my abilities, my talent, and my drive for accomplishing things. I took care of all arrangements necessary at home: childcare, grocery shopping, cooking, and paying the bills. I approached my responsibilities at work in the same manner. Because of my self-imposed perfectionism, the pressures of my responsibilities, and my highly visible position, I focused more and more on my job. The new era of the I-Can-Do-It-All Woman seduced me— I would be an excellent mother *and* an exceptional employee.

Late one afternoon, I looked at the pile of work on my desk. My manager, Tom, looked up from a stack of papers and said, "What do you think?"

I said, "I think the president's going to want this paperwork finished tonight. Can you stay a little longer?"

"Sure."

It always seemed so easy for a man. My staying necessitated a phone call. "Klaus, can you pick up Ty from the babysitter tonight? I've got more paperwork. I'll fix dinner when I get home, okay?"

He grumbled about the terrible day he'd had and how often I came home late, but finally agreed. Hoping Tom hadn't been able to hear the other side of the conversation, I hung up and said, "Okay, let's get this . . ."

I stopped mid-sentence as a man I had never seen before paused by the doorway of my office. He was tall, slender, and smartly dressed, with a warm smile on a well-tanned face. I leaned back in my chair and tried to remember what I'd been saying.

Tom, following my gaze, said, "Hey, if it isn't Mr. Jake Collins.

All the way from the Yellow Pages world. Long time no see," then stood and shook hands with him.

"Hey, yourself," Jake replied. "Long time is right. Missed you at softball practice yesterday." Jake's glance shifted and locked on me. "Sorry for interrupting your conversation."

"No problem. Just hashing over customer complaints." I stood up, extended my hand and said, "Hi, I'm Jeannie."

I noticed his wedding ring, yet still hoped I hadn't left all my lipstick on the late afternoon's coffee cup. Tom made official introductions while Mr. Jake Collins and I shared a long handshake and a lingering look.

"Well, I'd best be going," Jake said. "Got to drum up more business so you guys can keep your jobs."

He walked down the hall with a cocky stride, heading back to his department. "Better see you at the next softball practice," he said over his shoulder before getting on the elevator.

He was speaking to Tom, but as the doors closed the last look was on me.

Klaus and Ty were playing with a bouncy ball outside when I got home after 7:00 p.m. I stepped out of my car, gave each a weary hug, and once inside the condo, after tossing my briefcase on the sofa, made my way to the refrigerator. I stared at its contents, wondering what I could prepare. Something quick—I wanted some playtime with Ty before getting my kiddo ready for bed.

Klaus was usually too busy with office problems to pitch in. He had left Western Electric and taken a position with a large insurance company where, after being promoted to a supervisory role in data processing, it became clear that management was not his strong suit. As I pulled a few cans from the kitchen cabinets, I heard Klaus come inside and set Ty in the playpen before joining me in the kitchen.

After one look at his sour expression, I asked, "What's going on?"

He grimaced. "I do a good job and I'm the one who gets—how do you say?—dragged on the carpet?"

"'Called on the carpet.' What happened?" I was expecting the worst.

"They're all stupid. I didn't like that job anyhow. Stupid jerks."

"Did they fire you?" My voice wavered.

"No. They moved me to another position, but it won't be any better. I'll be working with a damned gook."

The accent made "gook" sound like "cook." I knew all too well what he meant. I'd heard the gamut of bigoted words and heard them all too often. Regardless, they still made me cringe. Before I could reply, he opened the refrigerator, pulled out a beer, and slammed the door shut. After attacking the cap with a bottle opener and exiting the kitchen, he slumped hard onto the family room loveseat and turned on the TV, volume high, shutting me out.

After I'd assembled a quick dinner, which we ate with few words between us, I played with Ty, then bathed and bedded him down. After that came laundry, kitchen cleanup, and paperwork, both household and office. I moved silently through the tasks, catching myself thinking about Mr. Jake Collins, my mind lingering on that earlier long handshake and those warm, kind eyes.

NINETEEN

Day 45

September 9, 1977, Nashville, IN

I felt like someone had thrown me a lifeline when a telegram appeared from Klaus's brother, Fredi. This unexpected contact included potentially valuable information, though the message was maddeningly brief: KLAUS CALLED SUNDAY LIVES FRANKFORT AUGUST 20. CHILDREN LOVEABLE.

Frankfort. The first real clue. So much for Sylvia's vision about Los Angeles.

I called Fredi every day thereafter with little success. The number belonged to his neighbors and though I left a couple of messages, they spoke no English and my German was lacking. Most calls were unanswered. With each unanswered ring, my hopes fell like shooting stars disappearing into the darkness. Fredi, the children's godfather, was the family member with whom I felt the closest tie. What if Klaus had convinced his brother that being away from me was best for the children?

Letter number four arrived on the heels of Fredi's telegram, and my hands shook as I read what Karen had received from Klaus. I had little doubt that he believed what he said: he was doing the right thing for the children; taking them away from me was his only recourse; I was not worthy and did not deserve to be their mother. He had sentenced me for the crime of divorcing him and dashing any chance of reconciliation by falling in love with another man. Klaus had plotted and planned, seeing himself as the children's savior.

September 1977

Hi Karen!

It has been over a month now since we arrived here and all of it has been fun. We just returned from Spain where my sister's in-laws live, they took all of us down there and Ty and Megan speak an English that consists of German, English, and a blend of Spanish—Mama mia! Confusion, for they do not know what they are speaking. I personally think they are making fun of the different languages.

Their behavior has been excellent, and their entertainment on the flight over here was first class— everybody spoiled them rotten. The family just adores both of them and the other kids in the neighborhood are constantly here to play with their "American friends." You can't imagine how Ty eats that up when I translate that to him. But you know what they like the most? Riding on a real train!

Well Karen, excuse my abrupt sentences but that is the easiest way to tell you a lot in a short letter. If you inquire about the behavior or effect of this trip on the children I can only reply in a very positive way. They are again behaving like a brother and sister should—they play extremely well together, they hug each other, they laugh at each other and protect each other the way it should be. They do fight with each other too. Well, as you can see, I am happy with the results thus far and regret only that I didn't do it earlier.

My future plans are currently stable for in two weeks, I start working in Data Processing again and my sister and sister-in-law who live next to each other will take care of the children. My hours are flexible and no Fridays, ever.

Let me close for now with the best wishes from all of us to you and you are welcome to write to us if you promise not to

write about the other person and her creep. Okay? Till the
next time. We love you,
    Ty, Klaus, and Megan

At first, each letter's contents dropped me down into a well of isolating grief. My body grew stiff, my heart raced, and the grief incapacitated me. Voices in my head reiterated what a bad person I was as his words created the intended pain.

I'd wait, cry, regroup, then attempt an objective read. Though the letters held numerous confusing discrepancies, they similarly described a joyous new life with Ty and Megan and Klaus's sense of noble self-sacrifice. I'd read them all, trying to imagine their new life as described, with the kids speaking multiple languages and popping down to Spain for a vacation.

Sighing, I slipped the letter inside an accordion document folder, which included everything pertaining to what we now called "the case." When my attorney and I met, I'd give him copies of the letters. Flipping through the growing stack of documents, I pondered again whether I deserved the sentence meted out. The voices in my head yammered, *he did love the children. He was a good father and treated them well.*

To help clear my head of self-deprecating thoughts, I reread the *Parents As Kidnappers* article from *Woman's World* and underlined phrases I'd missed. *"Any parent who really cares about the welfare of the children would seek to harmonize rather than exacerbate relations with an ex-mate, whatever his or her disappointments over the failure of the marriage. The children should come first."*

Yes, of course. Agreed. The children should come first. So why did it feel like the law was on the kidnapper's side? I moved to the newspaper, scanning it for any hopeful legal developments; Stockholm, Sweden, was hosting the annual INTERPOL meeting where they were crafting a resolution encouraging video piracy laws. What?

I grabbed my document folder and bitterly slapped the damn thing shut. The International Criminal Police Organization was duly concerned with people who copied or stole videos, while our local, national, and international authorities, without proper laws in place, allowed a father to steal his children—my children—without retribution.

twenty

A Different Path

1971, Indianapolis and Cumberland, IN

In the following weeks, Mr. Jake Collins and I somehow ran into one another all over the building. Hallway conversations turned into coffee breaks together and business discussions switched to personal topics. Jake was a few years older than I and several years into a marriage. I discovered I wasn't the only one with an unhappy home life.

When he suggested we meet privately somewhere, some evening, "just to figure this all out," I couldn't pretend to misunderstand him. I felt my body get warm even as a voice in my head said, *don't go down this path.*

I went. We borrowed a girlfriend's apartment. She had left a key under the mat and the apartment gently lit. My hand shook as I unlocked the door. Jake found a corkscrew, opened the bottle of wine he'd brought—he'd remembered me saying I liked red—and poured two glasses.

Still trembling, I lifted the wine to my lips. Jake sipped his, sat down on the sofa and gestured for me to join him. My fingers intertwined with his and I allowed his gentle pull and nestled down beside him. Without pausing, he leaned toward me and brushed his lips across mine ever so lightly.

Just the nearness of him excited me—and filled me with guilt. I had never pictured myself being unfaithful, yet I wanted him. *I can't let this happen.*

"Jake, I don't know what I—" A long serious kiss stopped me mid-sentence. The moment intensified as he drew me closer, arms enveloping me, and a hand softly rubbing the small of my back.

"Jeannie, I know we should talk. I just need you to know how much I care."

His embrace was as warm and soothing as the wine. Thoughts of guilt gave way to surrender, and I let myself slip into the inviting, loving world I'd been longing for.

Abruptly, he pressed back. "Jeannie, I didn't come prepared."

Prepared? Oh, right—that. We stared at each other and laughed for a second. Should we rethink the moment? We read the desire on each other's face. There was no stopping.

He left, quickly returning with a condom-filled plain brown bag from the nearest drugstore. More nervous laughter, more wine, more kisses. Jake paused long enough to slide one shoe off after another, completed the last kiss, then took my hand, and found the way to the bedroom.

Our house was dark when I entered through the garage door; Klaus was asleep. Breathing a sigh of relief, I took a long hot shower and crawled under the covers on my side of the quiet battlefield that was our bed.

I lay there wide awake, my thoughts consumed with Jake Collins. I could still feel him, smell the scent of his skin, and see the look in his eyes when he laid me down on the bed and covered my body with his. The embrace was unlike any other I'd ever known.

The memory of how he drew me closer would not let go. How he took me. How I had dissolved into his arms and welcomed the softness of his touch, letting my body respond, only to hear a rip in the bedspread as he entered me—my foot had caught on a seam.

It sounded like infidelity ripping my life apart. *Was this how my father felt when he betrayed my mother?* The startling moment had broken the spell; shame took hold, joy faded, and the evening ended. We had straightened up the apartment, awkwardly kissed goodbye after locking the door, and left separately.

Yet there was no stopping the alluring thoughts of passion in my mind. The memory of the hypnotic tenderness returned and remained. I knew I would be with Jake again.

I looked at the wall clock over the dining room table. 10:01 p.m. Finally, the awful TV program booming from the next room ended, replaced by the news.

I missed Jake and when he called, canceling our plans for an evening rendezvous, I found myself despondent. He had become like a seductive, irresistible drug for me over the last few months. Each time my house grew too cold, or when Klaus became too caustic, I left and secretly met up with Jake somewhere, anywhere. But Jake was as busy at work as I was—and had a wife who sometimes wondered about her husband's growing evening absences.

After more than an hour of distracted work, the pile of papers starring back at me was still daunting. Ty was fast asleep though, and if I stayed focused, I might finish documenting customer complaint resolutions and get to bed myself by 11:00.

Klaus turned off the TV set and stomped into the dining room. "I don't care how much Bell is paying you. You should quit."

I put my pen down and stared at him. "Excuse me?"

"You should quit. Find another job. Why do you have to spend so much time settling silly-ass customer issues? Those people don't deserve that much attention. What's the point, anyway? You're not making a difference."

"Okay. Enough. I've heard enough," I said, crossing my arms defiantly. "I'm so sick of your comments and your attitude. Ever since

I went back to work, you constantly find fault with me. Me, and the rest of the world, come to think of it."

"Well, if people here weren't so stupid, I wouldn't have anything to complain about."

That did it. "*Here?* Oh, excuse me, everyone except Germans. I can't believe you've been watching a program about Hitler again," I snapped. "You act like you're joking when you praise that madman's leadership and say how the Jews had it coming, but that's how you really feel, isn't it? Well, I'll tell you how *I* feel. I don't even know who you are anymore."

Maybe I'd never really known him. Starry-eyed when we married, I'd been so busy excusing any negative behavior, I'd never really explored it with him. I'd never asked how he truly felt. But at this point, I didn't care.

I left the room, not waiting for a reply, storming down the hall, too angry for tears. What a mess we'd created.

When he finally came to bed, I lay quietly, with my back toward him. I felt the weight of his presence as he lay down and pulled the covers over his shoulder. No touching, no apologies.

The silence was deafening, and forced me to look at myself and the protected, patriarchal, non-diverse world I grew up in, where little girls learned niceness and people-pleasing, where women didn't give voice, at least not enough, to the inequalities and inequities facing them. I could not live with his domineering, Aryan supremacist behavior.

I made up my mind: I was moving out and move out I did.

TWENTY-ONE

Day 47

September 11, 1977, Nashville, IN

I laid all of Klaus's letters on the kitchen table—his "farewell" letter to me, and the five letters family and friends had received since the kidnapping—and read and reread them, looking for clues. What finally struck me were the inconsistencies. I didn't know whether the man was brilliant, layering one inconsistency atop another, purposely creating confusion, or simply sloppy. Whatever the intentions, the conflicting stories were playing tricks on my mind.

I took a sip of my coffee and tried tackling the problem the same way I solved intricate issues at work—by studying the documentation.

"What are you up to, babe?" Haywood said, leaning over me. Dressed in Sunday morning's best—sweatpants and a T-shirt—he first looked at the papers covering the table, then my face, and had his answer. Wrapping an arm around my shoulders, he gave me a gentle kiss on the neck and left the kitchen without another word.

Refilling my cup, I sighed and kept at it.

In Klaus's farewell letter Big John had delivered on July 26, he wrote that they were in Germany. *Again, we are in Germany, happy and together, and in a place where you'll never find us.*

He had indicated Fredi was helping, and instructed me to communicate through Fredi. However, in the August 3rd telegram, Fredi seemed clueless. 'KLAUS ANNOUNCED TRIP VIA CANADA TODAY – NOT ARRIVED – AM UPSET – WILL SEND MESSAGE.'

In the letter to my mom, postmarked August 18 but most likely penned prior to the kidnapping, he'd written, *I am flying out of Toronto, Canada on 7-28 leaving my car and a few personal belongings with my uncle in Toronto.* He'd originally told Karen over the phone July 26 that they were boarding a ship the next day out of Canada. But in the late-August letter he said the kids entertained everyone on the flight to Germany. Did they sail or did they fly?

And in the letter to Karen, the story about starting a job in September was also troublesome. Were there family members supporting Klaus until then? Or had he already started work as he said in the letter received by a different family member?

And who was taking care of the children? A sister and a sister-in-law? The only sister and sister-in-law who lived close by one another lived in Hamm, three hours from Frankfurt, the city where he told Fredi he was living.

It all made my head hurt. Regardless of the inconsistencies, one thing remained clear and unwavering: hurting me was his goal, and taking the children out of the country was a foolproof way to do that. For all I knew, he planned the incongruities and intentionally meant to send me on a mental wild goose chase.

Or maybe it was all just smoke and mirrors. How could I have shared a bed and a life with this man for nearly ten years, yet knew so little about him?

One thing I knew: Klaus relished and prided himself on having the last word. Like a game of chess, he was a pro and knew the moves; I was at a loss. I took some aspirin, made a piece of toast, and holding a fresh cup of coffee, moved from the kitchen to the rocking chair on the screened-in front porch. Brilliant or otherwise, Klaus's plan had worked. He was oceans away *and* had the children. I gave up thinking, analyzing and dissecting. Instead, I rocked and wept.

twenty-two

Separation

1972, Indianapolis, IN

"I'm fine. She's the one with the problems," Klaus announced during our first counseling session. The therapist responded with an almost imperceptible smile.

I threw my husband a look of disdain, then turned away.

But I couldn't help wondering if maybe I had given up on my marriage too soon. I hadn't been a good wife—as defined by the culture and undoubtedly by the two men in the room. To them I was at fault: I'd packed up and left rather than stay and work things out.

Klaus hadn't believed I would make good on my decision, until he had come home from work and saw my bags by the front door, packed and ready. He yelled, then cried and pleaded for me to stay. I said we needed a break, took my son, and left.

I moved into a ground floor one-bedroom apartment much smaller than the Cumberland house we'd shared. It was nearer my office, which offered a big plus as I navigated an uncharted life as a single mother with a demanding job. Ty, now an energetic sixteen-month-old, loved his new babysitter, running to hug "Mama Joyce" each morning when I dropped him off at her house. Knowing he was happy and well cared for allowed me the chance to sort through my confused feelings about the marriage and my future.

Was I obligated to stay married to him? Our marriage was a disaster. Klaus and I were worlds apart in our thinking and our views on life. I didn't want the marriage, yet I struggled considering divorce.

Divorce felt like failure, and therefore I would be a failure, someone who couldn't handle difficult marital obligations.

Klaus called frequently, dropping by to see his son, giving Ty long wistful hugs, the two of them playing mournful games of bouncy ball in the apartment complex's small green space. He told me how quiet and empty our house now seemed, how hard focusing on his work was since I had abandoned him.

Even though I felt manipulated by Klaus's words, I grappled with the guilt every time Ty lit up at the sight of "Daddy!" Remembering my childhood, running after a father who always seemed preoccupied even when physically present, caused me to reconsider the current situation. Didn't Ty deserve a full-time dad, even if I had serious misgivings? And my parents, separated because of Dad's transgressions, had at least tried working things out before Mom finally closed the door on their thirty-seven-year marriage.

And being a single mother was hard. My work demanded much of my time, often spilling over into evenings, infringing on time devoted to Ty. However much Klaus had grumbled about helping around the house and with Ty, he had at least been there. Now, there was no one, just me with my son.

Jake was there, in theory, but he had his own problems, own job, own family—and his own guilt over our ongoing affair, although he handled it better than I. My current life exhausted me. Within six months, the guilt and life's pressures had worn me down. When Klaus suggested marital counseling, I agreed.

The therapist's non-judgmental demeanor influenced and softened my attitude. Klaus picked up on that and made an effort to listen and change. Shouldn't I at least do the same?

After several months of therapy, after endless talks, long discussions, after lots of blaming and even more absolving, I agreed I would go back, although I had some unfinished business to take care of first.

"Jake, we need to talk."

He had known and wanted no part of what was coming. Nevertheless, he agreed we could meet for a drink at a place on the outskirts of town. He slid off a soft-cushioned stool at the end of the bar and greeted me with a kiss. I perched on a stool next to his and realized we were the only patrons there. He ordered wine for us both and waited for me to say it.

So, I did. "This is a dead end, and we both know it."

"Please don't do this, Jeannie. I love you."

My hands were trembling, as they had the night of our first rendezvous. After the bartender set our wine on the counter, I took a shaky sip, tears welling up. "I love you, too."

"Then why would you even think of ending what we have?"

"Jake, we're filling a void, you and I. We've been unfaithful to our partners *and* our families. And you know what the worst part is? We haven't even been faithful to ourselves. We stayed in our marriages, yet chose to be with each other. And living in the constant fear that we'll be found out is really wearing on me. I've decided I need to at least try to make things work with Klaus."

We silently drank our wine. Finally, Jake reached for my hand, stroking the back of it, and lowered his head. "I didn't plan to fall in love with you, but I did, Jeannie. What do I do now?"

I forced the words out. "Go home, Jake. You need to go home."

He leaned forward and kissed me one last time, holding my hand in a lingering clasp. As he walked away, I moaned, closed my eyes, and wiped the wet streaks from my face. I would be forever beholden for the love and now the memory of one Jake Collins, but I knew I'd done the right thing, at last.

I woke up refreshed, for the first time in months, smelling coffee brewing as I stretched under Saturday morning sheets. Donning soft slippers and a plush white robe, I padded my way into a sun-filled dining room and found the table set and breakfast prepared.

Klaus stood beside a chair awaiting my arrival. I let him hold me and rested in his arms, soaking up the attention.

"Jeannie, I really want things to work. You've been different. You act like you care about me again and I know you're trying. We can do better together, right?"

I nodded.

"Let's sell the house," he said with a smile. "We'll get an apartment, a new place, start over. I know you like the complex where you've been with Ty."

My heart softened. I really wanted to believe things could work out.

Our therapist had advised me that confessing my affair served no purpose. The entire episode was behind me now, and my family was my focus. I felt a renewed sense of commitment to Klaus, and Ty, and to regaining my integrity. The game of hide-and-lie was over. On this sunny morning, with my husband smiling at me and breakfast waiting, it all seemed possible.

"It'll work," Klaus said. "You'll see."

"Okay." I lightly kissed his cheek.

He handed me the aromatic cup of let's-try-again. I took a sip and confirmed my response, "It will."

TWENTY-THREE

Day 51

September 15, 1977, Nashville, IN

On September 15, a 9x12 dark gray envelope arrived from CBS with a standardized enclosure of the transcript I'd requested. I opened the flap slowly and deliberately. If Klaus, as I suspected, had also contacted CBS requesting a copy of the May 1977 segment of *60 MINUTES* "Take the Children and Run," presented by Dan Rather, the pages I held in my hands might contain valuable insights into the plan he had concocted.

I read the opening paragraph. "You are looking at a man who took a little boy from the child's mother. Incredible as it seems, the man has committed no crime. He is the little boy's father."

The transcript, of course, had no pictures. I didn't need any. In my mind's eye, I could see *my* little boy, my Ty. I read on.

"Americans have always taken pride in the way they protect their children, but in the 1970s things are happening to American young-sters that make us wonder whether we do indeed protect them as well as we did in the past. . . . It's a story we first ran some months ago —a story about American kids who have become the innocent vic-tims of custody battles between their mothers and fathers. It's called child snatching or child stealing, and it's happening with alarming frequency to perhaps as many as 100,000 children every year."

In addition to a few individual kidnapping stories, Rather ex-plained that "countless other parents have discovered, it is perfectly legal to kidnap your own children, especially if neither parent has been awarded legal custody. And even if custody has been awarded, it isn't worth the paper it's written on outside the state in which it's been granted. Few other states will honor it. In fact, if a parent is disappointed with the custody decision of one state, he or she can simply grab the child and go 'custody shopping' in another state where they might get a better deal. But most parents don't know any of this when their children disappear, and they turn to the police for help."

Dan Rather confirmed what I had already researched, that what was surprising was "the state of the law, or rather the lack of it." He referenced the 1968 Uniform Child Custody Jurisdiction Act, which only eleven states (at that point) had adopted (Indiana was not one of them), and noting that a bill awaiting Congressional approval amending "the federal kidnapping statute to include natural parents," had "been languishing in a House Committee for more than three years."

The FBI and the Justice Department emphatically opposed the bill and wanted it to languish. Leading the opposition, Assistant Attorney General Richard Thornburgh said it was because the bill would have obligated the federal government to solve the problem. Even though the states had not acted, he didn't feel the child retrieval business was the job of the FBI. "It's a tough world and we can't solve everything by dumping it in the lap of Uncle Sam or the FBI," he told *60 Minutes*.

Dan Rather warned, "But, in the final analysis, this is not a story about law or about parents or about private detectives; this is a story about children. And we can't even begin to measure the effect of such experiences on them." Rather closed with, "Since we first broadcast that story last September, not one of the missing children in our film has turned up. Not one [new] state . . . has adopted the Uniform Child Custody Law. And that bill to amend the federal kidnap statute has spent yet another year bottled up in committee."

My stomach churned. I wasn't sure what I had hoped for when I ordered the transcript—perhaps a roadmap to the exact spot where kidnapping fathers would take their victims—but the report shed no new light on Klaus's intentions. The news was always the same about the current laws. Nothing. "They" could do nothing.

Even my lawyer, my advocate, sounded discouraged when I'd follow up with him, saying regrettably he'd made little progress in convincing the county prosecutor to issue warrants that would help us actually retrieve the children when we located them.

I sighed, set the transcript down, and skimmed through the rest of the mail. I pulled out an envelope from Big John. John had power of attorney for Klaus and had been handling the sale of our former condo. John had previously written Klaus and informed him that the jointly owned property had sold for $28,500. Enclosed was a copy of Klaus's response.

> *Dear John and Midge,*
>
> *Since I'd like to get this letter in the mail as soon as possible, I will only answer you in reference to the distribution of the proceeds from the sale of the house. First of all I guess that we both will be happy when this transaction is water under the bridge. Secondly, I would like you to take the total amount of the proceeds and pay same on the outstanding balance of my loan. As far as the $1000 is concerned, I will personally mail this amount to the party within forty-five days at which time I would also like to discuss the other question in your letter. I know the above situation sounds a little bit selfish, but when I give my word I stick to it even under this condition. In summary, take the proceeds, pay same towards my outstanding loan, forward statement with balance due to me for total payoff, inform the other party that a money order will be forwarded to you within the next forty-five days.*

*Should you encounter any problems follow the plan you
expressed in your letter. Now, should that be the case, do send
me a statement with the balance due from the bank after the
payment and I will complete the transaction myself. If we
have to go this route then any future discussion in regard to
the children and their immediate future is herewith
terminated. This kind of action might appear slightly strong in
content to you, but believe me John, I know what I am doing
and what I have to do after I take care of myself first. Since
we're on the subject of the children, they are both doing fine.
Ty is attending a private school over here (for Americans
stationed or living overseas only) and he is doing quite well, as
anticipated. Megan is also attending the same school, except
she is in Kindergarten. She has a five-year-old boyfriend who
brings her a candy bar once a week and she reacts like a
typical female — doesn't give a darn about him. Well, Midge
and John, I hope that everything is going well for you and
your family and that in the near future we can talk about
things that are not involved with items as the above. The
children do send you their love and a biggggggg hugggggggg.*
    Till the next time take care of yourselves,
    Ty, Megan & Klaus

So, taking the children wasn't enough. In addition, Klaus wanted
to finagle his way out of paying the $1,000 owed me from the sale of
the condo, and threatened all of us that, if he didn't get all the money,
there'd be no discussion of his returning with the children.

I grabbed the phone's receiver and called my attorney.

"Jeannie," he reminded me, "Klaus signed a promissory note for
the money owed you, so he can't have what he wants. The promissory note prevents the realtor from simply giving the proceeds from
the sale of the condo directly to Klaus."

I heard the words and put little stock in them. *He can't have what he wants? Oh, really?*

He successfully stole the children, and our divorce decree said he couldn't do that.

twenty-four

The Partial Woman

1973-1974, Indianapolis, IN

"If a woman surrenders her life to her husband, reveres and worships him and is willing to serve him, that is when she becomes really beautiful to him."

Is that so? I put the little paperback down and took a sip from the wineglass I held tight in my other hand and surveyed our new Tudor Park condominium. We hadn't stayed long at our third-floor apartment after selling the Cumberland house. We'd had a break-in, which left us both unnerved and anxious to find a better environment. Being in the new Tudor Park place felt refreshing, and I hoped being there would encourage me to fall in step with what, by all outward appearances, was the picture of a happy family.

The Total Woman, by Marabel Morgan, was a nationwide bestseller, but I was finding Morgan's tale a hard read—perhaps because I had so little time for actual reading. I arrived home from work before Klaus, even after picking up Ty from the babysitter. While Ty happily played with a new plastic dump truck in the living room, I had grabbed the chance for a few quiet moments with a book that, the author promised, would save my shaky marriage.

Morgan placed the responsibility for Happily Ever After squarely on the woman. The author claimed she had turned around her own failing marriage with her Total Woman methods. I thought it worth a try.

I read and reread the part about meeting your beloved at the front door, with a martini in hand, "dressed" only in Saran Wrap. I closed the book again. Is that what was necessary? I wasn't sure I could be such a "dutiful" wife, even if I wanted to take responsibility for my part in this marriage. My sense of self-sacrifice, however, had faded, along with the short-lived glow of the little honeymoon we'd enjoyed when I first moved back in.

The front door banged open then slammed behind Klaus, who shot through the living room headed for the kitchen without even a word to Ty. He used the N-word, grumbling about an employee who was causing more problems and headaches "than what he was worth."

I suppressed a groan hearing the racial slur, set the book aside and, though not wrapped in Saran Wrap, offered my husband a drink. Klaus ignored the offer, poured himself a glass from the wine bottle on the counter and said, through gritted teeth, "I'd like to kick his butt. He and Javier are too stupid to follow my instructions."

Clearly, I could have skipped dear Marabel's section about encouraging your husband to talk about his day. After the outburst, to show any interest at all felt like aiding and abetting a fresh round of prejudiced insults. The more his work responsibilities overwhelmed him, the more he regarded himself as superior to both the job and his coworkers. In our earlier years, I believed I could cause a shift away from his us-and-them world. I wasn't sure where a person learns such animosity. Surely, I thought, being on a campus as large and diverse as Indiana University would offer a course correction in his thinking. Later, I'd hoped actual life experience would open his mind.

It hadn't. This constant racism felt like a cancer spreading into our family life. Ty, so close by, could hear every word his father said.

"And those people from the finance department are no better," Klaus droned on. "That one guy, the asshole spic who thinks he's smarter than I am? He is going to hear from me soon."

He looked at me.

According to the book I still held, surrendering my life to this man was the objective. I spoke before I thought it through. "Klaus, can you hear yourself? Where is this coming from? If you have issues with the work somebody is doing, that's one thing. But to call people names and denigrate them because of their skin color or nationality, is . . . well, it's just *wrong*."

Oops—there went Morgan's advice about never contradicting him. If I had any hope of becoming a Total Woman, I obviously had some work to do—on both myself and my marriage.

Our daughter Megan was conceived in the fall of 1973. October 12, to be exact. 1:30 in the afternoon to be even more precise. We were celebrating Ty's third birthday at the lake cottage owned by Karen's parents on Koontz Lake. I came out of the bathroom and made a beeline for Klaus, still sitting on the deck overlooking the lake after lunch.

"Klaus. Now," I said.

"Now?"

Dr. Bob, his wife Lois, and Karen lifted their heads and looked at me from their lounge chairs, squinting into the sun.

I said, "Now. The temperature is perfect, and you, uh, wanted to go for a walk. This would be the ideal moment. I just need to change clothes. You ready?"

Klaus was ready.

"Have fun," Dr. Bob said, leaning back in his chair for a nap, while Karen and Lois smiled and continued their conversation.

I'd been tracking my temperature and knew the exact moment I'd be at peak ovulation. Forget that it was midday. Forget that we'd just taken abrupt leave from friends on the deck; we locked the bedroom door behind us. A second child would give us a second chance at happiness. Having a baby was certain to fill the emptiness inside of me, fill my need for love and affection. Painting the happy family picture in my head made me believe I could create a dream that would work. A baby was the answer.

Stripping from the waist down, I bent over and leaned my forearms on the bed. Klaus completed his manly duty and smiled as he pulled up his pants. I laid down and curled up into a fetal position, praying the emptiness would end, praying the Happily Ever After story would finally be mine.

He sat on the edge of the bed, watching me for a moment before resting his hand on my back. "Can I get you anything?"

"No," I murmured, feeling the emptiness inside me expanding rather than receding.

He didn't embrace me and didn't notice my eyes filling with tears.

We'd been husband and wife seven years when Megan was born the summer of 1974. Being happily pregnant diverted my attention from being unhappily married. Like the memory of the pain associated with childbirth, the memory of our marital storms faded with this new baby girl.

Her jaundiced condition at birth caused us to spend two anxious weeks waiting for her to stabilize. From her first moments, Megan had us smiling. She was a contented baby with an infectious giggle, and easy to love. She weathered the jaundice, which made me bet that her strength and fortitude would serve her well as an adult.

While she nursed, I studied a steady stream of books on improving relationships until I reluctantly returned to work for financial reasons just five months after her birth.

With our growing family, we sold the Tudor Park place and moved into a three-bedroom, two-story condo on the upper west side of Indianapolis. We found a nearby home-based daycare run by Chris, an efficient, caring mid-thirties German mom. She and husband Tom, eight years her junior, had met in Germany when Tom's US Army platoon was stationed there. They returned to Indianapolis where she provided a safe, loving space for a brood of six or seven plus her own two, prepared all their meals and maintained a spotless, nurturing home. My kids loved her.

Klaus moved on from the unsuccessful manager role at the insurance company and began working for Indy's Mercedes Benz dealership. On our two incomes, we were not only able to furnish but to *decorate* for the first time. The whole thing though felt unreal, as if Klaus and I were playing house, playing at being a family. Playing at loving each other.

Playing at loving someone and the joy of decorating faded quickly. The counseling, having another baby, reading relationship books, trying to buy into the "total woman" mentality, moving, decorating, making more money—nothing made a lasting difference in the relationship. Nothing filled the emptiness, and the marriage continued unraveling. The house grew cold as we spiraled downward.

Back at Ma Bell, I threw myself into my work. Maternity leave hadn't affected my career trajectory—my new position as the general commercial manager's executive assistant felt like a definite step up; a challenging one, yet one I could handle. Although I'd had only one high school semester of typing, I proved to be an administrative wonder.

My new boss called me into his office. "Jeannie, nothing is sacred in here. Look at anything, study everything so you can get the lay of the land. When I return in a couple of weeks from New York, I expect you to be well familiar with projects, needs, and functions of this office." I felt important, part of an inner circle of confidentiality.

I loved the job and quickly made myself invaluable to my boss. What a heady experience, and a stark contrast to my attempted happy homelife. Although I never tried the Saran Wrap trick, Marabel Morgan might have been proud of how I ran up and down the stairs at home, retrieving socks or a wallet for Klaus, how I cleaned and cooked. At the office, however, it was my opinion that mattered, and subservience was not on the menu.

"Jeannie, what's for dinner tonight?" Klaus said as he walked in the door.

"I just got home. I have no idea," I shouted from the upstairs bedroom. "I'm changing Megan's diaper."

Coming down the stairs, I could hear him rummaging through the refrigerator and adding, "Doesn't look promising."

"Why don't we go out? I'm tired," I said.

He got comfortable on the sofa after kicking his shoes off and hitting the remote. "No. I'm too tired. I'll wait while you fix something."

I set Megan down in the playpen and looked at him. "You work, I work. And I cook, clean, do the laundry. You watch TV. I change the diapers. You complain about, oh, I don't know, everything and everybody."

He glared at me with obvious irritation.

I had moved far beyond irritation. With my return to work, the homelife bubble had burst. How could I have thought having a baby would change all that was wrong with my marriage? And the Marabel Morgan approach had been like putting a Band-aid on a gaping, infected wound.

That very morning, her book had gone where such books belonged—out with the trash. I hadn't fully grasped the implications of the gesture until I stood staring at him. Then I knew. I loved my children, but I didn't love Klaus. And I didn't need him; I needed *me*.

"You know what?" I said, "I think the party is over around here. In fact, I know it is. I'm done."

And just like that, our marriage was over.

Almost.

TWENTY-FIVE

Day 54

September 18, 1977, Nashville, IN

The Sunday morning breeze cooled my tear-stained face as I wrote my son a letter. I prayed my former brother-in-law, Fredi, would figure out a way to get it delivered.

> *Dear Ty,*
>
> *I am sitting on our porch in Brown County. It is early and very quiet. The birds are singing and the crickets and locust are chirping. Cammy and Bobby's dog next door just barked.*
>
> *I wonder if the birds and crickets and animals miss you as much as I do? I wish you were here right now, enjoying this pretty morning with me, and I could hug you and tell you how much I love you and your sister.*
>
> *Only one time, when you were at Kingsdayle with Dr. Bob, were you away from me this long. I wish you and Megan were running around the yard right now, laughing and playing. I miss you and want to be with you.*
>
> *Please call me collect, Ty. Uncle Fredi can help you. You can call me at home or at work. Or write to me. Just please let me hear from you. Let me know how you are and how Megan is. I know you've had a wonderful vacation and you'll have lots of fun things to tell me. But I can't help missing you.*

All my love,

Mommy

xoxoxo

P.S. This paper is supposed to smell like cinnamon. What do you think?

P.P.S. Mama Cat had six little kitties. We're going to keep two of them if you want to. They are all black!

twenty-six

Accidents

1975, Indianapolis, IN

After I put Megan down for a nap late morning on a bone-chilling February day, I found my *Creative Divorce* book and headed downstairs. Reaching the landing at the foot of the staircase, I crumpled, depleted. Carole King described my marriage best: something inside had died. Our ten-year relationship had turned bitter cold, like a mid-winter house with frozen pipes and a cracked foundation. There wasn't even any friendship on which to build anew.

We had stayed together after the blowup at the end of 1974 purely for financial reasons; for all intents and purposes, we had officially separated. We were living under the same roof, but no longer sharing the same bed. The contrived arrangement strained family mealtime with the kids, with conversation almost nonexistent.

Slumped on the landing, I thumbed through the book, hearing myself sigh. Breathing in, breathing out.

I looked at my situation: twenty-eight years old, two kids, a dead marriage, missing my lover—or at least the intimacy—and alone with my if-I-stay-with-him-my-life-is-over thoughts. Why had I postponed moving on? When Klaus walked in the door, I was weeping.

"What's wrong?" he asked, with that vaguely irritated look he always got when I cried.

"What are you doing home?" I asked, drying my eyes with my sleeve as I slid the book under the stoop.

"I forgot my watch," he said, scanning the room, then looking back at me. He sat down at my side. "What's going on?"

Caught off guard, I let the words tumble out of my mouth as if stuffing them was no longer an option. "Klaus, I can't keep going on this way. Our worlds are so different. I don't love you and I can't make myself love you. It's time."

"Why can't you just be happy? I don't understand you. I need you, Jeannie. Things will change. They will." The words sounded flat, as if even he didn't believe them. *No*, I thought, *things won't change —unless it's for the worse.* Wordlessly, I shook my head.

He bristled and pulled away. "How can you break up our family?"

I had no reply.

"I'll never agree to a divorce, so don't even think about it." Grabbing his watch from the dining room table, he stormed out of the house.

Megan rustled in her crib, then quieted down and fell back asleep. I pressed my forehead in my hands, attempting to focus and figure out what I should do.

Karen. I needed my best friend. I navigated to the closest phone and called her at work long distance. "Hi Karen. I know you're probably busy, but could you talk for just a minute? I've hit the wall."

"Sure," she said. "Let me get someone to handle the front desk and I'll move into my office where I can shut the door. Can you hold a minute?"

I felt guilty pulling her away from her busy role overseeing the management of multiple apartment complexes. She could probably have used a mid-morning break, but instead she got me.

"Okay, I'm here," she said. "Sounds like things have gone from bad to worse."

"I'm so miserable and finally told Klaus I was done. I can't imagine staying any longer with things like they are. Karen, I feel like I'm dying. Klaus says he'll never agree to a divorce. The way things are is excruciating, and he acts so oblivious. He just doesn't get it."

"Oh, Jeannie. I'm so sorry. I know this hasn't been easy for you. What would you think about getting away for a few days? You and the kids could come up here. A weekend at the lake would do you good."

A getaway. I grabbed at the offer, as someone drowning grabs for a life preserver.

"Jeannie, it makes me so sad to think about the breakup of your beautiful family." Dr. Bob's voice was low and should have been soothing. We'd talked for two days and instead of gaining clarity, I felt lost.

I sighed and leaned toward the fire. I'd driven north with the kids to Walkerton to their lake house, hoping that a weekend with Karen and her family would help me decide what I could do. Once there, I realized his advice wasn't what I needed, much less additional time thinking or talking about the situation.

But Karen's psychologist father wasn't refraining from conversation on my last day with them. He poked the fire and continued, "Think about what this will do to Ty and Megan. Lois and I have had some rough times, but I would never leave my three beautiful children."

I looked around their warm, comfortable home and thought about my friend's family as I took another sip from my mug of coffee. Maybe all marriages were more like mine than I knew. Bob and Lois had rough times? They seemed like such an untroubled pair, and Karen and her siblings had turned out so well. Staring out the picture window, I watched Karen walk my four-year-old son down to the boat ramp for a farewell look at the long pier over the quiet lake. As much as I wanted to, I couldn't escape the emotional pull.

"Okay, Bob. I'll think about it. Thanks." It felt, however, like that's all it was—an emotional tug rather than reality.

I finished my coffee—I'd need the caffeine—and excused myself to pack the car. The trip home would take several hours, and the radio had warned that the roads could ice over soon. After loading the car, I got Megan, now seven months old, and Ty bundled up as quickly as I could. Based on the weather report, getting on the road before nightfall was important.

I was about an hour from Indianapolis when the dark Ford truck ahead of me stopped unexpectedly on the icy road. I hit the brakes too late and slid right into him. My neck whiplashed as my head slammed forward against the steering wheel. Lifting my forehead, I checked on the kids bedded down on the back seat.

"Ty, are you okay, honey? And your sister? Oh, thank God, she's still asleep."

"I'm okay, but Mommy, your face . . ." Ty said. I pulled down the visor mirror and gasped. Blood covered my already swelling nose and was splattered on my forehead. Ty climbed into the front seat with me and we held hands; we could hear the wailing sirens heading our way.

Bruised, battered, and unable to drive, I called Klaus from the emergency room.

"I'll leave right now," he said. "Give me an hour. Just stay put."

Arriving at the ER, he took me tight in his arms and held me, saying, "Jeannie, don't worry about a thing. I'll take care of you, okay?"

Shaken from the wreck, my body all but collapsed into his; I was admittedly grateful for the rescue. Klaus took charge of the situation, getting the kids tucked in the backseat of a rented Mercedes sports coupe and carefully placing me on the passenger side. When we reached our condo, he got the children ready for bed and settled in upstairs for the night.

"You're a mess." He sat next to me on the sofa where I had curled up in an old comforter, an icepack on my nose, tears still streaming down my cheeks.

"Klaus, I'm so sorry," I said, although I wasn't sure what I was sorry for.

He smiled with care and concern I hadn't seen in years, and said, "Be here with me tonight. Let me take care of you. Please."

Guiding me upstairs, he laid me down on the bed and covered me up. As I rolled on my side, he draped an arm over me and nestled in behind me. I turned back, facing him, sobbed and kissed him. "Oh, Klaus. If only . . ."

"Shh," he whispered. "Shh. You know how much I love you."

Each kiss weakened me, drawing me into the moment, and I let go. Because the flesh is weak. And when I went to the bathroom to wash up afterwards, I realized the condom was weak as well. Looking in the mirror at a bruised, swollen face and a pair of troubled eyes, I thought, *Oh God, what have I done?*

TWENTY-SEVEN

Day 59

September 23, 1977,
Indianapolis and Nashville, IN

"I can't believe I'm seeing what I'm seeing." I stared in disbelief and read out loud, "To any Peace Officer, Judicial Officer, Police Officer, Coroner, Sheriff of Marion County, Deputy Sheriff, Constable, Marshal, or any other officer authorized to serve Warrants in Marion County, You are hereby commanded to arrest <u>KLAUS MANTHEY</u> forthwith, and hold such person to bail in the sum of (<u>$5,000.00</u>), to answer at the present term of the Municipal Court, Room 10 of Marion County, in the State of Indiana, to an affidavit filed in said Court, for <u>CHILD STEALING</u>, and for want of bail, commit such person to jail of the County until legally discharged."

Throughout September Dennis had repeatedly met with and pitched the Marion County Prosecutor for warrants: child stealing and kidnapping. It was our understanding that obtaining such warrants for the arrest of a parent was a long shot, at least in the state of Indiana. As Dan Rather had pointed out in the *60 MINUTES* story, "Of all the components of this story, none surprised us more than the state of the law, or rather the lack of it. There are some efforts to make some of the present legalities illegal. But frankly, those efforts haven't gotten very far."

Dennis stood up from behind his desk as I jumped out of my chair and wrapped my arms around his neck. "Dennis, you did it!"

Haywood laughed, reached across and shook Dennis's hand. "So, did I hear you right that there are two official warrants?"

"Yes. Jeannie is holding the 'child stealing' one. Here's the other warrant, for 'kidnapping.' I can research it if you want me to, but I think they're unprecedented. The important thing is the court has issued them, and they're effective today, September 23."

Haywood grabbed and kissed my hand as I sat back down.

"Are you ready for the icing on the cake? Here's the third document." Dennis had requested the court consider my "plea" for a change in custody. The court had completed their review and agreed that Klaus took the children in violation of the court's decree, that his intentions were never to return to the United States, and that he had violated section 27 of the court's dissolutionment decree. The judge therefore granted me custody of Ty.

Not only did they award me permanent custody of both my children, they ruled that Klaus must pay $10,000 in attorney's fees for costs associated with obtaining custody of the children, and also stated "that the Respondent be restrained from ever visiting, talking to and otherwise seeing the Petitioner's children."

An unwelcome thought entered my mind. I hadn't imagined the scenario of "never" being one of the future options. My chest tightened as I read the words *restrained from ever visiting, talking to and otherwise seeing the Petitioner's children*. I let the thought sink in: Klaus was never to see the kids again.

Although I recognized that was exactly what he had done to me, I knew firsthand the heartbreaking prospect of never seeing my kids again. The court had handed me a gift, one that came loaded with mixed emotions. The joy, however, overwhelmed the ugliness that he had put into motion. There was no going back, and the court was doing its best to assist. Finally.

"I think this calls for a celebration. It's time, Jeannie," Haywood said, drawing me close when we got home.

"Time? For what?"

"Time for that honeymoon we didn't have. What say we go visit Louisville for the weekend and celebrate all this good news. You won, Jeannie! You won."

Those words brought on the tears. I was officially Ty's custodial parent—albeit "paper" custody. I confessed my mixed emotions to Haywood about the court's extreme ruling and how sick it made me feel.

He held me by the shoulders and looked me straight in the eye. "Jeannie, Klaus kidnapped the kids. He took them away from you—stole them from you. God, what he did was wrong on so many levels. Klaus thumbed his nose at the court and basically told you to go pound sand; this was not some noble act of love for the children. It was pure vengeance. I love you for being who you are, but your concern for that asshole right now is way off."

I knew he was right—about Klaus, about the kids, about the courts.

I rested my head on his chest and whispered, "What would I do without you?"

"Then let's not waste any more time. Let's pack and go celebrate!"

twenty-eight

Terminated

1975–1976, Indianapolis, IN

"Did the doctor say anything else?"

I knew what Klaus was asking. Sitting in a chair across from him in the living room, I nervously shredded the wet tissue I held in my hand and reached for another from the box on the coffee table. "Yes. I started crying when he gave me the news. That's when he told me we had options. There is a reputable clinic available to us, if that's what we want to do. He wished I had contacted him right away because there is a pill I could have taken."

If this had happened just a few years earlier, terminating the pregnancy wouldn't have even been an option. But in January 1973, the Supreme Court's landmark decision in Roe v. Wade had legalized abortion in all fifty states. Prior to that ruling, abortion was illegal in thirty states, Indiana included, and legal only under certain circumstances in twenty.

We sat in a brief silence, imagining another pregnancy, another baby, on the precipice of divorce. Though he stared straight ahead, I watched his eyes as he deliberated the impact of a third child. Biting his lip and shaking his head, he cast a clear vote. Anybody could read that face. Much as Klaus wanted us to be together, a third meant financial responsibility, not marital joy.

"Do you want me to call or do you?" he said, swallowing a sigh.

⁂

I stood at the curb a moment before I closed the car door and thanked Klaus for the ride. "Call me when you're ready and I'll come back and pick you up." As a chilly gust of wind whisked me into the building, my doctor's words still spun in my head. *I could have given you a pill.*

I looked around at the faces of the women-in-waiting. I hadn't turned thirty yet, but most of them looked impossibly young. My eyes met those of a nervous young girl no more than twenty. Long dark hair pulled back into a sleek ponytail flattered her high-cheekboned face, which registered surprise as she noticed my wedding ring. As a married woman, I was in the minority of waiting-room women ending pregnancies. I returned her smile, watching her process.

"Hi," I said. "Okay if I sit here?"

We exchanged first names, then low-voiced, she said, "I'm curious—can I ask you a question? You're married?"

I nodded. "I have two great kids and a not-so-great marriage. Bringing another child into this mess would be a big mistake." I sighed and added, "We all have our dreams, don't we?"

"Yes. I've studied ballet my whole life, and I just got accepted at the school I've been waiting to hear from for months. It's the beginning of the dream." Head down, she murmured as if the floor could process her words, "There's no room in my life for a baby. Not now."

We looked into the other's face, right before they called her name.

"Good luck," I said as she walked off.

"You, too," she replied.

When they called for me, I paid the receptionist $875 cash, and a woman who looked mid-fortyish escorted me to a small, clinical, but pleasant room where she said we could talk privately. Once inside, she closed the door, offered a firm handshake and introduced herself as Cynthia.

Based on her collared attire, I felt compelled to ask, "Are you a minister?"

"I'm an Episcopal pastoral counselor," she said.

We sat side-by-side on a window settee as she outlined her reasons for working at the clinic and supporting women's rights. Cynthia was in the forefront of a major controversy within the Episcopal church: she was seeking priesthood—a male-only option. I sensed her strength of character as she shared her story and felt comforted as she listened intently to mine. She told me the Episcopal Church supported abortion law reform and permitted the termination of pregnancy for a limited number of reasons: rape, incest, fetal deformity, or physical or mental health of the mother.

I didn't fit into any of those categories. There must have been some risk for Cynthia to even involve herself with an abortion clinic. It was clear she wasn't giving women a "stamp of approval." She was simply there, without judgment, for whatever counsel I needed. She looked at me, one woman to another, and we both knew the decision was mine: not the government's, not the church's, and not hers.

In the operating room, they gave me a type of twilight sedation before the procedure. I rested post-op in a lounge recliner with a warm blanket, a cup of cocoa, and a cookie.

And it was done.

Although Klaus and I slogged through another year, I knew the decision to terminate the pregnancy had clarified and cemented my decision to terminate the marriage. It was just a matter of time.

At the end of July 1976, I spoke the word divorce loud and clear and moved out for good. My exit was anything but graceful. Regardless, I thought it would be the end of things and I could move on.

TWENTY-NINE

Day 60, 61 & 62

September 24–26, 1977,
Louisville, KY, and Nashville, IN

"Haywood, this place is beautiful. Must have cost an arm and a leg. Did you rob a bank?" I teased when we arrived.

"I made some extra runs and have been stashing the cash waiting for this moment," was his proud answer.

We had left very early Saturday morning, toured Louisville, and checked into a stunning hotel overlooking the Ohio River. After getting dressed up, we drove to Kunz's The Dutchman, Louisville's famous steakhouse, known for both excellent fare and impeccable service. Definitely honeymoon material.

As we sat at our candle-lit white linen-covered table, I studied the menu, trying to focus on the descriptions of delicious food rather than the prices. Holding my hand, Haywood lifted his glass of iced tea and said, "Here's to you, Ty and Megan. When you're back home with your Mom and me, oh, the fun places we'll visit and the good times we'll have!"

The familiar sadness clutched at me, but I loosened its grip by clinking glasses with my husband and making a playful reply. "You'll need to be a little more specific than that!"

"Okay. When the kids are back, what's the first thing you want to do with them?"

I closed my eyes for a moment, remembering Ty's infectious grin, and the sweet smell of Megan's hair. My eyes watered as I thought about what it would be like having them back. "All I can think of right now is hugging them . . . loving them. Telling them they are safe."

He considered my words, and said, "Before or after the Rocky Road ice cream?"

We laughed out loud and couldn't stop, causing contagious laughter from others around us at the four-star steakhouse. Even the decorous waiter smiled and scurried over, taking part in the moment by quickly refilling our glasses.

Haywood had the touch. Even though this romantic getaway was only a temporary respite from the ordeal we were living through, he could lift my spirits like none other.

We spent the night in each other's arms, savoring a growing love and sense of mutual support, generated by our commitment to each other and the children.

On Monday evening, September 26, after the hour-long drive from work to Nashville, my steadfast carpool friend, Neil, dropped me off and headed home. I pulled two days' worth of mail out of the box and began sorting as I walked toward the house. The sight of a thin 3x6 inch envelope with German stamps, *Mit Luftpost Par Avion*, stopped me cold. The return address was A. Manthey, West Germany. Fredi had written. Even in his limited English, the message was obvious.

Sept. 20, 1977

Dear Jeannie!

Write this letter from my vacation place because last night our neighbors told me how often you tried to speak to me. In the week from 4th to 10th of September (2pm–4pm Indiana time) I too tried several times in vain to get a phone contact with you (dialed your number, hope was correct?). So let me tell what happened.

On September 4th got a message from Klaus that he lives in the Frankfurt area since August 20th or 21st. Am not quite sure about the date. During our fifteen-minute phone chat I told him off but he didn't react upon all I said. He strictly refused to give me his correct address and conveyed me his POB number only because he doesn't want anybody (even me) to know the place he and the kids are. He told me that the children are happy and in an excellent good condition and that he'll give me further information in some weeks.

I think he's very suspicious and he even doesn't want his sisters and brothers know what happened and the place he's living now. Am not to speak to you, Jeannie! I'm mostly sure he knows I did and do inform you and that can be the only reason he sent his message with this great delay. As he said, he's trying to get a job over here and a school for Ty and Megan. He's quite sure to get all.

So, Jeannie, that's all I know and all I can do is to transmit all his letters coming to my address. (I sent him Big John's letters!)

I'm sorry about this poor news but really hope to send you better information maybe in the near future. (Please don't tell anybody I gave you this.)

Love,

Fredi

I wrote back immediately, said I was glad he'd contacted me, and admitted I had worried he might not. Wanting Fredi to be in the loop, I enclosed a copy of Klaus's letter to Big John. My hope, I penned, was that we could keep the channels of communication open, and I would appreciate all news.

Questions—about the children; about who was taking care of them; about the Frankfurt PO box—filled my note. I expressed my fears that, with two months having gone by since their disappearance, I'd never see my children again.

According to Fredi's letter, he knew nothing of the kidnapping plans and found Klaus's actions upsetting, yet it was Fredi's address that Klaus told us to use. It all seemed so convoluted. Instinct told me I could trust Fredi, though there was always the chance that my former brother-in-law knew more than he was saying.

Even so, hearing from Fredi was far better than not, and added to the celebratory mood created by the surprise honeymoon weekend with Haywood.

I sat a little straighter, felt a little lighter, and felt a touch of hope.

thirty

A Room of One's Own

1976, Indianapolis, IN

With the divorce underway, I made my first solo housing decision and rented a second-story two-bedroom apartment in a friendly complex, inclusive of a playground and pool, less than ten minutes from our condominium. A place of my own which I could settle into and breathe.

Chris, our German babysitter for nearly two years, had found a good sales job and closed her daycare. I got lucky in my search for new home-based care; Lea and her husband Roger, my new twenty-something neighbors downstairs, were trying to have their own family and Lea loved the idea of babysitting for Ty and Megan. Her spunky, down-to-earth nature was appealing and undoubtedly a good match for the kids.

"We can't replace Chris, but this'll work," Klaus said, watching me pack my share of kitchen items at the condo. I wasn't sure if being supportive was his motivation, or making sure I didn't take anything he considered his. Whatever the intent, he acted momentarily convivial.

"Really?"

"Yeah. They seem nice enough, their apartment is clean, and Ty and Megan like them. It'll also be easier for the kids because it's close to the condo."

I paused, my favorite coffee mug in hand. I hadn't realized what that proximity might mean to my future privacy; my focus had been on Ty and Megan's emotional wellbeing. Megan was only two—she might come out at the other end of this unscathed. But Ty, almost six, had become detached and quietly observant over the preceding month; a darkness had settled over him and I felt the uneasiness at play, my son's and my own.

I carefully wrapped my mug, placed it with the other dishes, and taped the cardboard box shut. Klaus watched me set the box with the growing pile taking over the corner of the living room.

Switching gears, he said, "I hope you're not planning on me helping with your move. You're on your own. Just what you wanted, right?" Klaus waited for a reply that never came, then scoffed as he and his anger left the condo, leaving me alone to finish packing. My shoulders relaxed as soon as I heard the car pull away. Relief followed his absence, though the air remained thick with tension.

The children and I moved into our new place with help from friends on a Friday morning, and by Saturday afternoon, the three of us had most of the unpacking done. "Well guys, what do you think?" I said. The kids were running through the apartment, jumping on the beds, laughing as they explored each room.

Curled up on my recently purchased overstuffed sofa, sunlight warming my shoulders, I soaked up the spacious light-filled apartment and the simplicity of the space I had created. There was something rewarding about its newness: freshly cleaned carpets, fresh paint, with a few purchased green plants enhancing my current surroundings. I admired my modern floor lamp arced over the sofa yet realized even the old bentwood rocker that came with me had taken on a new life. I had brought very little and furnished the place instead by spending a few dollars: the lamp and the colorful contemporary bed linens and spread made it mine.

I inhaled deeply, claiming the moment, imagining my new serene life. Suddenly, Ty landed on the sofa, flopped on top of me and gave me an unexpected hug. His impromptu giggles, reminiscent of days gone by, were so contagious I laughed out loud.

My mind traveled back to earlier times when his antics had made me chuckle. At eighteen months, he inadvertently dropped scrambled eggs on the floor from his high chair. I had to muffle my reaction when he stared down at the eggs and startled me with a well-enunciated "goddammit." Another time, he couldn't have been more than four, he'd run into the kitchen before dinner and asked if he could have three cookies; I said no, only one. Later, realizing he had conned me into giving him a pre-dinner treat, all I could do was laugh and give the boy credit for a clever presumptive close.

Relaxing now on the sofa with my handsome son happily curled up in my lap, I said a prayer that my kiddo would weather the separation and the changed living arrangements. I tousled his thick brown hair and wrapped my arms around him, suddenly aware of how tall he'd grown. Being nearly six, and having already attended a nursery school for two years, Ty was ready for kindergarten in the fall. Considering the potential turmoil in the days ahead, I was glad he would be older than most of his counterparts.

Just from being in a place of my own, my self-confidence grew. Even though I was a good mother, I knew I could be a better mother now that I was coming into my own.

Ty needed his father, too—I got that. Klaus was physically demonstrative with his son—somewhat surprising to me, given Klaus's general demeanor—and Ty loved one-on-one time with him. Until Megan was born, Ty had captured and held his father's attention. When the baby sister came along, Klaus's interests shifted.

"Daddy, can we play ball?" Ty would beg.

"Not right now, son. Maybe in a while. Little Megan here needs us to take care of her. Don't you, my sweet girl? Ty, can you move over and make more room for your baby sister?"

I had watched that moment from the kitchen as Ty frowned and scooted over on the couch. Sharing Daddy's love wasn't easy for Ty, and Megan was a show-stealer. I wondered if the new living arrangements might cause Klaus to better balance the time spent with each of the children. I hoped he'd do that, however we worked out the divorce visitation.

Megan's voice interrupted my thoughts of earlier times. "Ty, find me!" she called. He wriggled out of my arms and dashed down the hall. I watched as they took turns playing hide-and-seek in the afternoon sunlight, and felt clarity within my bones: I had done the right thing. The kids and I would figure it all out as we went along.

"Who's hungry for a snack?" I said, happier than I'd been in a long while.

They came running, and we all headed into our new not-quite-unpacked kitchen in search of the Jif and jelly. Ty insisted, "Let me make them, Mom. I can do it. Just watch."

I put one of their favorite records on the turntable and we sang "Jeremiah Was a Bullfrog" as Chef Ty slathered peanut butter on slices of Wonder Bread and splotched the countertop with grape jelly.

"So, pizza later for dinner?" I laughed as they whooped and cheered.

THIRTY-ONE

Day 76

October 10, 1977, Nashville, IN

I turned on the desk lamp, picked up a pen and rolled it between my fingers. I sat down, closed my eyes and hoped the words I needed would come. In less than two weeks Ty would turn seven.

In the childless quiet of the evening, I composed a birthday note to my son. Regardless of whether he would receive it, the act of writing it felt like a connection. As a mother, I had to reach out.

> *Dear Ty,*
>
> *Happy Birthday, honey!*
>
> *You must know by now that it has been a very long time since we have seen each other. I miss you and Megan more than you will ever know. Please come home, son. Your Grandma Baker has been very sick because she cannot see her grandchildren. Everyone here misses you very much and wants to see you again. Even the kitties.*
>
> *Ty, I love you. You must always remember that I love you and you must know it has been very miserable (that means very sad) without you and Megan.*
>
> *I really hope you have a very happy birthday. When you come home, I'd like to have another party for you and give you your presents.*
>
> *I love you with all my heart,*
>
> *Mommy*

THIRTY-TWO

Day 80

October 14, 1977, Nashville, IN

"Haywood, I need help with this Passport Office letter. What do I say?"

He pulled up a chair next to me at the desk and looked over the document. "I know it feels intimidating and scary, but I think you're going to have to bite the bullet and say the passports are missing and you need new ones. Klaus had to get passports for the kids to take them out of the country. If we don't get replacement passports, we won't be able to get them out of Germany and back home."

The court's ruling weeks earlier had excited us, but we soon realized securing custody documents and warrants didn't bring us any closer to finding them. Actively looking for them in Germany seemed like the logical next step, so we were making our travel preparations. The idea of confronting Klaus on his own turf conjured up overwhelming odds and fears. I couldn't let those fears take over.

Haywood and I had lengthy discussions about the logistics of getting the kids back into the US, however, if we reported the kidnapping to the Passport Office, not only could they decline assistance, we feared they might refuse the issuance of new passports for the children. Haywood was right; best simply to report Megan and Ty's passports as lost.

The Department of State responded a week later with a request for more detailed information regarding the loss of the passports and the length of our proposed trip. I supplied believable details, informing them I'd lost the passports when moving from one home to another, that I had looked through important papers, moving boxes, etc. and couldn't find them. I told them our proposed trip was three, possibly four weeks.

I reread the form. *I have made a careful search for the passports and have not been able to locate them.* Heaving a sigh, I signed, stamped, and mailed the document. At this point, I had nothing to lose. Besides, they had only asked me if I knew where the passports were, and the truth was—I didn't know. They hadn't asked if I knew where my children were.

Haywood heard the screen door shut when I returned from the Post Office.

"Sit down, sweetie. Feel better with that done?" I joined him at the kitchen table without answering. He read my mind, something he was good at. "We can do this, Jeannie. We're going to find them and bring them back."

"I know. It's just tough doing stuff I've never done before, and I'm afraid I'll make some stupid mistake that would make this all blow up in our faces. And the thought of flying to Germany and wondering where we'll start, or how we figure out what in the hell we're going to do, it's just—"

"Jeannie, look at me." He cupped his hands over mine. "I love you. One step at a time. People are pulling for us and we'll ask for help to plan the trip. Okay? I'm here and we can do this."

His determination won me over and my fears left the room. Nodding, almost laughing, I threw my arms around his neck.

THIRTY-THREE

Day 91

October 25, 1977, Indianapolis, IN

A lice, a close friend at work, insisted I attend her church at lunchtime. I was Presbyterian; she was Catholic. Although the rituals were not part of my religious tradition, I anxiously mimicked her every move from genuflecting to crossing myself. I was desperate and prayed a preprinted prayer to St. Anthony, the patron saint of lost items or articles, beseeching aid in my search.

St. Anthony, patron and protector of all who invoke thee with confidence, behold me now at thy feet. I come to ask, not for wealth, nor for poverty; because I fear the one might lead me to vanity, the other to impatience, sadness or despair. But, for myself and for all dear to me, I ask for such things only as are necessary to soul and body. Come to our assistance, O thou blessed father of the poor, and deliver us from all danger. Obtain for us the accomplishment of our desires, and success in our undertakings. This favor I implore by the unfailing beneficence toward thy devoted clients. Amen.

I read the prayer, and in the silence moved to the front of the church and lit two candles, one for Ty, one for Megan. Klaus's words, "You'll never find us," kept reverberating in the back of my mind. Kneeling at the altar, I whispered, "Please. I'm not Catholic. I don't feel like much of anything these days. And I don't know how this works, but if my praying to you is all right, please hear this mother's prayer. Please help me find my children. Please. Thank you. Amen."

I wiped my wet face with the back of my hand and repeated, "I ask for such things only as are necessary to soul and body." Though I wasn't sure I believed in the power of prayer, I believed in the powerful love I had for my children, and that love mattered.

Later the Franciscan monks of St. Anthony's Guild wrote thanking me for a small donation I sent them. *We are praying every day that you will have continuing courage and that the children will be returned to you.*

They were praying for me. Who was I to turn down such love? It had to help.

thirty-four
***

Manthey v. Manthey

1976-1977, Indianapolis, IN

"Would you *please* pass the salt?" I repeated for the third time, voice raised.

It was December, four months into our separation. Klaus looked at me, reached for the saltshaker and, with a wordless smirk, slid it across the table in my direction. We'd met for a family dinner at a local steak house to review the Christmas '76 holiday calendar for shuttling the kids back and forth between my apartment and the condo.

"Thanks." I threw Klaus a sarcastic smile, hoping the kids didn't catch it. "Ty, how's your hamburger, honey?"

"Great. Can I get some more fries, Mommy?"

"I think you've had enough. Why don't you finish your burger?" I said.

Klaus, eyes still on me, motioned to the waitress and addressed Ty. "I'll get them for you, son. Just let me call the nice lady over."

"Okay, Daddy," Ty said, though he read the displeasure in my expression and squirmed in his chair. "Mommy?"

"It's okay, babe," I said.

"Why should you get the kids next weekend?" Klaus said dryly.

"Because I asked you last week if that'd work for you and you said yes, so I made plans."

"I don't remember that conversation."

"Oh, come on. So now you expect me to change my plans? This is nuts," I said.

"Your plans don't interest me. I don't care what you think. And since this is all your idea, I don't feel like playing according to your rules."

Ever since I had contacted a sorority sister's attorney-husband and started the divorce proceedings a few months earlier, Klaus had stopped playing by any rules—mine or those of the legal system. According to the existing separation agreement, Klaus should have been paying $60.00 per week child support and $125.00 per month maintenance payment, but no checks came after the first month. The court's convoluted procedures for garnishing wages were so daunting, I'd gritted my teeth and done without.

Like nails on a chalkboard, his nasty tone sent an unpleasant shiver down my spine.

"Why do you insist on making this so difficult?" I asked.

"*This* is all your fault. You don't care about me, you don't care about the kids, you don't care about our family. You're the one tearing our lives apart, not me."

Before I could reply, he threw in, "And the more I think about it, the less I want to sit back and take it. I thought you'd come around."

"Come around? There's nothing to come around to. You saw to that. You don't realize what it was like for me, living with you. Nothing is your fault; nothing is your doing. You are a hateful . . ." I stopped short.

Out of the corner of my eye, I saw Ty watching the verbal ping-pong. Megan didn't look up from her coloring book, but her furrowed two-year-old brow revealed her discomfort.

"We'll talk about this later," I said.

When the children and I got back to the apartment complex, they bounded up the stairs ahead of me and waited impatiently while I unlocked the front door. Once inside the Klaus-free environment, I did what I had done my whole life thanks to my musician dad—I cranked up the music. What a release and a surefire balm. *Jingle Bell Rock* filled the room as I turned on the tree lights and shouted, "Get those shoes off and let's dance!" Ty and Megan wiggled and jiggled and sang while I shook and shimmied, working on an attitude adjustment after the last two hours of chain pulling. This French fry incident was only the latest of many moments over the past few months involving the children: Klaus allowing them to do something I had told them not to, blatantly spoiling them, playing the good cop.

The kids and I had collapsed on the living room floor, laughing and breathless, when the music ended and the phone rang.

"I'll get it, Mom," Ty said as he bounced up and answered the call with a bright hello. "Hi, Daddy. Guess what? Mom put on some Christmas music and we've been dancing. It was really fun." After an abrupt pause, he added, "Okay."

Dragging the extension cord across the living room, Ty handed me the receiver. I nodded my thanks.

"Hello," I said in my best monotone, still out of breath.

There was no dancing on the other end of the line. "I've decided we don't need to have any more conversations," he said. "Glad you're getting to have fun with the kids. You can have them next weekend but, after that, we'll see. They're my kids, too, and don't you forget it."

I winced as the sound of a slammed receiver reverberated in my ear. Was he blowing off steam or was that a threat?

I tucked Ty and Megan in bed and turned in myself. Restless, I awoke within a few brief hours in a sweat, anger invading my sleep. What was he threatening? Was he planning on making life miserable for us? I knew being a single mom would not be easy, but I loved the life I was making for the three of us and I wasn't about to let his aggressive behavior deter me. I had to face the fact I would need financial support for the kids. Klaus's salary as the Mercedes-

Benz dealership service manager was ample; there was no point waiting any longer.

The next morning, I called my lawyer. "Dennis, after the holidays, let's get this over with."

When my copy of the attorney's letter to Klaus arrived right before New Year's, I slit open the envelope immediately. The letter pressed him to settle things and move toward a court date. The proposal seemed reasonable enough: I would have custody of the children and Klaus would have flexible visitation rights. Dennis had skillfully added, "Jeannie has called my attention to the fact that you have not paid the $60.00 per week, nor have you been making the full $125.00 per month maintenance payments that she is entitled to. It is not our intention to enforce the payment of the arrearage unless we cannot make a reasonable custody and property settlement agreement. If I do not hear from you by January 7, 1977, then I shall set this case down for a contested hearing."

My phone rang twenty minutes after I'd finished reading it. "I got your attorney's letter. We need to meet," Klaus barked into the phone.

I replied with an agreeable yes and made arrangements for Lea to keep the kids. *Calming the waters would be best,* I reasoned. *I can do this.*

Over breakfast at a small neighborhood restaurant the next morning, I reiterated the details of the settlement. Taking issue with each point raised, Klaus finally threw up his hands and said, "I'm not putting up with this. You're dreaming if you think I'll agree to let you have your way. I want custody of my kids, and I *will* get them. Just watch. Tell Dennis I'm hiring my own attorney. I'll see you in court." He pushed his chair back, threw a ten-dollar bill on the table and added, "My treat. Happy New Year."

He stood up, glared at me, and strode out of the restaurant.

The waitress walked over and offered, "More coffee, miss?"

I leaned both elbows on the table, my fingers interlaced under my trembling chin. I took a deep breath, one long inhale after another, afraid if I didn't, I'd lose it.

Shaking and unsure of what to do next, I just sat there, like a prisoner chained to a chair.

"Make me another White Russian, would you, Joanne?" I said, sniffling.

It was almost midnight, and the kids were asleep. As my sister handed me our favorite New Year's concoction, she laughed. "You should see yourself. You're a mess. You look like a raccoon."

She tossed a box of Kleenex in my direction. I took a large swig of my drink, then wiped my tear-filled eyes.

"Oh, that helped. Those mascara smudges aren't really your best look," she said, a futile attempt to get a laugh out of me.

I continued my diatribe. "He'll never let me out unless I agree. Can you believe he wants full custody? And he's hiring the 'right' lawyer to make that happen. What do I do then? What if he wins? I cannot believe this is happening. Why did Mom bring us up to be so damn nice? I'm sick of traveling down that road and falling into every pothole. I don't know what to do, Sis. If I stay, I'll be miserable the rest of my life. But to get divorced, I'll have to give up my kids!"

My sister nodded and mixed another White Russian for herself, then tripped á la Dick Van Dyke style over the ottoman, spilling some of it. The laughter that followed ended my rant.

After I got her upright, she hugged me, still smiling, and said, "We'll get through this, Jeannie. Mom may have taught us to be nice, but you can't blame her. You're forgetting what she went through divorcing Dad; she ultimately taught us to play our cards right. You need to hang in there. It's time—for both of us."

Joanne was also having a tough time, on the verge of ending her twenty-year marriage. After they'd adopted a baby five years earlier, her husband, Mark, after so many years of no kids, found being a dad wasn't his calling.

"I guess you're right about Mom," I sighed. I thought about the thirty-seven years she spent with our father before she finally divorced him. I still wondered how she felt after the first time she left him and then agreed to go back. Dad's heart attack during that separation, along with Dr. Bob's advice, changed everything. Dr. Bob, ever the counselor ready to expound on what was proper, had told her my father could actually die without her love and support. So, of course she reconciled; she didn't want him to die and didn't want the blame if he did.

Ever my mother's daughter, I wanted out of my marriage though didn't want the blame resting on my shoulders. I was twenty-nine and wanted Klaus to understand and not hate me. He felt no such compunction. My attempts at explaining or justifying the divorce had only incensed him. We were at war and his latest mantra was that he'd see I got nothing.

I set down my empty glass. "Sis, we'd better make a pot of coffee."

Early on a mid-January Friday night with the divorce hearing approaching, Klaus ordered me over to the condo. "Have Lea keep the kids. I need to talk to you. Alone."

Still believing I could keep the waters calm and attorney intervention would only fuel things, I blindly went. Klaus offered a deal: he would agree to the divorce and back off the court battle if we split everything.

Everything.

I sucked in the cold air from the chilled reception as my mouth fell open. "You're . . . you want . . . you're not really suggesting we split the kids, are you?" I said in disbelief.

"One is a better offer than none. Unless you'd rather give me full custody. It's up to you."

Two options. Only two. Blindsided, I could see no others.

Exhausted, dumbfounded, and knowing we were down to the wire, my customer service training conspired with my nice-girl default and I heard myself say, "Okay."

We would split everything: the dishes, the silverware, the children. Klaus insisted on no attorney involvement, so we met and laboriously went through item by item, every detail, every stick of furniture. My mantra: *Be nice, be fair, and he'll let you go.*

As I sat in my car with a severe headache after forfeiting my plans, my thoughts spun in two different directions. I could hear, *but I'm their mother! Children go with the mother*—thoughts contradicted by *is that fair to their father? The one you betrayed? The one who doesn't want the divorce? The one who is a "good" father?*

I started the engine and backed out of the driveway, my heart hurting worse than my head.

When I got home, I looked at my reflection in the bathroom mirror and exhaustion and fear looked back at me—I feared the fight; I feared his anger, and most of all, I feared losing.

I would learn years later of Gloria Steinem's coining of the term "female impersonator," referring to our male-dominated society's socialization of young girls. Men determine what is feminine and girls, at age twelve or thirteen, wanting approval, change their behavior to suit the male rather than developing their own definition of what being a female means.

I had learned early on to play the role of the pleaser, which came with its own internal dialogue of self-criticism. What I had trouble learning is that if you're always trying to be what someone else wants you to be, it's never enough. *Never enough,* the internal critics whispered—*not smart enough, not good enough.* The charges were a dissonant chorus of voices in my head as I tried to please my way through life. And here I was, wending my way through a divorce, wanting to stand my ground, and those voices were still dictating my decisions.

"Want me to swing you higher, Ty?" I asked.

"Yeah, Mom, like Dotti is doing for Megan," he shouted, looking out over the park.

Dotti, once my phone company trainer, now my close friend, tried consoling me while we continued swinging the kids. "Jeannie, I know this is a black day for you. I can't imagine separating my kids any more than I can imagine cutting them in half. I've never heard of anyone doing this split custody thing. Klaus must have one hell of an attorney. Do you really think the court will agree to it?"

In the 1950s and 60s, divorce courts awarded most mothers custody of the children; the father had visitation rights and paid support. By the 1970s, ideas about motherhood and fatherhood were changing. Although not released until two years later in 1979, the movie *Kramer vs. Kramer* encapsulated a cultural shift that had already begun. The film told the story of a couple's divorce and its impact on everyone involved, including their young son. Mostly based on the assumption that a child is best raised by the mother, the court awarded custody to the mother. But then, in a turn of events, she realized that the sanctity of motherhood, in her case, did not outweigh the relationship her child had established with his father. A new equality had emerged. Ultimately, she gave full custody to her former husband.

This cultural shift meant a woman could fight back and win financial concessions in a divorce. However, it also meant she might *lose* custody of the children, depending on the judge's decision about which parent would better raise the child. Caught between the familiar roles of my mother's generation and the upheaval of the 1970s, I was navigating uncharted waters.

"Dotti," I said, watching Ty push Megan on the merry-go-round, "I just don't know what the courts will see as fit at this point. My guess is though, if we've made it look like we've worked out the custody arrangements in advance, the judge has less to figure out and would go along with it."

She sighed and hugged me as she said, "Just remember, I'm here if you need me."

Later that evening, I called Dr. Bob for counsel. Klaus might listen to him—Bob was, after all, a man.

"Jeannie, I know it's been difficult for you. We all go through rough patches. But I'm sure you two can work things out. You need to think of the children. The marriage doesn't have to end."

"Dr. Bob, the marriage *has* ended. You know we've tried. Good grief, we had Megan hoping to save the marriage. We have reached a point of no return. It's over, and no matter what I do or say, he's angry. I thought maybe you could talk with him, you know, maybe make him realize that it's not the end of the world. There's no reason for him to be so hateful," I pleaded.

"Jeannie, you know I think the world of you, but you don't know what you're doing. I think where you went wrong was not giving Klaus his due. Klaus just needed to know he is the man of the house, that his rights were accepted and acknowledged."

I fell back into my chair as if I'd been sucker-punched and let out a groan. *Klaus just needed to know he is the man of the house?* I had no words for a moment, then the words came. "I am not going back."

"Well, if you insist on going through with this, Jeannie," Bob intoned, "the very least you can do is make sure that this is a divorce of integrity. I suggest you sign a moral agreement as part of the property settlement. I'll draft the document."

Integrity. How do you say no to that? It still felt like veiled bullying. My voice sounded small and defeated as I agreed to the command.

A few days later, I sat with Klaus in Dr. Bob's office reviewing the "moral agreement."

We, Klaus Manthey and Jeannie Manthey, on this date do hereby enter into this moral agreement for the spiritual and emotional wellbeing of our children.

We do hereby agree that our relationship with our children will never deteriorate to the point that the children are treated as pawns in a game between parents, and we will as parents support the integrity of the other.

As parents, we recognize and value the individuality and uniqueness that exists in each other and hereby agree to protect the parental image of each other even when we disagree.

"Integrity?" Klaus's tone sounded respectful, so Dr. Bob may have missed the sarcasm. I didn't.

Leaning back in his imposing leather chair, Dr. Bob assured him that if the divorce was indeed inevitable, this agreement would be a bulwark against the ill will that could negatively affect an estranged couple and damage the children.

Klaus looked at him for a moment, displaying deference to the older man's patriarchal control. Perched on the edge of an uncomfortable chair, I watched as something unspoken passed between the two men. I would learn Klaus had only nodded in agreement to appease Bob, giving the appearance of male solidarity. What I witnessed was actually two men posturing. Klaus submitted his signature as a courtesy; the vow meant nothing to him.

Klaus said, "Of course, sir." He picked up the pen and, in his orderly German way, signed and dated the agreement.

It proved to be as worthless as Bob's advice.

When Karen answered the phone, I fell apart.

"Karen, the divorce is less than two weeks out and he's still making demands. I cried all day yesterday—at work! I should have called you over the weekend, but I was so upset with your dad, I didn't know how to handle it."

"Oh no! What happened, Jeannie?" she said.

"We met at your dad's office last Friday and he had us sign a 'moral' agreement, but Karen, it was obvious he wasn't in my corner. The whole thing felt like some kind of setup. We both signed the document, but I was to be the compliant one and give in to Klaus's demands. I thought we'd *finally* gotten through everything, and then Klaus said he wanted me to take back my maiden name, and that is not what I want right now. That would mean the kids' last name would be different than mine. Do I not have any say in this? Your father just sat there."

"I'm so sorry. My father can be overbearing, I know. I've watched my mother over the years bow to his requests because, well, he wears the pants in the family," she said. "But you know what? Klaus can't force you to go by your maiden name. Just stick with the court date. It'll be over soon."

"I know. You're right. I'm just beside myself right now. What I should do is focus on Ty and prepare my son as best I can for this God-awful custody arrangement. That's really what's eating me up."

"Yeah," she said. "That will be a tough conversation."

I felt the tension in my neck release as I talked on. I could rest in Karen's presence, even over a long distance call. By the time I hung up the phone, I realized she was not just the loving force on the other end of line; she *was* my lifeline. We had what we joked was a DNA friendship—two lives that were so intertwined over time that the friendship took on a life of its own.

Before sitting down with my son, I chewed a couple of Tums and took the last of the aspirin. The lump in my throat, along with the headache, wasn't helping the situation. "Ty, come here, honey. I need to talk to you."

He grabbed the toy truck he was playing with and plopped down on the sofa.

Deep breath, Jeannie. "Ty, you know that Mommy and Daddy aren't living together anymore. We've decided to keep things that way. I'm going to live here at the apartment, and Daddy will live at the condominium. But we had a problem. Daddy wanted both you and Megan to live with him, and I wanted you and your sister to live here with me. We couldn't figure out what to do at first because we both love you so much. What we thought would work is to have you stay with Daddy, and Megan will stay with me here." I waited a minute, watching him, letting him absorb the information, and then asked, "How's that sound to you?"

His response was quiet and composed for one so young, but that was his nature. He looked down at the toy truck and slowly turned the wheels. "I guess that's okay, Mommy. But when will I see you?"

I spoke slowly. "Daddy and I have that all worked out, sweetheart. You can come see me and be with me pretty much whenever you want. Daddy and I will talk about it first, and then one of us will get you over here. You'll still be at Lea's every day with your sister when you're not at school and you two will be together every weekend either at Daddy's or here with me. You think we can try that?"

I reached out and touched his pensive six-year-old face. Leaning into me, he snuggled close as I wrapped my arms around him, tucking his head under my chin. We sat that way until my eyes watered and forced me to tilt my head back to quell unstoppable tears.

"I know this must be hard. It's hard for Mommy, too. But we'll work things out, and you can call me anytime if you're upset or sad or just want to talk." I rocked him for another minute then choked out, "You know how much I love you, don't you?"

He nodded, pressed his head against me, and said, "I love you, too, Mommy."

After Klaus and I hammered out the last of the property settlement, his new demeanor was obvious. Short of getting me back, he got everything he'd asked for, gotten everything he wanted—it was a successful power play. As the victor of round one, he became temporarily congenial. I turned the paperwork over to my attorney.

"Jeannie, I realize getting out of this marriage feels like life or death. Believe me, I totally understand your situation, especially after having met and dealt with Klaus," Dennis said. "But, just hear me out. You are agreeing to things I'm afraid you'll regret—seriously regret—down the road. I mean, my God, you've split custody of the children!"

"Dennis, it's taken months to get to this point. I know it's an unusual settlement, but I've got to make it work. The draft calls for open visitation, sharing the same babysitter, and the kids will be together on weekends with one of us, right? It's not perfect—not even close—but it's what I have to do. I'm afraid I could lose custody of both of them."

"Jeannie, we can fight him."

"Dennis, he has worn me down and worn me out. I don't want to fight him anymore. I just want this over."

Though dismayed, he acquiesced and drew up the agreement. Klaus signed it.

On the morning of January 31, 1977, Dennis and I, the only ones whose attendance the court required, made our way into the courtroom for the 9:30 a.m. hearing. Klaus was not present. The judge asked a few questions—if reconciliation was possible, if I was pregnant—then granted the divorce. Considering the preceding months, it felt joyously anticlimactic. No big court scene, no visible battle. Judge Gerald Zore named us each a fit and proper parent and decreed I was the custodial parent for Megan, and Klaus custodial parent for Ty.

The split custody arrangement was if nothing else unusual in Indiana's history. My intuition proved correct. Because we had negotiated our own parenting plan prior to the divorce hearing, the court considers it more likely to work out than a custody decision imposed by the court. Though our solution required approval by Judge Zore to make it legally binding, Klaus and I had negotiated a custody agreement "with one eye on the law" to make it acceptable to the court. Relieved as I was that the judge put his stamp of approval on the arrangement, I wondered if it'd really work. Regardless, with the judge's agreement and the divorce granted, I could only hope for the best.

Klaus called that afternoon. "Would you meet me later tonight? We need to put this behind us. Let me buy you a birthday drink. Why don't you meet me at TGI Fridays, okay?" Saying no didn't feel like an option. I was on the verge of a new life; better to end the old one with a toast.

"I think this will all work out, don't you?" he said as we sat at the bar.

I cocked my head and said, "Sure," not knowing what "this will all work out" meant. "I'm just glad we were able to settle things and get the divorce over with. Who knows, someday it might make it easier for us to get along."

"The divorce doesn't even matter," he said, as if this were some temporary arrangement that would calm me down and cause me to see the error of my ways. "You just need some space, some time."

Startled, I thought, *Time for what?* Did he not realize that this time there would be no going back? I sipped my drink, maintained a minimum smile and hoped my internal reaction didn't register on my face.

By the time I finished my heavy pour of wine, I didn't care what he thought. This was the day before my thirtieth birthday and in my purse, I had my papers, my birthday gift: "The marriage of the parties is irretrievably broken and is therefore dissolved."

We picked up the kids and went our separate ways. At last.

Home in my apartment, I rocked Megan a bit and put her to bed. I smiled as I brewed a cup of spiced tea and enjoyed a barefoot saunter across the living room carpet to my sofa. A birthday card had arrived from my sister, who was back in Florida following through with the overdue closure of her own twenty-year marriage. She and I had talked about the possibility of living together, of raising our two boys and Megan in a happy family setting. I opened her card and drank my tea while I read and reread the message she included. *"It's time to dream a new dream, Sis. And we women have the power to make those dreams come true. So, happy birthday to you and all your dreams."*

I walked into Megan's bedroom where she lay sleeping and stretched out next to her. I whispered, "Let's dream big, my sweet girl," and wrapped my arms around her until I drifted off and slept, too.

thirty-five

Haywood and the Kids

April 1977, Indianapolis, IN

T y and I were busy making dinner while Megan played in the living room. We could hear her singing along with Sesame Street music while we got ready for our company. Tonight, there would be four of us. Haywood and I, now several weeks into our relationship, had agreed a meeting with the kids would be okay. Was I moving too fast? Was it too soon? I thought about my friend Dotti's warning about the rebound effect. Her words swirled around in my head. *Try to pace yourself. Considering you're just coming off the marriage-go-round from hell, I don't recommend jumping on the rebound wagon. Been there. Done that. Those blind rebounds are usually more like suicide with Novocaine—we don't feel a thing.* But I felt so good, so happy, and safe with Haywood. I smiled, certain that my needs outweighed what would, in any other situation, be good logic.

No, this was different. After what I'd been through, I wasn't about to lose this opportunity.

The doorbell rang. "Ty, why don't you go answer the door. Our company is here. Just remember, ask before you open it," I reminded him.

"Wow, you're tall!" Ty said, looking up at Haywood after practicing door-opening protocol. Megan trailed behind her brother, then stood with her mouth open and craned her neck to check out this new friend I had told them about.

"Ty, look! A puppy!" she squealed. Haywood had borrowed his father's Shih Tzu for the kids to play with.

"I think Bennie likes you two," Haywood said, dropping to the floor with them. I perched myself on the sofa, watching this big kid, disguised as a twenty-seven-year-old adult, laugh and roughhouse with my children. Haywood had a way with them. The mood of the moment was so different from the tension I felt coming from the kids when Klaus was around. My perspective affected how I viewed things, but they just seemed more carefree without Klaus's temperament affecting things, and admittedly, without the tension between Klaus and me stressing them. With Haywood, we were all somehow able to breathe easier.

"Your kids are really something," Haywood said after helping me tuck them in bed. They were asleep before the covers touched their chins.

As we relaxed on the sofa, I said, "All that roughhousing knocked them out. They had a good time with you tonight."

I could not believe another man had entered my life, fallen in love with me *and* my kids, and willingly accepted the precarious backdrop of my ex-husband. Haywood gave me the opportunity to trust again. He knew what I had been through, and it hadn't fazed him when I shared the details about my marriage and the contentious divorce.

"I'm still concerned," I said. "I never know about Klaus, and his behavior has grown even more erratic over this last month. Time, in this case, does not seem to be healing all wounds."

"Don't worry, Jeannie," Haywood said. "Nothing's going to happen that I can't handle."

Haywood had the gene I was missing: he was fearless.

thirty-six

Chaos

April 1977, Indianapolis, IN

"Who the hell is Haywood?"

This was one conversation I wanted to postpone. I should never have answered my office phone minutes before heading out the door for the evening. "Excuse me?"

"Ty told me he had fun with Haywood last night. Who is Haywood?"

My neck tightened. Klaus's intense breathing held my tongue captive for a moment before I replied, "He's a guy I'm dating."

"Well, that changes everything. Since you want to date around, I don't want to see you anymore. And I'll be making other arrangements for my daughter."

From the sound of his voice, I pictured him reddening in an apoplectic fit. "What are you talking about?" During the two-and-a-half months since the divorce, we had been together a few times for dinner with the kids. That apparently equated to dating in his mind, regardless of my refusals to see him socially. The post-divorce "you just need some time and space" birthday drink he'd bought me was code for his certainty we'd date and get back together. I politely refused each subsequent request, and his frustration caused him to vacillate between being loving and bitterly sarcastic, a tiring navigation for me.

"Never mind." Click.

And what did he mean by making "other arrangements" for Megan? I dialed the babysitter. "Lea, do not release Megan to anyone. I'll be there as quickly as I can."

When Haywood picked me up, he listened to my story and reassured me repeatedly during the thirty-minute ride home. "We'll work through this. Take a deep breath."

There it was again: the fearless gene. It was among the many things I liked about him.

According to society's rules and timelines, Haywood, this man who had an amazing capacity to love not only me but life itself, had come into my world at the wrong time. There should have been a decent interval between my escape from a terrible marriage and the appearance of this ridiculously brave, kind, solid guy. Haywood, though, didn't play by such rules—and made me want to be equally fearless. We spent every minute we could together and, whether or not Klaus approved, the kids were crazy about him.

It had happened so fast, yet it had happened. What the outside world thought mattered not. I planted my feet. I wanted to be with him, and I was keeping him.

Once we arrived at the babysitter's and I got my arms around Megan, my breathing relaxed. She looked at me, puzzled by my tears of relief. After Haywood's softball practice, we played at the park before driving to his duplex so he could shower. I checked in with Lea and found out she had heard Klaus pounding on my apartment door before he showed up downstairs at her place to get Ty.

Oh, God, I thought. *And I'm supposed to attend Dru's wedding with him. Another regrettable agreement made under duress.*

Karen's sister, Dru, was getting married within a couple of weeks and Ty was the ring bearer. Given this new turn of events, spending five minutes with Klaus, much less the planned five days of celebration, would be challenging. I sat on Haywood's living room floor, my back against the sofa, and mulled over the situation while hairdresser Megan brushed my hair. Impulsively, I reached for the phone and called Dr. Bob. I decided that Bob, as the mighty psychologist and author of the moral agreement, might be of help by keeping Klaus in check.

Bob reported that a "very hurt and angry" Klaus had already contacted him. He had calmed Klaus down and told me I should act as if nothing had happened. "You and Klaus and the kids need to make that trip together up here for Dru's wedding." In Bob's opinion, the Walkerton trip with the children would do Klaus good and provide some time for us to talk through our situation. "It would behoove you to show a little empathy."

Klaus had told Bob he couldn't sleep until he spoke with me. "Why don't you call Klaus and ask him over to your place for a talk? He's okay now," Bob insisted.

The voice in my head said *don't do it,* but the louder voice of deference won. "Okay. I don't want things going from bad to worse. We're at Haywood's now, so I'll call from here."

Klaus's phone rang and rang. No answer.

Tired, I asked Haywood to take Megan and me to our apartment. When we got home, Haywood waited until we were safely inside before driving away. As he pulled out of the parking lot, I recognized the rumble of a diesel car engine nearby. I looked out the window and saw Klaus in his prized 240D Mercedes follow Haywood. As Klaus turned the corner, I gasped when I spotted my son in the passenger seat. Not wanting to alarm Megan, I soothed us both with a bedtime story. She was soon asleep; I was not. I paced the apartment until Haywood called twenty-five minutes later.

"God, tell me Klaus didn't follow you," I said, continuing to pace, dragging the extension cord behind me.

"He didn't follow me; he *chased* me. When I realized Klaus had Ty with him, I figured I should just ditch him. He got stuck at a light, so I turned into a subdivision. I took the first side street, then parked in an alley and turned the lights off. He missed the turn and never saw me. I'm fine, but you'd better be careful, Jeannie. Is he coming over there? I think I should come back."

I thought it over, picturing the two of them in the same room, and Ty in the mix. "No. I'll call if I need you. Thanks."

"I don't like it, but okay. Let me know if you change your mind. I can be there—twenty minutes, tops."

After I hung up, I sat and stared at the phone; I jumped as if I'd heard a gunshot when it rang. Klaus was calling from a pay phone, and asked if he and Ty could stop by. "Sure," I said politely. I waited until I heard the click and dial tone before I slammed the phone down.

When they arrived, Ty looked at me without saying a word. His eyes, full of confusion, told me all I needed to know. I hugged him before tucking my bewildered six-year-old in my bed, then closed the door and headed into the living room.

"I spoke with Dr. Bob and he said you'd let me come over, so I hope it was okay that I called," Klaus said. "And I'm sorry about the earlier phone call. I was just really upset. Jeannie, you have to know it's because I still love you."

Sitting apart from him on the sofa, my arms crossed and locked tight, I stared into his face for a few seconds before saying, "I don't want any trouble."

"I want you back so badly. Could we please at least still go on our trip to the wedding?" Even as angry as I was, I nodded an okay. *Don't make waves.*

"Please let's get back together. We can make this work." He scooched closer to me and reached for my hand.

Startled, I pulled back. Keeping my voice low and measured, I said, "But I don't love you. I don't want to be married to you anymore," and waited.

His shoulders slumped. Rather than respond, he changed topics. Questions about Haywood followed—how old was he, where had I met him, where was he from? He glanced at the new rough-sawn wood coffee table and asked if that had come from Haywood. "Is he a carpenter?"

"Well, yes, in a manner of speaking." That Haywood was a truck driver was none of Klaus's business. I sat straight-shouldered and redirected the conversation. "Klaus, why did you follow him earlier tonight?"

"Follow him? What are you talking about?"

"I saw your car. I saw Ty was with you. What were you thinking?"

He stood up, indignant, and moved across the living room, then changed his mind and sat back down, shifting uncomfortably on the couch, sighing. "I really am sorry. Please, can we just talk about the wedding trip?"

I stiffened. "Not now. I need some sleep."

Still acting conciliatory, he said, "Sure, sure," and with that, he gathered up Ty and left.

I locked the door behind them, closed my eyes and pressed my tired head against the door. Only then did I let myself react. My body trembled, and I realized I was afraid of him.

Later that week, I received a late morning call at work from the babysitter. "Lea, slow down. I don't understand. You gave Klaus the key? To my apartment?" Through her profuse apology, she explained Klaus had brought Ty to her apartment rather than send him to school because Ty had a stomachache. He asked if she'd watch him for about an hour so he could deal with a problem at school.

"I said sure, and that's when he asked me for your apartment key, so he could get Ty's pillow. He said they'd left it by mistake last weekend. I'm so sorry," Lea said tearfully. "I figured it'd be okay because I was right here, but when he took the key and dashed up the stairs, I realized how stupid that was. He's up there now." Despite all her unabashed spunkiness, Klaus had caught her off guard.

I hated having my messy life involve others. "It's okay, Lea. Just call me after you get the key back." Per her report, he'd stayed in my apartment for fifteen minutes then, with a pillow under an arm, returned the key.

I waited about thirty minutes and called Ty's school; the teacher confirmed my suspicions. Klaus had not been at the school for a meeting with her or anyone else—not the other teachers, the counselor, or the principal. There were no problems with Ty. I explained the situation with Klaus and asked if she'd please call me should Ty say anything to her, or if problems arose.

Nothing was out of place when I got home that night, though it didn't matter. I felt violated just knowing he'd been there. At my bidding, the apartment management installed new locks on the entry door.

The Mercedes dealership had laid Klaus off at the beginning of April, which only made matters worse. Dr. Bob had offered him a job at Kingsdayle Academy, the youth and equestrian camp Bob operated on property adjacent to their lake house. Klaus and the kids headed up there for the weekend so he and Bob could discuss the opportunity. Meanwhile, Haywood had garnered two Friday night tickets to an Indianapolis Racers hockey game.

Lea called me at work again Friday morning. Before leaving for Dr. Bob's, Klaus had given her a letter for me. I hesitated even taking it from her when I got home that night. I couldn't imagine its contents and let it rest on the dining room table while I got dressed for my evening with Haywood.

Once I was ready for my date, I finally opened the envelope, revealing a one-page missive written on old stationery. My stomach churned as I read, "I wish that all the problems we're facing now would vanish in thin air, there would be no one to bring us any harm, because we could walk again arm in arm," and, "I know I love you from the bottom of my heart for the wonderful person you are. . . . I need your warmth, understanding and your strong friendship . . ." and on and on.

His behavior vacillated between being in hot pursuit of the man I was dating, the next minutes being remorseful; one minute breaking into my apartment, the next being polite; one minute threatening me, the next sending me a love letter. I slipped the note into its envelope and groaned.

From the sofa, I scanned the apartment, still feeling violated by his presence. Besides a pillow, what had he taken?

"God, this is sort of bloody, Haywood." As I watched a fight break out, I decided this would be my first and last hockey game. I winced and turned my head away from the players and saw Haywood watching me, not the game. Apparently neither of us were into hockey. I pointed to the two well-padded jocks battling on the ice below.

He glanced at them, then back at me. Three deep breaths later, our eyes still on each other, he said, "Will you marry me?"

The game faded into insignificance. Only he could take such an unlikely moment and turn it into a romantic one. Haywood felt like a never-ending breath of fresh air, living life with undaunted joy. We'd known each other for just four weeks; I didn't feel a shred of concern.

The first time around, I'd done everything by the book—the extended, parentally approved courtship with every socioeconomic box checked, every red flag ignored—and the fairytale had collapsed around me. Then, against all odds, I had found a man unlike any I'd ever known: a loving, down-to-earth, brave, blue-collar guy who was big enough—in every sense of the word—to save me.

With Haywood, there was no pressure, just relief; no stress, just fun. Just love. How do you say no to everything you think you need? Klaus had suffocated me; how could I—*why* would I—reject this gift of oxygen?

The ice rink's crowd roared its approval as I took a deep breath, crossed my fingers for good luck, and said, "Yes."

He took my hand, kissed it, and led me out of the arena. The game continued, but we were long gone.

Back at Haywood's 100-year-old duplex, I wrapped myself in an oversized navy terrycloth robe and created a candlelight dinner of scrambled eggs, toast and bacon. We talked through the messiness of dealing with Klaus as if we were discussing somebody else's troubled situation. Haywood's demeanor convinced me we could handle this.

He told me about his past and things he had overcome, stories of what a happy childhood looked like growing up on the wrong side of the tracks, and sharing details about an earlier bankruptcy following a back injury. "I'm not great with money but sure like helping my friends out when I can. I've run up some debt, but I've got some good ideas and I'm a hard worker, so no worries there." A give-you-the-shirt-off-his-back kind of guy who admitted to being long on ideas but short on follow-through was refreshing.

Because the kids were at Dr. Bob's for the weekend, we made an impromptu decision, packed a bag, and left Saturday morning for St. Louis to enjoy a quiet celebration of our engagement.

Bob answered the phone when I called the next evening from our St. Louis hotel to check on Ty and Megan. "Hey Bob. How are the kids?"

"They're dead," he said.

The ringing in my ears grew loud as my chest tightened. The air felt thin. My breathing stopped. "What?"

"No, they're fine," he chuckled, sounding amused. "You would know that if you were here. I'll get them."

I tried to hide my stress when I heard Ty on the phone at last. "Mom! Guess what? I got to ride Lancelot today and then we got to go swimming." I could hear Megan in the background, "I want to say hi to Mommy. Ty, I want to talk!"

"He said *what*?" Haywood was incredulous when I repeated Bob's words, my heart still pounding and my body trembling as we sat on the edge of the bed. "Come on. You need some food."

Over dinner, he spoke clearly and decisively. "Jeannie, I know he's Karen's dad, but from all you've said about him, and now this, you need to rethink this guy. This is bullshit."

Hearing the obvious struck a chord. As I sipped wine and studied my fiancé's candlelit face, I reconsidered Bob's intimidating, arrogant style. He was my best friend's father. He had been my counselor. He was not my friend.

With Haywood by my side, sleep came easily that night. We spent the next day exploring St. Louis. By the end of the day atop the Gateway Arch, life had taken on a new view and my resolve had gelled. We could, *I* could, take on whatever was ahead.

Back home on Sunday evening, I fanned through the mail and opened a card full of sisterly support from Joanne, now newly divorced. Her note echoed Haywood's sentiments. "It's time for us to be strong, be invincible, Jeannie. We are WOMAN, and if people don't like it, tough shit." Helen Reddy's lyrics had struck a chord with Joanne and an entire generation of women. The postscript on her card read, "My horoscope said I should practice being strong and assertive today. How am I doing?"

When I shared her message with Haywood, we laughed and shared a high-five. I felt infused with courage.

To bolster that new courage, I attended a psychology class Monday evening regarding understanding people's behavior. Transactional Analysis (TA), a theory of personality and systematic psychotherapy for personal growth and change, had grabbed many of us with its promise of self-awareness and improved personal interactions. After class, my first stop was the condo to see my kids and take Megan home after their long weekend with Klaus. There were hugs and kisses all around, but something felt different.

Megan returned to Klaus's side. "It's okay, sweetheart. Daddy's right here," he said, patting her head. She wrapped her arms around his leg and clung tight. A faint smile crossed his face as he watched for a reaction, like a cat eyeing its prey.

Without the TA training, I might have fallen victim to his ploy. Instead, I focused my attention on Ty with big hugs and asked about the weekend.

"Mom, riding Lancelot was so much fun!" referencing his favorite horse at Dr. Bob's camp.

"I bet when you grow up, you'll have a stable of horses all your own. Wouldn't that be something?" I said. I moved toward Megan, who was now on the couch with Klaus. "Come on, honey. We better head for home."

Pulling back from me, she said, "Daddy cry if I go. I can't leave Daddy alone."

"You'll see Daddy soon," I smiled and assured her.

She hugged Klaus goodbye adding, "I never leave you, Daddy."

I wanted to vomit.

In the following days and weeks, interactions with Klaus became more difficult, with the children suffering the ugliness. During dinner one weekend when Ty was with me, I asked if he wanted to go to the movies. "Will the creep be with us?" As soon as the words came out of his mouth, he lowered his head and with raised eyes said, "Daddy won't let us say Haywood's name or talk about him."

"Really? And how do you feel about that?" I asked.

"Not very good, Mommy. I'm sorry."

Though Transactional Analysis could help me recognize and handle Klaus's manipulations, the training hadn't yet given me any clues on countering them. I took the only course of action I could think of: I started keeping detailed records of my ex-husband's behavior.

thirty-seven

Tripping

May 1977
Indianapolis and Walkerton, IN

T he night before leaving for Dru's wedding, Megan and I prepared a picnic dinner and headed for Haywood's, taking a
back route around the apartment buildings for fear of being followed; the memory of Klaus's car chasing after Haywood's kept me
on edge each time I left the complex. As I turned the first corner
and scanned the area before driving through, I caught sight of a car
hidden in an alleyway near a building under construction. Klaus lay
in wait. He hadn't seen me yet. *Should I leave or confront him?*
Screw this. I pulled up next to his car and rolled down my window.
Looking up, his startled expression was telling. My eyes fell on the
car's young passenger, whose troubled face mirrored my own. *What*
must you be thinking, Ty?

"I, uh," Klaus stammered, "I forgot to tell you I left Ty's new
clothes for the wedding trip at Lea's."

I glared at him, not even masking my disbelief. "Right," I replied.

"Okay. Well, we were just out for a ride in the neighborhood."
Although Klaus had been unemployed for over a month, he hadn't
taken Dr. Bob up on the job offer at Kingsdayle and apparently had
time for super-sleuthing.

I nodded. "I love you, Tyger. You take care. See you soon." Driving away, I steadied my hands by gripping the steering wheel. I kept

picturing Ty's face, wondering how many evenings like this he'd spent hiding with Klaus. As Megan and I headed down the road, I checked the rearview mirror again and again, expecting to see Klaus's car tailing me.

Haywood greeted us at the door and when we got inside, I blurted out the story of the evening's encounter with Klaus.

"Jeannie, I'm really concerned about your trip tomorrow. I feel like I have no way to protect you. Is there any way you can get out of this wedding?"

I shook my head. Though a regrettable agreement, I couldn't change the plans without creating more turmoil: Ty was so excited about being the ring bearer, others were counting on us, and letting Klaus take the kids without me wasn't an option.

On the three-hour trip up north the next evening, Klaus exuded pleasantries while irritating me by over-indulging the children. Although happy to be with Ty and Megan, the situation wreaked emotional havoc on me and the sharp pain over my temples promised an all-night headache. We had planned a Brookfield Zoo excursion for the kids so we checked into a nearby Chicago area hotel, got a room with two queen beds and I slept with Megan, Klaus with Ty. I fell asleep filled with trepidation and Tylenol.

The next morning, Thursday, was zoo morning. The fresh air, and watching the kids have fun, helped; being with Klaus exhausted me. I counted the hours until I would see Haywood again. Strolling through the zoo, I attempted a civil discussion about better arrangements for the children—setting up more definitive and equal visitation times. Klaus stopped walking and said, "Why don't you just give me Megan? What can I give you in exchange? Would you trade her for the condominium?"

I clenched my teeth. "Not funny."

"Don't get upset. I was just kidding."

The headache took hold with a vengeance.

On Friday, before we left the hotel, Klaus found my pen on the floor. As he placed it in my open purse, he carefully reviewed the contents, spotting some keys, and asked. "Your keys?"

"It's my purse, so yes," I hissed. They were my keys—to Haywood's duplex.

We went shopping at a local mall and split up so he and Ty could look for a toy while Megan and I searched elsewhere for a wedding card. Before we could decide on one, Megan tugged on my jeans. "Mommy, need to potty." While waiting in the restroom stall with her, I searched my purse for a mint and discovered the keys—all the keys—had disappeared.

"Omigod," I gasped out loud. I quickly left the bathroom, child in tow, and searched the mall. We checked the dime store. No, no one had been there for new keys. We arrived at the area where the four of us were to meet. Klaus and Ty had just returned.

"Did you find the toy?"

Klaus replied, "Yeah, at Sears, but it was too expensive."

Sears. He duplicated the keys at Sears. *Goddammit.*

"Give me my keys. Give me all of my keys—including the ones you just had made."

He stared at me, then pulled them out of his pocket and handed them over.

I took Megan by the hand, found a card shop, bought the damn wedding card and we all left for the car.

"I'm sorry," Klaus said. "It was a dumb thing to do. The devil made me do it." Making light of it infuriated me even more.

I slammed my butt in the passenger seat before slamming the door shut. The four of us rode in silence to Walkerton, with me processing the troubling effect this was having on the all-too-quiet children in the back seat.

Once we were at the lake house and Ty was off at the wedding rehearsal, I pointedly spent the rest of the weekend with Karen, the kids and other wedding guests, pretending to enjoy the festivities. Klaus remained politely aloof. I didn't care.

When we got home Sunday early evening, he dropped Megan and me off at the apartment. Relieved and relaxed back in my own space, I called Haywood, who arrived within thirty minutes with open arms. Several hours later, after a soup and sandwich dinner and playing with Megan, the phone rang.

"Hi, Pamela. What's up?" Haywood said to his sister-in-law, Bill's wife.

"I just got a call. From Klaus. He gave me some fake name, but based on what you've told us is going on, it was easy to figure out who it was."

"Wait a second, Pamela. Let me put you on speakerphone. Okay, go ahead."

"He said he was in the construction business and needed good carpenters, and asked if I knew you. He wanted your phone number and address," she said. "When I asked him where he was from originally, he said, 'Oh, my accent. I'm Hungarian.' Do you believe that?" Although Pamela knew what Klaus was putting us through, she said he sounded so pathetic she felt sorry for him. "I finally said, 'Isn't this really all about Jeannie?' which got him completely flustered. I ended the conversation by saying I'd need to get the information and he'd have to call me back."

"Sorry, Pamela. This is over the top. Hope you don't hear from him again," Haywood said.

"Wait," she said. "That's not the end of the story! After we hung up, I looked up Jeannie's number in my address book, not realizing it was her old number, and got Klaus at the condominium! I asked for

Jeannie and he told me she didn't live there anymore. God, it was absolutely embarrassing. It was so obvious he was the same person I'd just been talking to. Anyway, Bill had Jeannie's new number, so I thought I'd better call and let you know what was going on. Good luck, you guys. Keep us posted."

"Jeannie, if he's called my brother's house, he's probably called every Ware in the book, including my parents. I better check with Mom."

Sure enough, they'd heard from Klaus.

After story time, hugs and bed for Megan, I collapsed on the sofa. Haywood kneeled in front of me and cupped my face in his hands. He had an I'm-taking-charge smile on his face. "We've got to put a stop to this. He needs to hear from me. Are you okay with that?"

"Yes, do it."

After reaching a busy signal for fifteen minutes, Haywood tried one last time and got through. Mr. Hungarian Accent answered. "Hello."

"This is Haywood Ware. I understand you've called my family looking for me."

"I don't know what you're talking about. I haven't made any calls."

"You didn't call my brother or my mom?"

"No! I've been in the shower for the last two hours."

Haywood covered the mouthpiece and whispered, "He says he's been in the shower for the last two hours." Not laughing was difficult.

"Well, if you say you didn't, then you didn't. I'm not looking for trouble and I don't want any trouble, Klaus. What I'd like is to keep everything above board from here out."

"Are you at Jeannie's place now? May I speak to her?"

"I am. Just a minute." Haywood held out the phone.

I took the receiver, stood up, and exhaled a cold "yes" into the phone.

"Jesus Christ, Jeannie." Klaus sounded tearful. Or scared. I couldn't tell which. "What is going on? Nobody believes me. I haven't made any damn calls."

"Pamela said she called the condo to talk to me and she got you! And it was the same voice!"

"There must be a hundred guys in the city with accents like mine."

As I paced back and forth, I thought, *who said anything about accents?* "Look, it doesn't matter at this point. Let's just move on. You know, I'm not trying to make things difficult for you. Things don't need to be difficult between us. If you want Haywood's address, telephone number, whatever, just ask."

"No. Well, maybe a phone number—in case of emergency."

Haywood nodded an okay.

"Now, can we agree to move on with our lives?" I said.

"Sure. You can live your life, and I'll take care of my plan. Good bye." Click.

"Well, what did he say?" questioned Haywood when I hung up.

I sat down on the sofa, pressed my forehead into my hands and quoted Klaus. *What the hell? What plan?*

thirty-eight

Breaks and Break-Ins

May 1977,
Nashville, Friendship, and Indianapolis, IN

I t was just Haywood, me, and the kids the next weekend, and our chance to tell them about our wedding plans. We had decided we'd have the ceremony at the weathered white country home on Jackson Branch Road we had recently rented for $150 a month where we'd be Grandma Lee's next-door neighbor. Saturday was wide open, so we piled into the TR7 and hit the road. Nashville was little more than an hour south of Indianapolis. We knew relaxing at Brown County State Park would restore a level of sanity. After showing the kids the rental house, we hiked at the park, finding the perfect spot where we unloaded our picnic basket, and watched the deer and wildlife over lunch. Ty and Megan's obvious delight with all of nature, away from the war zone of their parents' fractured relationship, reinforced my commitment to myself and my future with Haywood.

But the battle scars were evident when Megan whispered, "Daddy don't like Haywood," as she leaned into me.

"I know, sweetheart. It's okay. I do."

She cupped her tiny hands around my ear and laughed, "Me, too!" then hugged me tight. Somehow, when away from Klaus, she could cut right through the mess and find her own feelings. I loved her innocence. She made life simple.

Ty piped up with, "I think Daddy would feel better if he had a girlfriend."

We nodded and told them about our June wedding plans just weeks away. Ty catapulted off the picnic blanket, jumped up and down and asked, "Mom, can I be in the wedding?"

"Would you like that, honey? I bet we could arrange it."

When we got back to Indianapolis that night, we stayed at Haywood's place. Ty phoned his dad to check in and I overheard the conversation. "We had so much fun. We're staying at Haywood's, I mean, we're at you-know-who's." If the day hadn't been so idyllic, I would have considered grabbing the phone and ending the call. I tamped down that emotion.

The kids fell fast asleep after story time and, with our wedding now four weeks out, we spent the rest of the evening talking through the plans, keeping them simple.

No one minded when the alarm went off early Sunday morning. Our destination for the day was Friendship, Indiana, the home of a famous flea market, about two hours southeast of Indianapolis. Shortly after the sun peeked over the horizon, we got dressed and bounced out the door. Surrounded by southern Indiana hills, Friendship remained quiet for most of each year, but alive with excitement each spring and fall, hosting the National Muzzle Loading Rifle Association's Black Powder Shoots, one of the world's largest. Thousands of visitors would arrive to experience the shoot or simply enjoy the hundreds of booths and vendors, spread out as far as one could see.

The Friendship experience was new and exciting for the kids and me; not new for Haywood. I watched him confidently joke and barter with the vendors as he found and paid for one deal after another. Haywood—bargain hunter, rifle owner, and food lover—had frequented the flea market for several years. This year, though, he beamed and relished sharing the day with the kids. He used the last of his cash so they could experience their first horse-drawn carriage ride before we headed back to Indianapolis for another workweek.

When we got home, I bedded Megan down, and Haywood stayed at the apartment while I took Ty to the condo. The sunset carriage ride had made for a late return, so I braced myself for his father's irritation and interrogation. When I got there, Klaus hit me with the anticipated barrage of complaints and petty requests as we stood in the living room. Ty scurried upstairs to get ready for bed.

Yes, I said, I was sorry we were late getting back. Yes, I would provide addresses of Haywood's parents and brother. Yes, I would pick up the last of my stuff. Yes, I would get the cat. Yes, yes, yes.

Sullen, he continued goading me and told me about a job in Kokomo he'd interviewed for but didn't get, intimating the loss was my fault.

"You're saying you lost the job, and it's my fault?" I said, "How is that?"

"The guy who interviewed me didn't like the fact that I was divorced."

The babysitter had already shared the bad news with me about the interview and I had called Klaus's employment counselor, a mutual friend, and delicately asked what had happened. In the counselor's opinion, Klaus blew the interview. "When somebody says they're not good at nor interested in sales during an interview for a sales-oriented job, what do you think the outcome will be?" he said.

I'd asked about divorce being an impediment. He carefully generalized his response and said he'd had two other recently divorced clients, but they'd both welcomed the sales opportunity. Reports from past employers were also a factor. The counselor admitted placing someone like Klaus wasn't easy.

Now Klaus and I stood face to face, with the blame for his bad luck meant to burden my shoulders.

"Well," I said, avoiding the intended confrontation, "I hope you find something you like." I paused, swallowed hard, and attempted a stance of confidence as I dropped the inevitable news. "By the way, I want you to know about our plans. Haywood and I are getting married next month." I wiped my palms on my jeans and waited. I didn't know what he'd do.

"Huh," he grunted and strode into the kitchen. After popping the top off a cold beer, he leaned his back against the counter, took a big swallow and said, "Well, if you can't take the cat, I'll take care of it for you. Then there'll be one less stupid cat in this world."

I stared at his beer a moment, fearing the mounting anger behind the bitter response. "No. I'll be taking the cat. In fact, I'll take her now."

Klaus had the kids the following weekend. A few days later when I arrived at the babysitter's after work, Lea took me aside and blurted, "I just wanted to update you on a couple of things." Since he'd lost the job at the Mercedes Benz dealership in early April, Klaus usually arrived earlier at Lea's than I did, and she would get an earful. Each night when I picked Megan up after work, Lea disclosed the evening "news" relaying Klaus's comments from that day. To me it felt like Klaus was trying to flaunt his power, to manipulate and control things. His efforts to muddy the waters played on me and wore thin, yet I was also grateful to Lea for pipelining the daily buzz.

"Megan's now saying that Haywood isn't her friend anymore. Klaus is filling that little head with such mean garbage." Lea went on, "Remember I told you last week that he's kept Ty out of school a couple of times for no apparent reason? Well, I've convinced him that's not really good for Ty, but I sure haven't changed his mind about Haywood. The things Klaus says are so hurtful, and *scary*. Roger, tell Jeannie what he said last night."

"Well, he tried to make it sound like a joke," her husband said, after making sure that Megan was out of earshot, "but he said he'd give me fifty bucks to get rid of Haywood."

I gasped. "Say what?"

"I told him he shouldn't be joking about stuff like that, so he said, 'Okay. How about $125?'"

Lea said, "I told him to hush up, Jeannie, but he said it didn't matter because he was going to take you to court."

"What? For what?"

"Cohabitating mainly," she said. His diatribe included anger over having another man raise his kids, and concerns about Ty having to compete for my attention.

Cohabitating? "You're kidding," I said, incredulous. Before 1960, laws against cohabitation had been common in the United States. But this was 1977—*and* I was thirty years old, an adult. Were there still laws on the books that could dictate with whom I slept?

When I told Haywood that evening, we both shook our heads and agreed for the time being, he should go home for the night.

"Sadly, all we can do is make note of these threats," my attorney said when we spoke the next day. "If he's potentially threatening a lawsuit or custody battle based on cohabitation, the best advice I can give you is don't cohabitate."

Adding to the cohabitation lawsuit threat, Klaus had informed Lea he was thinking about filing for custody of Megan. An attorney allegedly advised him that contacting a detective agency and making use of tape recordings and pictures would aid in a custody hearing.

My legs weakened at the thought of some detective sneaking around, snapping incriminating photos of me and Haywood, or getting recordings of . . . what? Taken out of context, Klaus's side of the story would present a wronged father whose wife had abandoned the family and was whoring around. And I couldn't help wonder where the money was coming from for attorney or detective costs. As far as I knew, unemployment was his only source of income.

"I don't want to scare you, Jeannie," Lea said, "but he also mentioned he's planning a trip to Germany. I wouldn't have put much stock in it, but later Ty told me, even though he wasn't supposed to tell anyone, that they were going to Germany maybe next month or the month after."

"Germany?" I fumed. "If Klaus thinks I'd allow him to take the kids out of the country, he's nuts." I was furious, but knew that confronting Klaus would only intensify the situation and increase my blood pressure. Haywood suggested I call the attorney and see what my options were. We decided against quizzing Ty about the "secret." Stressing my six-year-old further made no sense. Also, he'd likely confess to his father we had talked about it. We didn't want Ty placed in the middle of things or have such information going back to Klaus.

With only three weeks before June 10, focusing on wedding plans felt impossible while dealing with all of this. The kids spent the weekend with Klaus. I spent it sick to my stomach.

Lea opened her front door with a smile. "Good news!"

"*Good* news?" I asked. "What's that?"

"Klaus is having date number three with a lady doctor. She's going to his place for dinner. But the really good news is that he's decided not to take you to court. Somebody, I guess that attorney guy, told him if he does the court thing, you might both lose the kids. He still doesn't like Haywood and sure doesn't want Ty to, but he was in a great mood and has a job interview scheduled for Thursday and one Friday. Maybe he's lightening up."

"Maybe," I said. "But I feel like the pressure cooker lid is shaking, and it's about to blow."

"Well, maybe the burner's finally off. We can hope!"

Haywood and I took the kids and drove out to Danville later that week for dinner with Big John. As we visited over a glass of wine,

I told John about Klaus hiring an attorney to get custody of both kids, and how volatile he'd been since Haywood had entered the picture. "I'm sure this is difficult for you, too, John, hearing from both parties," I said, "but at least Klaus appears to be dating now."

"What say we head into the dining room and I'll serve up my specialty." After he plated the meal and joined us at the table, he said a prayer and added, "With Midge out of town, salmon is the only thing I trust myself to do a decent job of without her help."

We had a good laugh and John continued our conversation about Klaus. "I'm glad to hear he's seeing someone. It might help with the depression."

Depression. I took a bite of my salmon and processed that perspective. Until that moment, I'd never considered Klaus as depressed. It gave me a grudging sort of sympathy for his situation. I had destroyed his happy-marriage dreams, different as they were from mine. I thought about how my relationship with Haywood had upended Klaus's world and affected his behavior. No matter who was at fault for our failed marriage, it no doubt devastated Klaus to see me moving on with such apparent ease. I could almost feel sorry for Klaus— until I reminded myself of all he'd done. I abhorred and feared his patriarchal behavior because, at the core, it supported neither the children nor me. We were possessions.

Over dinner, Ty said, "Wouldn't it be nice if Daddy would like Haywood and you would like Daddy's girlfriend? You could all be friends, and then I wouldn't have to be in the middle."

I cringed. Hearing my six-year-old's commentary on negotiating between two parents' worlds pained me. For him it was like being a chameleon, a different person with your father than with your mother.

I hugged him. "You know, he's never met Haywood. Maybe when they meet, he'll like him."

⁂

Klaus and I arrived at Lea's at the same time; it was Memorial Day weekend and he had asked to have the kids. He was in a foul mood, and the sliver of hope I had allowed myself on hearing Lea's recent report faded. Apparently, his job interviews had not gone well, nor did the dinner date with the doctor. When I mentioned that I'd had a conversation with Ty's teacher who informed me about an upcoming school picnic, he snapped, "I hadn't told you about it because I'm his guardian and I didn't want you there."

Dumbfounded, I said, "Oh for God's sake, I'm his mother. I'll be at the picnic, Ty."

Klaus picked Megan up with one arm, grabbed Ty's hand with the other and barreled off.

Haywood and I drove to Nashville for the long holiday weekend. Our wedding was less than two weeks out, so we took a breather at our Brown County house, and spent some time with Grandma Lee covering last minute plans.

That Sunday, we heard on the radio that A. J. Foyt chalked up his fourth win at the Indy 500 and Janet Guthrie, though she didn't fare well in the race, became the first woman to qualify for the previously all-male race.

"Hear me roar!" Haywood joked. I laughed and switched off the news. Feminist milestones aside, the quiet of the country held much more appeal than the Indy race hoopla. Traffic was as bad as expected heading back to Indianapolis Monday night, and exhaustion hit when we finally arrived.

Something felt odd the moment we walked into my apartment. As I stepped through the door, I noticed a chair cushion out of place and the throw, originally on the sofa, hung over the rocking chair. The mail I left on the coffee table now rested on the kitchen table.

Someone had been in the apartment.

"What the hell?" I said and began pointing out the oddities.

Haywood shushed me, putting his finger to his lips. "Don't

move," he mouthed. After checking the living room, dining area, kitchen, bathroom and Megan's bedroom, he called me into my bedroom. "Well, whoever was here is gone, but they left your jewelry box open." Whoever sifted through the contents found and removed the engagement ring Klaus had given me. They also had stolen the box with my former wedding dress in it off the top shelf of my closet. Odd things, too, like magazines, appeared combed through and some were missing.

"This is nuts," I said. "You know it was him. The thought of him here again, rifling through stuff and taking..."

"Yeah. This *is* nuts. I bet the kids innocently said something about you and me being gone over the weekend," Haywood said. We both silently deliberated the situation, letting the whole thing soak in before he addressed an even more troubling thought. "If Klaus was crazy enough to break in here, I'm wondering if he got into my place."

We hustled over to Haywood's duplex and found the front door unlocked and ajar. We went inside and he immediately looked behind the door.

"He stole my shotgun."

"Oh, my God." My jaw dropped and fear caught in my throat. I blinked hard, trying to stop the panic, but it was too late. We surveyed the rest of the duplex, downstairs first and then up. Nothing else was missing.

What was Klaus thinking? We looked at each other, having the same thought. Was he planning to show up at the wedding? At the moment, all we could do was call the authorities and report the gun and the diamond as missing.

"Yes sir, it's a twelve-gauge J.C. Higgins shotgun, single barrel. It has a little lever on the side next to where you break it down. The stock is scratched. The ring was a yellow gold band, four-prong, one-third karat diamond. Simple, plain, made by ArtCarved."

As Haywood gave the officer our contact details, he watched me. I stood in the kitchen, moved to the couch, couldn't sit still and got up, choosing to pace instead.

I couldn't stop shaking.

thirty-nine

Games

May 1977, Indianapolis, IN

The kids and I used the drive-thru at McDonald's, picked up some hamburgers and headed for Haywood's softball game.

"Mom, has Daddy said something to you about Haywood conning me?" Ty asked when we were further down the road.

"No, honey. What do you mean?"

He choked up. "I'm not supposed to say anything."

"Ty, it's okay. You can tell me."

"Daddy said if Haywood tried to give me any presents, just to say 'no thank you' because Haywood was just trying to con me to be his friend. Is conning a bad thing, Mommy?"

"Ty," I said, composed, "Haywood is your friend because he likes you. He doesn't have to give you presents to be friends. Conning is like tricking you into being his friend, and he's not doing that. It's okay to be friends with Haywood and love Daddy, too. Daddy loves you very much. He's just having some problems because I love someone else. I love Haywood, honey. He makes Mommy happy and hopes you're happy, too."

We reached the ballpark and when we got out of the car, I said, "Let's go have some fun, Tyger." He hugged my waist, then darted off to the ball field.

After the game, Haywood and I drove separately to his duplex. The kids piled into the TR7 with him, fun for all three of them; a big guy with a little car; a big deal for two little kids. Megan giggled as she lay flat on her back on the parcel shelf behind the back seat where she fit as if it had been made for her. Haywood smiled at my clever two-year-old and slipped her to a safer spot in the backseat. He glanced at me as I was getting into my car and said, "I'm not trying to be a hard-ass. There ought to be a law. I'm not comfortable with her up there while the car's moving."

I smiled. One more reason to love him.

At the duplex, Haywood instigated a hushed kitchen conversation while the kids played in the living room. "Well, Ty just confirmed what we heard from the babysitter. He told me in the car he wasn't supposed to say anything, but Klaus is taking them to Germany, maybe next year."

"Mom! Mom! When are we going for the ice cream?" Ty said, popping into the kitchen.

"I promised ice cream, didn't I?" Haywood smiled. "Let me get cleaned up and we'll go, buddy."

As he left the room headed for a shower, he whispered, "Let's hope your attorney can nip this in the bud."

Startled out of a sound sleep that night, I glanced at the clock as I reached for the phone and mumbled hello. The response: silence, heavy breathing, click. Thirty minutes later, another call.

I lay there, wide awake, until after 2:00 a.m., my skin feeling as thin as the sheet covering my weary body. Exhaustion finally helped me drift off.

Arriving home from work the next night, I discovered a note stuffed in my mailbox:

hey lady
while you were fuckin that man in the honkey TR car last

*nite, three black dudes tried to steal the tires from that car but
they saw me in the window and left. Did you enjoy the
screwing that dude gave you? Is he as good as the other guy
who picks up your kids? I bet if he knew that you were fuckin
round he would kill you. Send one of them over to me you
honkey whore.*

A neibor

After the initial shock, I made my way up the apartment's exterior
staircase, inconspicuously checking the neighbors' windows. I dropped
the key twice, trying to unlock my door. Once inside, I locked it and
secured the deadbolt. Dropping my briefcase on the living room
floor, I kicked off my shoes, sat down on the carpet, and anxiously
examined the note.

The longer I stared at it, the more incredulous I felt. It didn't
take much for me to puzzle out that a neatly typewritten note from a
neibor asking about *the screwing* made no sense . . . unless the author
was a dialect-challenged ex-husband.

I picked Megan up at Klaus's without mentioning the *neibor's*
note, then stopped for hugs from Ty at the condo's playground. He
wouldn't look at me.

"I don't want to go with you if you're going to be with, you
know, him," were his hesitant words.

"I don't think I'm hearing my son talking." I kneeled beside him,
but he kept his head down and shuffled his feet.

"You know, Ty, Daddy doesn't have to like Haywood. What I
need to know is how *you* really feel."

"I don't know. I'm confused."

Too tired to press him and too mad at Klaus, I squeezed Ty
goodbye, left with Megan and drove away. On the way home, she,
too, made disparaging remarks about Haywood, things that obviously
didn't originate with my sweet two-year-old.

"Now Megan, listen to me. I think we have a lot of fun with Haywood. Remember when we went to the ballpark, then went for ice cream the other night? Wasn't that fun?"

"Uh huh," she said. I could see her confusion as she tried to reconcile her affection for Haywood with whatever negative ideas Klaus was feeding her. Keeping my eyes on the road was difficult as I painfully watched her struggle. Finally, she whispered the words, "I like Haywood."

"He likes you too, honey, and that's a good thing." Though tempted, I resisted spitting, "And don't let anyone tell you it isn't!"

By the time we got home, I was seething. The whole situation had grown untenable: the *neibor's* note, Ty's growing resistance, and Megan's brainwashing eclipsed my tiredness and my fears. I dropped her off at the apartment with Haywood and blasted the ten minutes back to Klaus's, ready for a confrontation.

Seeing me at the door, his face registered surprise. Face to face in the living room, Klaus denied my accusations of manipulating the kids, blaming me for their unhappiness. I brought up the calls to Haywood's family, and the complete nonsense of "the caller" thinking Haywood was a carpenter.

"You told me he was a carpenter!" Then, quickly realizing the hole he had dug for himself, changed the subject 180 degrees and brought up Ty's issues at school. "It's your life that has messed up the kids." The teacher had mentioned trouble with Ty telling some stories a few weeks earlier, but she assured me it was normal for his age and nothing serious. Still, Klaus blamed me for Ty's confusion and lying at school.

"Klaus, my loving Haywood is not the cause of Ty's problems," I said.

"Well, you must have been messing around with him while we were going out after the divorce. Otherwise I bet we could have worked things out, had a fresh start."

"God. That is not true. I didn't meet Haywood until April." Angry tears ran down my cheeks.

"He's not my concern. I can say whatever I damn well want about him. I won't talk against you to the children and you are not to talk against me, do you understand?"

"I never have," I asserted. "But please, stop this negative talk about Haywood."

"I won't." He wagged a finger at me. "Not until you have a ring around that finger! And those kids are not to speak his name. I won't allow it," he shouted.

Ty returned from the playground, ending our conversation. I dried my eyes, gave my son a kiss, and walked out toward my car with Klaus on my heels. As I slid behind the wheel, I said, "What good does your hatefulness do for anybody?"

Red-faced with fury, he looked as if about to slug me. Instead, he stormed back into the house and slammed the door.

I sat in the car, momentarily gathering my wits, and left. Back at the apartment, I found Megan and Haywood curled up on the sofa together, engrossed in a story, one where everyone undoubtedly lived happily ever after. My mood lifted when we decided eating out was a good idea. Haywood was short on cash, but I didn't mind paying. Being happy with him was so easy. After dinner, his goodnight kiss lingered on my lips as Megan and I watched him pull out of the parking lot and head home.

But the moment I walked back into the apartment, the phone rang. Klaus had called with a directive. "I just talked with Dr. Bob. He wants you to call him. Now." Hearing his caustic voice sucked all the pleasure from the evening. I had no desire or energy to talk with Bob, but begrudgingly made the call anyhow after Megan was asleep.

Forty-five minutes later I was still on the phone with Dr. Bob, whose sympathies clearly resided with Klaus. During the call, however, something changed. After the day's events, I'd had enough. My voice grew firm, and my sense of commitment to my children and our lives came through with a new sense of clarity. Bob reacted with surprise.

I pointed out that Klaus's attitude and state of mind were infecting all of us, particularly the children, and read the obscene mailbox note as an example of Klaus's increasing instability.

Bob told me Klaus had mentioned receiving a similar note on his windshield.

"Bob, really? Give me a break. Let's think this through," I said, tramping back and forth on the living room carpet, careful not to get caught in the long extension cord. Klaus's story was ridiculous. We didn't even live in the same neighborhood. So, if Bob believed Klaus, some deranged person would have to travel from neighborhood to neighborhood, leaving obscene typewritten notes in mailboxes or on windshields. Or, the deranged person must have been watching us specifically, following our routines so they could write crazy notes for some unknown reason.

Or . . . the pathetically logical explanation: Klaus had made up what seemed like a smart cover-up story in case I accused him of typing the note I received.

"Well, your explanation does make more sense," he eventually conceded.

Just as my forcefulness caught Dr. Bob off-balance, his unexpected agreement took me by surprise, I pressed the momentary advantage. "Bob, he's made many statements that really concern me, several times mentioning some 'plan,' and talk about going away. And Ty told the babysitter he'll be going to Germany, but it's a secret, which in and of itself is completely unnerving. I'm sure Klaus knows I'd never agree to him taking the kids out of the country. But given his state of mind, I'm afraid he'll simply grab them and go."

"Jeannie, I'm sorry to hear about this turn of events, but I can't see him doing anything so rash. I'll tell you what, Klaus was initially lukewarm about the job at Kingsdayle we discussed, but I'll get in touch with him and reiterate the offer. His concern really is for the children, I'm sure, and his ability to provide for them is a big part of that."

That gave me pause. Was it my turn to make a concession? Klaus hadn't lived in Germany for decades—for most of his adult life. The best job prospects were in the United States. Even with the support of family, the transition back to his former country would be financially and emotionally rough on Klaus, and on his thoroughly American children.

He must realize that, however angry he was with me.

Despite everything, Dr. Bob must be right. I needed him to be.

"Okay, Bob," I said, "Please do make that job offer again. There must be a way to make this work out."

In the morning, I'd call my attorney, set an appointment, and apprise him of everything. I already suspected Dennis would say what I'd heard several times before, that there wasn't much we could do, "but I'll look into it."

The note from my *neibor* lay on the kitchen table where I had left it. I wished I had immediately tucked it into my desk, out of sight. The crumpled single sheet provided a revelatory glimpse into my ex-husband's troubled interior landscape—a dark place I had no desire to probe further.

forty

In Sickness and in Health

June 1977
Indianapolis and Nashville, IN

Haywood and I focused on our plans for the wedding, nine days away. We were keeping things simple and the guest list short: local family members, friends from my office, and Haywood's closest friends. Grandma Lee took care of several critical items—like baking the cake and working with a local deli to cater the event. She also connected us with Sam Rosen, Brown County's Judge Pro Tem, who agreed to perform the ceremony.

A colleague helped me find a gown befitting of Brown County's country setting. I chose a simple white-eyelet floor-length dress, bought Haywood a white knit shirt, and wedding outfits for the kids. All I needed now was a good haircut. The friend who approved the dress had given me the card of a new local hairdresser. When I made the appointment, I mentioned the upcoming wedding, and was happy to get an appointment for that evening.

Sitting in Ron's dimly lit, less-than-upscale garage-turned-salon, I adjusted the black plastic cape and sipped on the glass of red wine offered. I watched in the mirror as this dark-haired Jesus Christ Superstar doppelgänger examined my hair, though his piercing brown eyes lingered longer on my face than my locks. With a deep, almost caressing voice, Ron asked only a few questions about my style preferences. After pouring more wine, he softly pushed a strand of hair from my cheek and started cutting.

While he cut, I sipped. Though unnerved, I sat as still as possible. Faking a sense of calm and attempting to appear composed, I struck up a conversation, my mouth loosened by the wine, and blathered about my past life and newfound love.

"Considering all that's happened, I am a little, you know, nervous. I know it looks like we've jumped into this marriage pretty quick, but I love the guy." Ron offered a throaty judgmental "hmm" and nodded.

He moved closer and trimmed the hair framing my face; I closed my eyes as instructed, allowing him to finish the bangs. I could feel his breath on my face as he leaned in and, without consent, pressed his lips on mine, softly at first, then with intention. In heady shock, I allowed the moment, but within seconds, when the fear and confusion registered, I abruptly leaned back in the chair, ending the uninvited kiss.

"Are you sure you want to marry this guy?" he asked, his words as sensual as the kiss.

I responded with an artificial laugh. "I appreciate the concern, but I think we're through here."

Trying not to appear shaken as I removed the cape, I pulled cash from my purse, set it near the empty wineglass on the counter, and made my exit.

"I like the haircut," Haywood said, walking into the kitchen. I put the dishes in the sink and looked up at him. Rather than blurt out details about what had happened, I hesitated, searching for the right words, but none came. "Jeannie, what's going on?"

I didn't answer.

"I'm not surprised, honey," he said, as if reading my mind. "I'm guessing you've got cold feet."

"Don't you?" I asked, still flustered from the Ron episode.

"No," he laughed and pulled me close. "This time I got it right and I know it. But we can wait if you're not ready. What do you need from me?"

"You just gave me what I needed," I said, leaning into him with a tight hug.

"So, that means you want to wait?"

"No! No, I don't. I'm ready. *You* are what I've been waiting for. I just needed to think things through, that's all."

The "Ron episode" took on a new perspective: I didn't have to fall prey to an ego-driven manipulative man who thought he had a home court (in this case, a garage/salon) advantage. Bottom line: I got a good haircut and an education.

I planted a serious kiss on Haywood's smiling lips. "Guess you are ready," he said with a relieved grin. "I'll keep those feet warm, you know, if they get chilly again. No extra charge."

"Don't tell the kids I'll like him someday! Don't tell them that! Leave me out of the picture! Do you hear me?" Klaus yelled through the phone.

Another day. Another angry call. I said nothing.

Infuriated, he asked, "So, when are you getting married?"

"The wedding is Friday, June 10."

"I'll give it two years, tops. Just give me the kids when your problems set in. I hope you're planning on changing your name. I don't want you keeping mine."

"You can't wish me well, can you?"

"I'm not the guilty one. If I were, maybe I'd feel differently. No, I can't wish you well." I winced when he slammed the phone down.

Haywood's twenty-eighth birthday the next day brought news from Lea. Klaus had busied himself researching information on my fiancé: the details of Haywood's divorce, ex-wife, debts, and obligations. Setting that aside, Megan's questions to Lea about learning German if she lived over there were of more concern.

On Sunday, with the wedding five days away, out of desperation, I called Dr. Bob, wondering what he knew. "I'm even more uneasy about Klaus. Did you make that job offer again?"

"Yes, I did," Bob said, "but since he couldn't bring both kids, taking a job up here wasn't realistic. He said at this point saving money for his plan was his only option."

"His plan. Did you press him on that?"

"I asked, but he just brushed it off. Said it was no big deal and changed the subject."

"Not a big deal? Ha! He's playing us all, setting the stage, wanting to intimidate me, create more fear that he'll take matters into his own hands by taking the kids to Germany. Then where are we? Are these just idle threats? He's so angry, there's no telling what he might do."

There was a moment of silence on the line. Bob confessed, "I'm afraid you may be right. Have you considered postponing the wedding?"

"Postpone the wedding? Are you serious?"

Another pause, and then he said, "Klaus is obviously feeling frustrated, but if you're sure you want to go through with this, I would hope he wouldn't do anything that rash."

I ended the phone call even more determined. Klaus was not going to ruin or even delay my chance at happiness.

When Klaus called on Monday ranting about Ty being in the wedding, and talked about changing the current visitation agreement, I refused getting drawn into the argument. I fired back that instead we needed to talk about his breaking into my apartment. After calling me crazy, he hung up.

The next day, Lea, unnerved by Klaus's increasing agitation, told me he talked about going to Brown County for some weekend target practice. He'd said he was over being dumped but couldn't put up with my stupidity.

My stupidity? I had run the gamut of emotions during the past weeks, but when I heard Lea's words, I felt suddenly and fiercely angry. Klaus seemed intent on destroying my chance at starting a new life. Before I had time to second-guess myself, I was at the condo, leaning on the doorbell, defiant.

When Klaus opened the door, I brushed past him, and went straight up the stairs and down the hall into Ty's room. My son dropped his new Slinky and looked at me, surprised and a little alarmed. "Hi, Mom."

He looked over my shoulder, knowing that any moment Klaus would storm in after me.

For Ty's sake, I acted much calmer than I felt. "Hi, Sweetie. I wanted to remind you to get packed for Thursday night. I'll pick you up at 5:30 p.m., okay?"

Klaus reached the top of the stairs, apoplectic with rage. "Aren't you going to speak to me? I'm the father around here!"

"I'll pick Ty up at 5:30 Thursday," I repeated, headed down the stairs, and walked out.

After I got home from work Wednesday night, Lea provided more disturbing information. Ty told her he and his dad had been to Kokomo. When Lea asked what they'd done there, he confessed that wasn't actually where they'd gone. "I'm not supposed to tell anybody, but we went to Nashville because Daddy wanted to see the house where the wedding's going to be."

"God, Jeannie, with the wedding almost here, this must really freak you out."

After I thought for a moment, I said, "No, I'm not freaked out, Lea. I'm exhausted. I'm going to bed." Thinking about Klaus's effect on Ty by forcing him to lie, teaching him to hate, to keep secrets, filling his head with loyalty issues, driving a wedge between my son and me . . . I needed sleep. Rather than buying into the madness, I figured I'd confer with Big John the next morning.

"I'll invite Klaus to spend the weekend with Midge and me here at our place. But regardless, I really don't feel Klaus will interfere with the wedding. It wouldn't help his situation with the kids," John said.

We agreed that potential post-wedding actions were of greater concern. John recommended I contact the judge and request changing the current custody arrangement. "I know it seemed like a fair and equitable plan at the time of the divorce, but now, under the circumstances, maybe it would be best if you had custody of both children, rather than just Megan. It might slow Klaus down."

It might slow Klaus down? I heard what John said—and what he didn't. My good friend the reverend was looking out for the children's best interests, *and* knew more than what he could share. His cryptic advice meant one thing: he was facing a confidentiality quandary.

On the morning I should have been attending to last-minute wedding details, I was instead on the phone with my attorney reviewing options to protect my children.

"Dennis, things are really getting scary. I cradled the receiver between my shoulder and my ear, freeing up both hands to pour another cup of coffee. "I doubt Klaus would do anything crazy at the wedding, but I absolutely believe he's planning to take the kids out of the country under the guise of a trip within the next month or so."

He thought for a moment. "Jeannie, I think hiring a private detective is your best bet right now. Klaus has been clever in that he's not done anything legally wrong, or at least not gotten caught doing it. I've got a couple of names I could give you."

I tucked away the detectives' information for future reference. For wedding day security, we opted for local help. Haywood contacted Brown County authorities and requested whatever help they could offer. For additional support, we visited Judge Sam Rosen that afternoon at the courthouse. Judge Rosen already knew we were under some stress since we mentioned it when we'd met with him a week prior regarding the ceremony details. Being with Sam was like being with a trusted, long-lost uncle. When we updated him about new concerns, Sam alerted the sheriff's department and also suggested Haywood contact Dave Anderson, a detective with the Indiana State Police.

Haywood returned from the meeting with Detective Anderson, feeling upbeat about the response he'd gotten. He told me the Indiana State Police would cover things for us, that they'd have several officers patrolling the area, "just to be sure."

"That sounds wonderful," I said. "but how can we afford them?"

"Sweetie, we don't pay. Dave told me, not to worry. He said, and I quote, 'It's what we're paid to do.'"

"*Dave?*" I asked. "Are you two already on a first name basis?"

"Sure. He's a great guy," Haywood grinned, "and I just know he'll take good care of us."

I had to smile. My husband-to-be couldn't leave the house without making a new friend. The anxiety that had gnawed at me faded away. The future still held all its unknowns, but trouble on our wedding day was no longer a concern.

There were no cold feet the night of June 10, 1977. Haywood and I married, surrounded by twenty-five local friends, the kids, Haywood's family, and of course best-friend Karen, all gathered together in the country house on Jackson Branch Road—with six officers outside patrolling the area. If Klaus was anywhere near the wedding, he did not make his presence known. My Florida family members— Mom, Joanne, and my dad—sent cards and flowers, and I received a tender call from my Birmingham brother. "Here's to a happier ending this time around, Sis."

"I know, Jim. Do you remember our 'wedding' dance ten years ago? I knew then that, for whatever reason, you had 'unspoken' concerns about Klaus. If only I'd known then what I know now . . ."

"Hey, none of us knew how things would turn out. I'm just sorry you were so miserable for so long," Jim said. "Well, on a brighter note, you sound happy now. Seems this Haywood fellow took my little sister by surprise and swept her off her feet, didn't he? Enjoy every moment of some well-deserved happiness." He laughed and added, "Just be sure and tell him what I told you back then. I'll always look out for you, so if Mr. Wonderful ever gives you any grief, he should expect a call from me."

When the esteemed Sam Rosen arrived with Mrs. Rosen and another couple, we made introductions all around. Haywood turned the party music off, pulled me close, and surprised me with a long-stemmed red rose. We grinned, kissed, and the ceremony took place without further ado, right there in the simple setting of our living room.

"Friends, out of affection for Haywood and Jeannie, we have gathered together tonight in a spirit of peace and happiness to witness and support their marriage," Judge Rosen began.

I leaned into Haywood and tightened the grip of our joined hands.

The judge closed with a reading from *Between Man and Woman* by Shostrom and Kavanaugh, which sealed the deal. "Love gives all, risks all, holds nothing back, . . . It lets go, it releases, it dissolves. It can live anywhere, survive any threat, endure any pain."

The ceremony ended with a kiss, applause, and a wave of spontaneous laughter. We all indulged, what with the great spread of food, cake, and wine before us, while the music played on into the night.

Though there was no honeymoon, there were no complaints from either the bride or the groom about having a house full of family post-ceremony; Haywood's mom and dad spent the weekend, as did the kids. We loved watching them entertain one another with jokes and silly conversation—pure joy.

Everyone else left, including Karen, who headed back to Indianapolis and stayed at our apartment so she'd be fresh the next day for her drive home. She told us days later that she had received numerous phone calls that night, which she suspected were from Klaus. Each time she answered, the caller hung up. "I finally got to sleep, but the calls were disconcerting," she said. Another unsolved behavioral mystery.

On our wedding night, though, you'd never know we were in the midst of a looming personal hurricane. I curled up on Haywood's lap, enjoying the moment, feeling safe and happy. Once everyone had gone, and the kids and his mom and dad were fast asleep, Haywood dropped a 45 of Leo Sayer's "When I Need You" on the turntable, lifted me off my feet for a hug before gallantly inviting me for our wedding dance. I smiled, reminiscing about our first date, when the song had played on the radio during the drive home from Nashville. A mere ten weeks had passed from the time we had met at the phone company, thanks to his brother, Bill. It was hard to comprehend all that had happened during those two-and-a-half months.

Now, in the darkened living room, he pressed me close as we danced, kissing away any lingering fears I had about retribution from Klaus. This moment, at least, was ours.

forty-one

Everything Changes
July 1977, Indianapolis and Walkerton, IN

June came and went which, besides the wedding, included Klaus's thirty-ninth birthday, June 20. I didn't send a card.

The kids told me he finally sold the beloved 1969 Mercedes and bought a used BMW, which made economic sense; he was still unemployed.

A few days into the warm month of July, I received a surprise call. "I ran into Klaus at the grocery store," said Chris, Ty and Megan's former German babysitter. "He says he's selling the condominium, going to Canada and taking both kids. What is he talking about, Jeannie?"

Klaus had alienated Chris right after finding out Haywood and I were dating. Per Chris, Klaus called her, expecting a supportive ear, and had ranted about how, at thirty, I was dating a twenty-one-year-old. Besides being factually incorrect—Haywood was twenty-seven at the time—Klaus had forgotten about the age difference between Chris and her husband, Tom, eight years her junior.

"I wasn't very nice, certainly not sympathetic. He's obviously upset about your new life, but this is crazy. Is there anything I can do?" she said.

I thanked her for the offer. Klaus, in a continuing effort to create fear, used the opportunity to plant more confusing seeds. It didn't seem there was anything anyone could do.

Later that night, Klaus called. "We need to talk about new arrangements and visitation. By the way, I'm sending Ty to Dr. Bob's, to Kingsdayle camp for three or four weeks. The kids and I are going up there tomorrow morning to talk over the details with Bob and Lois."

"I hear you're planning on selling the condo and changing your residence. Is that why we need to discuss visitation?" I asked.

"I'm not moving, and the condo is not for sale. I don't know where you're getting your stupid information, but your sources are wrong. I have to go," and he hung up.

Bob and I spoke that weekend while Klaus was there. Bob remarked about Klaus's lack of parental guidance, that the kids weren't being disciplined and were hyper in the ensuing chaos. "Klaus is detached, even cool, around Lois and me."

Translation: Bob didn't have the control over Klaus that he once had.

Why would Klaus act cool toward the Rosses? Klaus had always been so deferential to Bob, even if I sometimes noted an underlying sarcasm the older man didn't pick up on. I wondered if Klaus felt, with me remarried, staying in their good graces was no longer necessary. Whatever the reason, the relationship between the two of them appeared to be waning.

Bob surprised me by recommending Haywood and I bring the kids back up the following weekend. We could spend the Fourth of July with them and come up with some kind of plan. Karen, who agreed with her parents, would join us at the lake for the holiday weekend. "We just can't let things go on this way. From what my parents have said, he's alienating Ty in particular, making him a robot. It's cruel and heartbreaking," she said.

⚬⚬⚬

217

Lois greeted us with a kind smile at the door when Haywood and I arrived with the kids Friday night just in time for dinner. Bob rose out of his living room leather chair as Ty and Megan ran toward him.

"Well, well, look who's here!" Bob exclaimed, hugging the kids. Haywood extended a hand, receiving a hearty introductory handshake from Bob. "I guess congratulations are in order," Bob said.

"Thanks. I'm a lucky guy. I know you've sort of been in the thick of things and just looking out for the kids' best interests. Probably hasn't been easy, has it?" Haywood said.

I watched Bob nod and raise an eyebrow in agreement, while assessing Haywood.

Haywood smiled and said, "I got a package deal. These kids are something, aren't they?"

Bob smiled back, and I watched an ease set in between the two of them.

"Hey, where's my hug?" I said, approaching Bob. While garnering a fatherly hug from the good doctor, I whispered, "I just want you to be happy for me." He looked at me and nodded.

We heard the bang of the screen door. "I hope I'm not too late!" Karen said as she dragged her suitcase in. I ran toward her for a hug and a quiet second with her.

"Your dad seems different, almost sympathetic to our situation. Maybe I've misjudged him," I said, waffling.

Sitting around the dinner table after the meal, Bob gave us his professional opinion of the situation. "Klaus feels he lost the first battle when you two got divorced, Jeannie—lost you and life as he knew it. Then he lost his job, which is always a blow to a man, and then yet another battle when you remarried. He is adamant that he will not allow another man to act as a father to his children, and will not lose this battle. I'm afraid he's said he will get his kids, one way or another."

"I am so sorry for all that's happening," Lois said, unexpectedly sharing her thoughts. Being Bob's wife, she normally remained quiet and gave him center stage, tamping down her own opinions. "The thing that gets me as a mother is the way Klaus's bitterness toward you was so obvious in front of the kids last weekend. Oh, Jeannie, it's so hurtful and affects everyone's relationship and it's got to be confusing for the children. I overheard Ty say that he doesn't have a mother anymore. Klaus has fed him that information on purpose. It's awful. Bob and I tried to talk with Klaus and shift things, but . . ." Lois stopped and just shook her head.

Karen got up to answer the phone. "Jeannie, it's Klaus, for you."

Surprise registered on everyone's face. Walking into the bedroom to take the call, I could hear the kids playing in the living room; I breathed a happy sigh, relieved they were here with us and not Klaus for the weekend.

After a few awkward preliminaries, Klaus admitted he was considering a move, an admission I found surprising, considering the denial when I confronted him earlier. Then I realized it wasn't an admission; it was a negotiating tool, and we were playing chess. He would stay in Indianapolis if I agreed to give up custody of Megan in exchange for unlimited visitation. He explained it was in the best interests of the children, and he was willing to sacrifice to keep them together. I counter proposed that I, too, would sacrifice and made the reverse offer: he could give up Ty and get unlimited visitation. Otherwise, I maintained there was no need to change the custody. I had already sacrificed by being forced into a split custody compromise, and he already had access to both children. Though the current arrangement displeased both of us, it worked.

Stalemate. He uttered a cold *okay* and hung up.

"Let's not jump to conclusions," Bob said, "but why don't you call your attorney, Jeannie. My guess is what we're all feeling is the growing fear that he'll up and take them. However, for right now, the kids are safe here with you and Haywood, so let's get some sleep. We've got a long weekend to figure out what's best to do, okay?"

Having Bob in my corner, at least for the moment, provided a measure of relief. After further discussions, we agreed Bob would work on Klaus and I would call the attorney to determine if he could offer any safeguards.

By Monday, after exhaustive conversations, we needed to shelve, at least temporarily, all our concerns and enjoy the holiday. From our blanket on the deck beside the lake, we watched the sky fill with ooh-ahh fireworks. The expressions on Ty's and Megan's faces were priceless.

"Mom—isn't that cool!" Ty yelled, as an especially spectacular cluster of starbursts rained down. Megan squealed and pointed from her perch on my lap.

"It's wonderful, Tyger—and so are you and your sister," I told him, as I gave her a big hug.

"You, too, Mom," he said. They both appeared as relaxed and happy as kids ought to be on the Fourth of July. As Haywood took my hand, I reminded myself of exactly what we were fighting for: their right to be kids, not pawns—loved, not used.

When morning came, we'd head back to Indianapolis. Work and calls to the attorney awaited me, and Megan's birthday was coming up the next weekend. My soon-to-be three-year-old delighted in the plans for her very own party. The week would be busy and, as always, I wondered what fresh trouble Klaus might serve up. But in this moment, watching a shower of white sparks fall into the lake, I reveled in the joy and prayed for peace.

Two weeks later, July 17, as I dropped Ty off for the coming week, Klaus came out to meet me on the front porch of the condo. He was smiling.

How odd, I thought.

"Thanks for coming over. I wanted you to know I got a job and start next week, so I'd like to take the kids to Six Flags this next weekend."

"You got a job?" I said.

Nodding, he said an opportunity had finally come through, and had made a big difference in how he felt. I stood there, cocking my head in disbelief. His entire demeanor was different, though, and he really seemed happy, something I hadn't seen for a very long time.

"I know I've been angry, and really rough on you. I was so mad about the way things had turned out. It felt like everything had gone wrong for me. I was in a really bad place when I called you at Dr. Bob's over the Fourth. But now, with this job, and . . ." he paused, "I've met someone, so things are different, really different." He laughed out loud.

I blinked, speechless, searching his face for something that resembled truth. I wanted it to be true. But I could hear the attorney's recent words in my head. Klaus hadn't legally done anything wrong or anything we could charge him with, so there was little to do except wait and watch. I was waiting for the next misstep, not an about face.

"Well, that's great about the job," I said finally, "and about finding someone."

Neither one of us spoke for a few seconds. I could feel an overwhelming pull of *wouldn't it be nice to lay down the past and let go of it all.* I had prayed for this moment. Was it possible? At last?

He continued talking, apologizing at length, and appealing to my softer side, the one easily hooked by "I'm sorry. I'm so, so sorry." He acknowledged the custody request he made the Fourth of July weekend was foolish, and he'd worked that all out now.

Ah, at last he's seen the light of day. The fantasy of a truce grabbed me and I let down my guard. "Okay," I said, and let out a long sigh. "I've been hoping for this. I'm happy for you, really I am, and, if you mean this, I'd be so glad if we didn't have to fight with each other anymore."

I knew his used BMW's reliability was questionable and, as a peace gesture, offered my car for the four-hour trip to Six Flags in St. Louis.

"Thanks, but no need," he said. With the new job on the horizon, he'd had repairs made.

"Good. Well, I'm sure the kids would love Six Flags. I'll pack a bag for Megan and have her ready. So, I'll see you on Friday."

I awkwardly offered a handshake, but he pulled me close and hugged me, saying, "Things can work out now. You'll see."

FORTY-TWO

Day 101

November 4, 1977, Indianapolis, IN

The search continued into November. We planned as much as possible, despite all the unknowns. The children's three-month temporary passports arrived, issued as "replacements for lost/stolen passports" with a January 31, 1978, expiration date. I requested an official leave of absence from my job. On the request form, I guesstimated the dates: November 11, 1977 - January 1, 1978. The reason given: "Extremely Confidential. My ex-husband kidnapped our two children on 7-26-77. I am going to West Germany, find them and bring them home. I have legal custody of both children."

The phone company upper management and executives supported and assisted me in numerous ways. On November 4, 1977, Tom Berry, Indiana Bell's Vice President-Operations, summoned me to the eighteenth floor where the top-level execs resided. As my boss's boss, Tom knew of my credentials and was the one who requested I oversee Bill Ware's work for the company. He had also been briefed about my personal situation. Tom's secretary, seated outside the VP's large office, announced my arrival by phone. Appearing in the doorway, he motioned to me and said, "Come on in, Jeannie."

Walking on the thick carpet, I followed him. "Good morning, Mr. Berry."

"I must unfortunately get off to a meeting but didn't want to wait to get this to you." He handed me a piece of paper from across the desk. Tom had contacted Senator Birch Bayh's office seeking political intervention regarding my case, and the note gave me the contact's name and number.

I stammered a thank you. Almost as an afterthought he added, "You might go down the hall and talk with Shannie Bibie as well."

I had had some interaction with Shannie, once when she first came on board at the phone company and later consulted with her regarding legalities surrounding a couple of customer complaints received through my boss's office. On the outside chance I might catch her, I made my way there and popped my head in her office.

Shannie Bibie, a beautiful, softly flamboyant attorney, was, in 1977, the only female on Indiana Bell's high-ranking executive floor.

She invited me in with a warm smile and a firm handshake. I did not mistake her quiet demeanor for meekness; she was without question in charge. Although tasteful suits graced her wardrobe, she did not strive to be one of the guys. She maintained both her feminine qualities and success within her profession. I admired her chutzpah; she was 100 percent Shannie, and a force to be reckoned with.

Given full rein to decorate her office, she had made it into an invitation. An art deco painting of a woman on one wall, the print of which I had at home, created an immediate connection. The office colors were various shades of blue, purple, tones of rose and hints of pink. The sofa, definitely not brown leather, was soft and plush, the kind you can sink into and feel safe. On her uncluttered desk, pictures of her young daughter were prominent.

We talked at length, and what began as a "hello" became a shared experience of story. After hearing my plight, Shannie offered the services of her brother, who was attached to the Air Force as a translator through some kind of agency. With enough information, he could determine Klaus's whereabouts in Germany by checking with the American embassies, local officials, and possibly churches in West Germany and Austria.

I told her all I knew at that point: Klaus Manthey, no middle initial, five foot ten, one hundred eighty pounds, short brown hair, blue eyes, thirty-nine years old, social security number; allegedly working for an American company as a systems analyst, Monday through Thursday, thirty hours a week. I shared what information I could about Klaus's brother, Fredi, and supplied their mother's location and address as well.

As she hugged me goodbye, my shoulders relaxed, and I again allowed myself to feel the slightest bit of hope.

FORTY-THREE

Day 107

November 10, 1977, Nashville, IN

The world news did little to maintain, much less raise my spirits. Sitting on the sofa, relaxing after a long day at the phone company, I shivered as I read a disturbing newspaper article. The remains of a well-known West German business executive had been found. The victim of a September kidnapping, they discovered his body a month later, after the German government wouldn't negotiate with the terrorists involved.

This politically motivated crime had no real parallels to my situation. It unsettled me to read about any kidnapping ending so tragically—especially in the very country where we'd be searching for my kids. Reports like these, of such hate and anger, created a depressing string of wild head thoughts. Dropping the paper onto my lap, I stared off into space, thinking about Klaus's fury when he first heard I was dating, and the surreal car chase as he sped after Haywood, with Ty right there with him.

And then, the letter Klaus sent immediately afterward, professing love for me.

I had tried to convince myself he'd been—except for being indulgent—a responsible parent, that my concerns for their care weren't reasonable, wherever he'd taken them—but that assumed he was behaving reasonably. Now, with all evidence to the contrary, I feared for the mental and emotional well-being of my children.

I reached for Klaus's post-kidnapping letters on the coffee table.

Rereading them yet again, I could feel the palpable anger toward me, and total hatred of Haywood. *I have decided that no judge can tell me what to do with my children nor will any one of my children be raised by some non-related creep.* Klaus would see that I pay for dashing his dreams. And if he didn't get all the proceeds from the sale of the condo? The threat was clear: *If we have to go this route then any future discussion in regard to the children and their immediate future is herewith terminated.*

It all played in my mind: the hateful, contentious divorce; lying to the babysitter to gain access to my apartment; stealing all my keys; hiding near my apartment building with Ty in the car with him, and stalking me.

All of this for *love*?

Dr. Bob had said, "Klaus didn't feel he was given his due," as if it was a man's right to steal and hide the children, or chase and harass Haywood, or use the children as pawns.

The darkest thought crept into my mind. What else might Klaus do for *love*? Karen's mom had told me over the July 4th weekend she had overheard Ty say he no longer had a mother. I could only imagine what poisonous lies Klaus was feeding them. Were they being told that I no longer loved them, that I had willingly given them up? He had ripped Ty and Megan from everything familiar—all they had at this point was Klaus, their father, the man who considered himself their savior, the only one willing to sacrifice for them.

I tried imagining how Klaus must have prepared for the kidnapping, the trip, the whole undertaking—how being so driven by hate and anger evolved into feeling righteous and privileged enough, that taking the children and running wasn't just an option, it became his duty. Married to Klaus for almost ten years, and I didn't see it coming—that he was capable of using his children and could call it love.

Actually, I *had* seen it. I simply hadn't believed it.

The newspaper was still on my lap. I looked down at the face of the dead man, a pawn in a game of politics I understood even less than I understood Klaus. The victim held a crudely lettered sign that read, "Seit 31 Tagen Gefangener." (Captive for 31 days.)

It had been three times as long for my kids.

Drowning in hate and anger wasn't what I needed or wanted. I wanted my children. My fears fueled a new fierceness. My job as a mother was to focus on and be responsible for my children's well-being, and by God that's what I would do.

FORTY-FOUR

Day 108, 109 & 110

November 11–13, 1977
Indianapolis and Nashville, IN, and Birmingham, AL

On Friday, November 11, Shannie called me to her office; news had come from her brother.

Her office, with all of its soft touches, was such a place of peace. And not just the physical space; I found her very presence comforting, even with her seated behind her desk. She stood and greeted me with a warm handshake. "Hi, Jeannie. Please, sit down. I heard from my brother late last night, and I have to tell you, this whole scenario has given me quite an unexpected education. I'm glad I can pass along what I've learned. Here's what we know." She explained that Klaus, by virtue of becoming a US citizen, forfeited his German citizenship, and could not have returned to Germany and simply set up residence. People entering Germany intending to stay, she relayed, must either register with Einwohnermeldeamt (the Residence Registration Office) within a week of finding permanent residence, or register as an alien, in which case the consulate would gather necessary information and arrange for registration. To remain in the country and/or work, this registration must take place within thirty days of arrival. Without such a revised visa, one could only stay for a month. Shannie's brother determined through the American consulate that no such registration took place. Klaus had not applied for a new document, nor had anyone issued a work permit in his name.

"So that means . . ." I said.

Shannie nodded confirmation. "Klaus is not in Germany."

I sat perfectly still, absorbing the information, feeling happy yet confused and unable to discern what in the world should happen next. We had been ready to fly across the Atlantic and search. They're not in Germany? The overarching question: where then? Where were my children?

"So, her brother is pretty sure of this?"

Haywood was processing my earlier afternoon's conversation with Shannie. I'd only been home from work a few minutes when I had heard his car pull into our gravel driveway. I raced from the kitchen at the back of the house with my news. The poor guy couldn't get past the front porch. "Klaus and the kids aren't in Germany! They can't be!"

"Whoa. Slow down. What's going on?"

I took a deep breath and explained, "Klaus hasn't registered with the authorities there. The Germans are real sticklers for everyone having approved documents and paperwork. Basically, if he's living there, if he's working, if the kids are attending school, Klaus would have to have registered. And he's not!"

"You're kidding me, Jeannie. This is big!"

"Yes, that's what I'm saying!"

Dizzy with the news, Haywood and I agreed we needed a break to think things through, and getting away for a few days might settle our exhausted nerves. "How about we go visit your brother and his family?"

"Really? I'd love seeing Jim and Paulette right about now. But, Haywood, it's at least a seven-hour trip to Birmingham."

Mr. Truckdriver laughed. "Seven hours is a piece of cake for me, and you've told me what a good guy Jim is. Why don't you call and check if it's okay, then pack a bag? I bet he'd love to see his little sister and finally meet her new husband."

Though we arrived after 2:00 a.m., Jim was at the door with hugs, a welcoming handshake for his new brother-in-law, and helped us get settled in.

The breakfast table buzzed with conversation after we all got a good night's sleep. Jim's wicked sense of humor was apparent when told the story of Klaus and the car chase incident. "What did Klaus think he was going to do if he caught up with you, Haywood? He apparently hadn't gotten a good look at you."

Haywood grinned. "I wouldn't have hurt him."

"Probably not, but I wouldn't want to meet you in a dark alley," Jim laughed.

"All kidding aside, the fact that Ty was in the car is so disturbing," my sister-in-law Paulette said. "How could he do that to his son? And these letters from him you brought, they take my breath away."

We hashed through the events, the terms of the divorce, the split custody arrangements, trying to find clues that might reveal their whereabouts, and combed through the letters, reviewing the inconsistencies. The weekend provided no answers, but the brainstorming and support were just what we needed. Jim's upbeat spirit and positive ways inspired us to stay the course.

"And don't waste time blaming yourself or thinking Klaus's actions are justifiable. You don't have time for that. Ty and Megan need you, Jeannie. They love you and you *will* find them and bring them home."

His loving words ran deep. Despite everything, I knew how lucky I was. The family support increased my determination and courage. As we left, Jim said, "You've got me fired up now. I'll call you if I think of anything that might help."

Garnering a big brotherly hug, I told him how much I loved and appreciated him.

"I love you, too, Sis. We're here for you. You stay strong."

FORTY-FIVE

Day 113

November 16, 1977, Nashville, IN

I abandoned my heels and poured my evening glass of merlot, aware of the house's emptiness. Haywood's last truckload of steel was an out-of-town delivery and he wouldn't be home until after 9:00 p.m.

I marked an X through another day on the kitchen calendar. One hundred thirteen days. Without them. While relieved that Klaus hadn't taken the kids to Germany, and encouraged by the previous supportive weekend's visit with my brother, one fact remained: my children were still missing. Their absence was an ache that never subsided, and evenings were the worst.

Picking up my glass, I wandered from room to room, knowing full well they weren't there and looking for them anyhow. The old country house couldn't contain my grief, and I found the quiet deafening.

I shook my tired head. Nearly four months with this gaping emptiness inside. Four months that felt like decades. Another glass of wine might blur the edges a little, but the emptiness would remain. When I was busy at work, or the recipient of Haywood's boundless optimism, I could temporarily escape the desolation. When I was poring over letters, telegrams, and documents, I could deny its existence. On this November evening, however, with the trees bare and forlorn, and the early 6:00 p.m. darkness, I was defenseless against the thoughts that crowded out reason as I stood in the room that would be Ty's.

His window faced east and caught the morning sun. I stood at that window and tried picturing how it would look on a summer morning once Ty was back with me, when the cardboard boxes that lined the far wall were unpacked and the favored Star Wars sheets would outfit the now-bare mattress.

My imagination failed me. All I could see in the darkened window glass was my reflection, tall and slim, weary shoulders slumped. A woman, a mother—a mother who had failed to protect the ones she loved most.

To be a mother, my reflection whispered, *involves sacrificing personal needs and desires for the good of your children. Where is your willingness to sacrifice?*

"I am willing to sacrifice," I said aloud.

How much? she whispered. *Didn't you put your own happiness, your own fulfillment, above their need for an intact family life? Whatever his failings as a husband, Klaus is their father.*

"Yes," I admitted, "but how happy can the children be, with a mother who's miserable!"

How happy can they be with a father who is miserable and alone? she continued. *You did that. You left him. You broke your vows.*

"Yes, I did that—because a marriage without love is no marriage at all," I told her. "But I love my kids, and I'd do anything to protect them."

You would . . . but did you? Protect them?

I thought of my brother's recent admonition, "Don't waste time blaming yourself or thinking Klaus's actions are somehow justifiable." Those words had sounded so reasonable at the time. Now, alone in the darkness, all I could hear was the wind stirring outside, scraping a branch against the windowpane, making the silhouette in the wavy old glass move. Her shoulders were shaking, as if she were laughing. Or crying.

FORTY-SIX

Day 115

November 18, 1977, Indianapolis, IN

"Sis, I know you're at work, but I didn't want to wait to talk to you. I think I've got something. Do you have a second?" my brother asked.

"Sure, Jim," I said, pushing a stack of papers aside. "What's up?"

"Last weekend when you and Haywood were here, you told me Klaus took over the credit cards in the divorce settlement. But before that, you were the one who paid all the bills, right? I was thinking, if you kept any of those old credit card statements, you could contact those companies and you might be able to find out where the monthly bills are being sent. What do you think?"

The credit cards. For a minute, I couldn't breathe. "Oh God, Jim —I think you're brilliant."

In the divorce settlement, Klaus retained the credit cards. If I, though, as keeper of the records prior to that, had kept at least some of the old statements with account numbers and billing information, *and* if he'd left the accounts open . . .

After Jim and I said goodbye, I immediately called Grandma Lee for help. It would be hours before I could get home to Nashville and check the records. Although eccentric and a bit crazy, our seventy-five-year-old neighbor was nothing if not trustworthy.

I had locked the house, but when the feisty septuagenarian heard my request, she gladly agreed to the important document-retrieval mission. I could picture her stubbing out her cigarette, rising from her country porch rocker and heading to our house. Grandma Lee, gutsy old broad that she was, would have no problem hoisting her buxom body through an unlatched window.

She called me back, excitement in her gravelly voice, after scouring my desk and locating the crucial manila file. In it were the prized old checks and listed on one of them she found the MasterCard account number.

After I looked up MasterCard's customer service phone number, I sat motionless, staring at the notepad on my desk, heart racing, palms sweating. What would I say to the person on the other end of the line? I could easily screw up this call. Taking a deep breath, I picked up the receiver and dialed.

"Customer Service. May I have your account number, please?"

Giving her the number, I added, "I just need to check on our bill. I, uh, haven't received it and wanted to make sure we made the payment."

"I can help you with that, ma'am. Your name, please?"

I inhaled and, on the exhale, said, "Jeannie Manthey."

"Thanks, Mrs. Manthey. I'll be right back with you, okay?"

I waited.

"Well, ma'am, we show the billing address as 2150 W. Crestview Avenue, #2025, Anaheim, California 92801. Is that not correct?"

My body vibrated as my heart rate shot up. Gathering my wits about me, pen in hand, I asked if she could repeat the address, capturing it as legibly as my trembling fingers allowed, and said, "Oh, that's right. We changed it to our summer place. No problem. Thanks for checking."

Good God. My mom's psychic friend, Sylvia, had been right. Germany was a total ruse. Klaus had taken the children and fled to the West Coast L.A. area just as Sylvia said months before.

Without even putting the phone back in its cradle, I called TWA and booked a 9:15 p.m. flight from Indianapolis to Los Angeles via Kansas City leaving that night. The only seats available on the connecting flight were in the smoking section. I was so elated over getting a flight, I didn't care. It didn't matter that we had no plan and no idea of what we'd find. I just knew we were going, despite the warning offered moments later on the call with my attorney.

"Jeannie, this is not how it's done. Let's wait until tomorrow. I'll make some phone calls to the California authorities and we'll do this the right way."

"Dennis, there is no way on God's green earth that you could stop me from being on the next plane to California. I'm not waiting another minute. Just bill me for services rendered and I'll stay in touch with you."

"Are you sure? I really think ..."

"I've never been more sure of anything in my life. I promise I'll call you."

"Okay, he sighed. "Good luck. Please be careful. You just don't know ..."

But I didn't hear the rest of his warning. I'd already hung up. I needed to reach my carpool buddy Neil so I could get home, and also make a quick call to Haywood to get packed.

I had found my children.

FORTY-SEVEN

Day 116 & 117

November 19-20, 1977, California

The plane landed at LAX at 1:00 a.m. Saturday, November 19. Exhausted, starving, and edgy, we rented a car, a Thunderbird. Haywood had visited California before and said a Thunderbird was the way to go. Too tired to argue finances with him, I let it go. We instead focused on calming each other's nerves over a middle-of-the-night breakfast of bacon and eggs at a small diner, hoping to quiet our adrenaline levels.

Thirty minutes later, we reached and drove through the large apartment complex matching the address provided by the credit card company. There were over twenty separate buildings, each with its own courtyard parking area, and courtyard after courtyard proved to be a dead end.

Until the last one.

There it sat, Klaus's BMW, identifiable by its distinct Indiana plates. I scanned the nearest building but I couldn't read any apartment numbers. Behind one of those dark windows, I imagined my children, sleeping. Oh, how I longed to beat down every door, find them, and gather them into my arms.

Instead, we left, and at 3:00 a.m. checked into a Garden Grove motel, less than fifteen minutes from Klaus's apartment. Though physically exhausted, my body felt wired, as if I had had caffeine pumped straight into my veins; so tired but wide awake with my heart racing. *Inside an apartment, in this very city, less than ten miles away, my children . . .*

After a few brief hours of restless sleep, we grabbed a quick breakfast and decided the next step was to determine Klaus's routine and where the kids went during the day. We contacted an assistant with Indiana Senator Bayh's office and asked for the name of a private investigator, someone who could follow Klaus on Monday. The staffer on call tracked down a local California contact and gave us the number. Once we called and hired him, Haywood contacted the Orange County Sheriff's Department and found out it would be Monday before we could meet with the appropriate local authorities.

"Why would the sheriff take the weekend off?" I fumed. "Criminals don't. Kidnappers don't!"

"Honey," Haywood said calmly, "we're not talking about the sheriff. The deputy I just spoke with said that Detective Harrison is the guy who handles these things, so let's do this right. I know you're frustrated, but we can't do anything before Tuesday anyway—the private detective needs Monday to figure out where the kids are during the day. You know we can't risk a direct confrontation with Klaus."

"You're right. I know," I agreed. "I know we can't."

Leaving the area for the weekend was our best bet. We both feared if we stayed in Anaheim, we might run into Klaus, or let the temptation to investigate on our own override common sense, and somehow tip him off to our presence. Saturday noon and we were already feeling crazy. Where could we go until Monday morning?

I called old family friends living in San Diego. Relief filled my bones when they extended an invitation for dinner that night, which would give us an opportunity to relax with trusted others, talk about our story in a place of safety, and gain some confidence for what lay ahead.

We needed comfort and support. Now that we were actually in California, the reality of retrieving the children seemed like a monumental undertaking. Because it was. Airing our fears and concerns, we made the two-hour trip down the coast to San Diego, then checked into an area motel before arriving at their home.

I gave them the short version of our crisis and watched the shock register on their faces. Talking with them over dinner helped clarify ways we could handle things when we returned to Anaheim. I also shared an unsolved mystery brewing in the back of my mind. Klaus needed Fredi's help but didn't want Fredi to know specifically where he was, only that he was in Frankfort. If Fredi believed Klaus was living in Frankfurt. Someone else in Germany was "processing" the mail because Klaus was not in Frankfurt; he was sending mail to Germany from California. Fredi would have told me had he received mail with a California postmark. Although Klaus's mail "from Germany" carried Fredi's return address, someone other than Fredi was acting as the Frankfurt postmaster.

What I surmised was Klaus prepared letters to me, Big John, Dr. Bob, Karen, etc. and used Fredi's address as the return address. His letters to Fredi reflected a Frankfort PO Box return address. Klaus put those letters inside a larger envelope and mailed them from California to the rented Frankfort PO Box, monitored by an intermediary, a co-conspirator. That person then opened the larger envelope and removed the enclosed letters, facilitating Klaus's hidden California address by resending Klaus's letters to the recipients. If they were for Fredi, the intermediary put them in the Frankfort mail. If they were for me or others back in the States, the co-conspirator drove to the post office in Fredi's town and sent them from there.

When Fredi received mail *for* Klaus, Fredi would forward it to the Frankfurt post office box which Klaus had given him. The mystery person monitoring the PO box forwarded the mail on to Klaus's California address.

Someone in Germany knew exactly where Klaus was and was aiding him.

What's odd is Klaus never mentioned nor communicated with friends in Germany during our marriage. I suspected the co-conspirator was one of his other siblings, but I had no proof and would not compromise my good relationship with Fredi by accusing a family member. It would forever remain a mystery.

The next day Haywood and I attended a San Diego church, thankful for such supportive friends and also praying hard that a foolproof game plan would somehow materialize. Over breakfast at a local restaurant, we discussed different scenarios and made our list: check on airline flights; call the private investigator; buy sunglasses for Haywood; update our attorney, possibly call the Legal Aid Society, and definitely contact the Orange County Sheriff's Department; call Klaus's apartment complex and determine what elementary school children living there would attend. Having a to-do list made us feel we had some control over the situation.

Once we compiled the list, made some calls, and completed our purchases, there remained way too many hours to fill before we could take action. We headed north via a different route and found ourselves in the town of La Quinta, close to Palm Springs, where we stopped for a Mexican dinner at Las Casuelas.

As we sat with our margaritas, preoccupied with the unknowns of the coming day, a classical guitarist played *Recuerdos de la Alhambra*. I loved the reflective, soothing melody and asked the guitarist what the title translation was. "Some say Memories of the Alhambra, a palace in Granada, Spain. Or, it could mean souvenirs or keepsakes of the Alhambra." I wondered about the distance between California and the faraway land of Granada, feeling it could be no greater than the divide I'd experienced between myself and the children all these months. We had arrived and were so close, but the outcome remained elusive and unknown.

Instead of driving back to Anaheim, we decided staying in nearby Palm Springs made more sense. Before turning in for the night, we boarded the last aerial tram to experience the top of Mt. San Jacinto, traveling through five botanical and geological life zones in a mere fifteen minutes. It somehow seemed representative of the last five months of our lives. The view from the top was breathtaking and inspirational. It gave me hope the pinnacle of our trip was possible; we would get my children back. Breathing in the night air was a release and a relief, self-care preparation for what lay ahead.

We used a payphone to call the private detective to confirm our Monday morning schedule. There I was, in the crisp night air, in such a beautiful setting, on the phone leaving a message with a private detective. Haywood popped into a gift shop and bought a Palm Springs silver-dollar-sized lucky starburst coin. He grinned and pressed the coin in my hand, saying, "We're going to get them back, Jeannie. I'll make it happen; I promise you." And I believed him. The man was a walking inspiration.

FORTY-EIGHT

Day 118

E arly on the morning of November 21, Haywood and I began our own detective work from a sixth-floor Anaheim hotel room. Posing as a potential renter, I called the office of Klaus's apartment complex. I asked about availability, rental rates, costs, deposits and terms. "Oh, and one more thing," I asked. "We have a seven-year-old and need to know about schools. What elementary school would he attend?"

"Let me check," she said. "That would be Mel Gauer Elementary. It's not far from here. The address is 810 North Gilbert Street. Did you want to come look at the models? I'd be happy to show them to you."

"No. No thanks. Not right now. I'll get back with you."

The drive to the Orange County Sheriff's Department didn't take long. Detective-Lieutenant Thomas E. Harrison of the Fugitive & Warrants Bureau met with us in his office; I liked him immediately: composed, solid, straightforward. He listened intently while we told him the entire story and then inspected all of our documents.

"So, what do we do?" I asked.

I recounted the information I had gleaned about California earlier during our mid-August search, not realizing at the time how relevant the data would be. California, we had learned, had recently passed the toughest anti-child-snatching legislation in the country, making it a felony, punishable by up to four years' imprisonment, to hold or hide a child in violation of a custody order.

"So, you can help us, right?"

Detective Harrison broke the bad news. If bureau agents accompanied us to retrieve the children, the agents, bound by local laws, would take custody of them. He confirmed that California was one of ten states using the Uniform Child Custody Act whereby they refused to consider any case already settled in another state. Orange County courts had to enforce and not modify custody orders of a sister state; however, the Uniform Child Custody Act did not provide enforcement *procedures* for carrying out this requirement.

This meant my paperwork was valid, but how law officials processed the paperwork was up to each particular jurisdiction. In Orange County, kidnapped children, if recovered by the authorities, became wards of the state pending determination of their ultimate status. If that happened, we'd be among a growing number of cases and could end up in a long-term court battle, far from home and, even then, with no guaranteed outcome.

I realized what Detective Harrison was implying. He and I stared at each other for a long while. I knew Haywood and I had only one option: go it alone.

I let the "what ifs" bubble up and take over my brain. *Wards of the state of California?* If, in our retrieval of the children, we made one wrong move, if we didn't get cooperation from the school, if they requested the sheriff's office send someone to the scene, if they called Klaus, if, if, if . . .

We were so close, but one wrong move and "close" wouldn't matter.

"I understand. So, what happens to Klaus?" I asked hesitantly.

"We make an arrest and hold him. We then contact Indiana authorities to determine if extradition paperwork is in place," Detective

Harrison answered. "And by the way, that is something you'll have to set in motion through your attorney."

He waited for my reaction.

I looked at Haywood. Extradition was the last thing on my mind. I just wanted my kids back and hadn't really considered the legal hornet's nest I'd be jabbing by involving the authorities. My initial impulse? Just steal my children back and rely on Indiana laws for protection, but that ultimately left Klaus free, with the ability to immediately wreak more havoc. Extradition was apparently a wise part of the deal: without a commitment to extradite, California wouldn't be able to take any action against him.

I imagined Detective Harrison thought my hesitation strange, but requesting extradition scared me. In order to get my kids back and have at least some assistance from the legal system, I had to have my children's father arrested.

"Okay," I said at last.

"We'll need some time to process the extradition, probably until tomorrow night."

Haywood and I looked at each other, then nodded we understood. "Call me if you need me," Detective Harrison said in a quiet voice and handed me his business card as he shook my hand.

We contacted our attorney and ordered the extradition paperwork. We'd have to borrow the necessary $1,000, but we'd get it, somehow.

With that decision behind us, we returned to the hotel and discussed our next steps. We feared flying directly home—if something went wrong, if they didn't arrest Klaus and he discovered what was going on, he could intervene and would certainly check Indiana flights. When we'd left for California, we were so paranoid we informed only our attorney of our plans, rather than risk implicating others, or risk others alerting Klaus. We had no idea if he could stop the plane, or have California or Indiana authorities take action against us.

We booked a Tuesday afternoon flight to Birmingham, Alabama, where we could safely stay with my brother and family. Booking the Birmingham flight fueled the determination and the belief we would find them and take them home. Being on that plane the next day with my children became our driving force. We had a schedule, a deadline, and a specific plan. Returning to Avis, we extended the rental on the '76 Thunderbird we'd already put 495 miles on. We needed the car for one more day.

The countdown began.

The private investigator's office rang us at the hotel with a verbal report that afternoon, providing only one piece of valuable information: "At 7:10 a.m. this morning, Mr. Manthey came out into the parking lot with a young female child, presumably Megan, and drove through the complex on internal roads to the Child Care Center which is located directly behind the manager's office building. Mr. Manthey dropped off the female child and then drove off."

"What about my son?"

"I'm sorry, Mrs. Ware. There was no one else with him."

No sighting of my son. Not good. I started wringing my hands. "Don't go there, babe," Haywood reassured me. "We've gotta stay focused on what we know. We'll figure out the rest as we go."

FORTY-NINE

Day 119

November 22, 1977, Anaheim, CA

I awoke Tuesday morning, November 22, the enormity of the day pressing on me, a day with no room for error. Sipping my coffee after packing my bag, I stared out through the white sheers of the window overlooking Anaheim. The morning light fell on my face as I brushed the curtain aside and noted the muted traffic noise below. I'd dressed in my navy-blue pantsuit, hoping it would fortify me and give the appearance of someone worth taking seriously. I felt my heartbeat pulsating rhythmically, guiding me, poising me for what was about to happen. Arching my back, I practiced standing tall.

There were so many variables at play, and I knew the whole thing could blow up in our faces. I closed my eyes, gripping the sides of the paper coffee cup, and contemplated the odds. I picked up the custody documents, which felt heavy yet powerful in my hand as I mentally reviewed our checklist of the day's events. But what if it didn't work? What if we didn't get them?

Each move needed to be clean. We would get in the car and drive to Mel Gauer Elementary School first. We had no idea though if my Indiana paperwork would matter, and that thought terrified me. I'd rather already be back home in Brown County with the kids. I couldn't let fear take over. We'd come this far. I looked at Haywood, set the cup down, and reached out to him for a calming embrace. I laughed as he handed me part of a muffin for added sustenance.

"I know you're scared, but you don't need to be, and you don't look it. You have the strength in you to do this. Just keep focusing on the kids—not Klaus. You hear me?" he said.

I whispered a prayer. *Please God, please, give me the strength to go through with this. It's true; I am scared, but we're so close. Haywood is right. I need to be brave, fearless. I'll do whatever the day requires of me to get them back. Please watch over us, guide us, and don't let me make a mistake.*

The clock was ticking, and the return flight scheduled. We had to move now. Zipping up the suitcases, we left the room and the stark sound of the hotel room door closing behind us ended the planning stage and ushered us forward. *This is it; it's happening.* Moving quickly, as if to stay one step ahead of the fear nipping at our heels, Haywood took my hand and together we readied ourselves to do what we came to do.

Suitcases safely stowed in the trunk, I settled into the passenger seat. Haywood drove out of the parking lot and headed for the school, the school where my son had no idea what was about to happen.

We arrived unannounced at Mel Gauer Elementary at 10:00 a.m. and were escorted to the principal's office, where we introduced ourselves to Earl Fleischman. Mr. Fleischman was tall and business-like in nature and appearance: suit, tie, large square-framed glasses, thinning hair; not much of a smile, though pleasant enough, and a man of few words. I couldn't read him, but knew the gravity of his role in our lives. We had to rely on his willingness to hear us, believe us, and acknowledge my custodial rights. We had to rely on him to *not* contact Klaus. When he confirmed that Ty was, in fact, enrolled there, I breathed an initial sigh of relief.

We spent over thirty minutes telling our story. With little to no expression, he then methodically reviewed our documents. The surroundings felt like a foreign land: an unfamiliar public school, a principal's office, his bookshelves, the extraneous papers covering the desk, the sterile smells of an elementary school. How could I possibly have thought I could simply walk in and miraculously walk out with my son? Trying unsuccessfully to discern what Mr. Fleischman was thinking added to the intensity and anxiety of the moment. I was so distracted I missed the question he posed.

"Mrs. Ware?"

"I'm sorry," I said. "It's been a long four months and being here now, it's, well, it's unbelievably unnerving." I glanced at Haywood and reached for his hand, taking in the soft smile on his face. "I'm sorry, Mr. Fleischman, what was the question?"

"I was asking why Mr. Manthey would go to the extreme of kidnapping the children."

Breathe, Jeannie. Remain composed. Be clear. Be straightforward. You can do this. "Klaus was pretty much a loner, and after the divorce, he was certain we'd get back together again. Then he lost his job, I remarried, and he went off the deep end. The only way he could hurt me was to take the children away from me. With very few friends to turn to for support, the only thing he could control was the children."

Mr. Fleishman said nothing for a moment or two, then asked if we'd like to see the application Klaus filled out at the beginning of the school year, and handed me the document. The space provided for "Mother" was blank. I blinked back tears as I thought about the blank space in their lives . . . one day they were with their mother; the next day, not. Day after day without their mother.

He watched my reaction, then stared at his desk for a full sixty seconds, an eternity. When he lifted his head, his face was still unreadable. Lacing his fingers together, resting them on our documents, he spoke at last. "Well, all your paperwork seems to be in order." He removed and held his glasses in one hand while he rubbed his eyes with the other, holding back his own emotions. After clearing his throat, he added, "I'm sorry for what you have obviously been through."

This quiet man regained his composure, picked up the phone and called a staff member. "Get Ty Manthey, please, and bring him to my office." He looked directly at me and said, "Based on what I see here, I have no obligation to call Mr. Manthey, so I won't be doing that. I have a question, though. How will Ty react to seeing you? Might he run?"

Oh, my God. That thought hadn't crossed my mind. Why hadn't I prepared for that? A moment of panic took hold. "Mr. Fleishman, I don't know. Not knowing what Klaus has told Ty over the last four months, we honestly don't know." I stopped, remembering the depth of my son. I never questioned his love for me, and I wasn't going to start now. "No," I said with resolve. "No, I don't think so. He's a smart and brave little boy."

"I'll stay and help however I can."

I nodded a thanks and winced, noting my stiff neck. I dropped my shoulders to sooth the tension consuming every motherly fiber of my body and inhaled deeply to counteract my shallow breathing. *My son. My little guy is about to walk into this room. It's happening. Keep breathing, Jeannie. You've spent four long months of lost love awaiting this moment.*

I stood back out of view when I spotted him coming down the windowed corridor. He entered the room and an adrenaline rush like I'd never experienced hit me. I caught myself by leaning against a tall file cabinet. Witnessing my now seven-year-old son, I released the tiniest gasp as my jaw dropped open. I covered my mouth and braced myself.

He looked so different, thinner and taller than I remembered, and he'd lost his top two front teeth, with new ones barely visible. Without warning, I was awash with the wondrous feeling I had the night I gave birth to him, my firstborn, the one who gave me the gift of motherhood.

He saw Haywood and his eyes grew large, followed by a matching grin. Haywood swallowed hard, "Hi, buddy!" Haywood's enormous arms opened wide and enveloped Ty. They hugged and laughed, then hugged and laughed some more. "How are you, buddy? We've missed you so much!"

Ty said, "I've missed you," then stopped short and said, "Where's Mom?" As he scanned the room, I stepped out in plain view. All I could choke out was, "Ty," and wait, frozen in place.

"Mom!" he said and ran toward me. "Mom, you're here. You came!"

My son was in my arms. My body shook with the joy of actually holding him, and the tears wouldn't stop. "Oh, God, I can't believe I've got you. I thought I'd never see you again. I've missed you so much. I love you. Do you have any idea how much I love you?"

"I love you, too, Mom." He hung his head while holding tight. "I tried to call you, but I couldn't find you in the phonebook."

"Oh, honey," I released a comforting laugh. "There was no way you could reach us. California is a long way from Indiana." I dabbed my eyes while I tried putting his mind at ease. "I'm with you now. That's all that matters."

We thanked a smiling Mr. Fleischman, and asked Ty if he'd like to go on a little trip, and then questioned him about Megan. The clock was ticking, and we had little time to spare; moving quickly was critical.

"She stays there, Mom. The place where we live, the daycare at the apartment building," he said proudly, and agreed to show us the way.

Once in the car, a seven-year-old's questions began. My son was both happy and confused. And anxious. How did we find them? Should he call his dad? How long would we be gone? Did he have to finish his lunch he'd brought along, or could we get something else? Was he going back for afternoon classes? We assured him we'd take care of things, one at a time. I dried my tears and squeezed him close.

We received a different reception at the daycare center. The reaction of the director was the opposite of the school principal. Mrs. Grenetka, a grandmotherly type, was pleasant but serious about protecting the young children in her care. Ty stayed with Haywood while she and I moved to a small children's table and reviewed my Indiana custody papers and the warrants.

"I'm sorry, but this is a private daycare center. Your documents have no standing here." My heart sank. Even knowing that the elementary school's principal had released Ty, she wasn't budging.

Although a great risk, I asked if we could call the Orange County Sheriff's Department for assistance. Detective Harrison, who had helped us earlier, was not in. Another man fielded the call and said, "You cannot just take the child without the daycare's approval, regardless of your paperwork. You know that, don't you?"

He confirmed with her we had in fact been in the Orange County Sheriff's Department the day before. That was the extent of what he was willing to do for us.

I sat there at a loss. Seeing my despair, Mrs. Grenetka began asking questions of a more personal nature, details about the kidnapping, about my background, about my relationship with my daughter.

"What prompted his actions? Why did your former husband feel the need to leave with the children?" she inquired.

There it was, that same question posed by the principal. I steeled myself and set aside the shame and blame associated with it. There was no time for that. I looked her in the eye, spoke from the heart and told her the story. "He left a letter saying he'd taken them to Germany, and we'd never see them again. As we all know now, it was a ruse. He moved here. Do you want to see the letter he left?" I asked.

As she read it, she looked up at me periodically, with thoughtful eyes, as if she were experiencing what I must have felt. Quietly, she folded the letter and put it back in the envelope. She held on to it as she sat and pondered things for several moments. Finally, with a new softness in her voice matching the gentleness in her dampened eyes, she looked at me while motioning for her assistant. "Go get Megan. Go get her daughter."

I stared into Mrs. Grenetka's face, then put my head down and closed my eyes. She reached for my hands and placed hers over mine. I lifted my head, face wet, and whispered, "Thank you." We smiled at each other and waited. I smiled at Haywood, standing in the corner of the room, and he drew Ty close.

A troubling thought entered my head, causing momentary panic. Would my daughter know me? She was only three years old. At seven, Ty had some comprehension of what had happened, listening to my side of the story as I shared it with Mrs. Grenetka. He knew they had been "taken" and realized they had been "found." Would Megan, at three, understand? Could she comprehend what had happened? Her mother had stopped existing with no explanation at all. Would she even know me?

As I waited for her to enter the room, I recalled a memory when she was seven months old. I had had a long day at work and was spending the early evening feeding her, playing with her, bathing her and putting her to bed. Standing crib-side with my arms cradling her, I pressed her to my chest and cupped her head in my hand, smelling her sweet hair, aware of the softness of her skin. It was a small, quiet but unforgettable moment. Just us. As I gently swayed back and forth, I whispered in her ear, "Megan, I love you so much."

I remembered thinking I needed to capture that moment because someday, all too soon, she'd be grown and gone.

And now, she was coming down a hall, about to be within reach in the same room with me. I wanted to run to her, even while I knew I must be cautious and take my cues from her. God forbid I should scare her. I could only imagine her confusion, what she'd been thinking, feeling. What had my daughter been told, she who was motherless these four long months?

The hallway door opened, and I saw her. She looked so tiny as she walked tentatively into the room, holding onto two fingers of the assistant's hand. Her curly light brown hair was now medium length, soft and tousled. She wore pink corduroys and a long-sleeved pink pullover cable-knit sweater, her brown eyes wide open as if she had just awakened from a nap. The assistant walked her over to me.

Megan stared up, and I gazed down. I held my breath as we looked at each other.

"Hi sweetie," I finally uttered.

She said nothing, staring at me, still. *Oh God, she doesn't remember me.* Very slowly, I crouched down, sitting on my heels in front of her, and looked into her eyes. The room faded away, and it became a small quiet moment. Just us.

"Megan," I whispered, "it's Mommy."

Still nothing. Only the stare. My mind was racing. Could she speak? What words did she know? Four months and I couldn't remember. How could I forget what words my daughter knew, what she could say?

In the next moment, without changing expression, without uttering a sound, she loosened her grasp on the assistant's hand and moved toward me. She raised her small arms and wrapped them around my neck. Releasing a sigh, she nestled her head in the crook of my neck and clung tight.

I clutched her as I stood up, crying and whispering in her ear, "Oh Megan, it's okay. Mommy's got you. Megan, I love you so much." I looked over at Ty, smiled and held out a welcoming arm. He sidled up to me and held on, squeezing me hard. God help me, we were together at last.

The daycare director passed out tissues to everyone in the room. She had made hard decisions that morning, life-changing ones, based on the wisdom of her years and her intuition. As we left, the only words I remember were those of this caring woman as she assured us, "I'll give you some time before I make any calls." I knew full well this woman could handle any legal ramifications that might follow.

I could not regain what I had lost: four months . . . seventeen weeks . . . 119 days . . . 2,856 hours of their lives; time and memories, lost forever. But here they were, Megan and Ty, in this moment, in my arms. I felt them breathing as I held them close, silently making them promises—*I will never take you for granted. I will care for you, love you, protect you. No one will ever take you from me again.*

Megan would remain nestled, arms around my neck for well over an hour, only releasing her grasp when we boarded the plane.

The drive to the airport was both exhilarating and tense. Our timing left no room for error. With Megan's head burrowed in my neck, my emotions were in my throat. Ty seemed to like the adventurous nature of all that was happening, though the stress of the circumstances was palpable.

"Mom, where are we going?" Ty asked.

"We're going to visit Uncle Jim and Aunt Paulette in Birmingham. They've invited us for Thanksgiving. Does that sound like fun?"

"Yeah. I just need to know when to call Dad."

"I know, honey. We'll talk about that after we get there."

"He's not going to be happy, is he, Mom?"

"No honey, he's not." I looked at Haywood. He patted Ty's knee. This poor boy, though happy we found him, was undoubtedly wondering what this would mean to life as he knew it. Unspoken concerns about the repercussions with Klaus plagued us all.

We returned the car and took the shuttle to the terminal. Two of us had flown into California. Four of us would fly out. At 2:25 p.m., family now intact, we boarded United Airlines Flight 896, scheduled for takeoff at 2:55 p.m.

We sat across the aisle from each other, Ty with Haywood, and Megan with me, safe. Breathing a sigh of relief, we buckled up the

YOU'LL NEVER FIND US

kids and immersed ourselves in conversation. It was well after 3:00 p.m. when we realized we had not taken off.

Finally, the stewardess made an announcement, frustrating for everyone, bone-chilling for me. "We're sorry for the delay, but we will be remaining on the ground for approximately fifteen more minutes. We apologize for the delay and we'll have you in the air shortly."

Haywood and I looked at each other, panicked. Could Klaus have found out? Called the school or daycare and discovered we had taken the children? Had he contacted the authorities and halted the plane's departure? Were they on their way?

I'd have taken extreme air turbulence over this emotional turbulence. We had successfully retrieved the kids. Sitting indefinitely on the tarmac was not part of the plan. There was no safety on the ground. God in heaven, get us in the air, away from Los Angeles. Let us get out of here.

We waited. Everything about the airplane fascinated the kids who had never been on an airplane and were oblivious to the delay. While they found delight everywhere—the seats, the trays, the magazines—we kept nervously peering out the windows. We watched the crew. And we waited.

The commotion at the front of the plane caused an immediate tightening in my chest, heart palpitations, and an inability to breathe. The stewardess made way for an unknown individual. I watched as they seated some veiled movie star (I swear she looked just like Barbra Streisand) in first class. I sank down into my seat and let the air out of my lungs, followed by a long deep breath of relief while the plane taxied down the runway. Gazing down at my three-year-old resting on my arm, holding my hand, I wrapped my other arm around her and whispered, "I love you, Megan."

"I love you, Mommy."

Goodbye, California.

FIFTY

Safe

Thanksgiving 1977, Birmingham, AL

For most of the other passengers, the Birmingham flight must have been like any other flight. For Haywood and me, it was nothing less than a miracle—two miracles, actually. One seated with him, the other curled up with me. I was afraid to close my eyes for fear I'd fall asleep, only to wake and find them gone. I thought back to that July night Big John brought me the letter from Klaus. *You'll never find us* kept repeating in my head, and all the subsequent nights without them when I'd all but given up hope of ever finding them. I looked over at Ty, who kept Haywood entertained with serious tic-tac-toe games. He saw me staring at him and said, "Hey, Mom. You should see the score. I'm winning!" and he lit up my heart with his special smile when I gave him a thumbs-up. I kept touching Megan, careful not to wake her from a nap, but feeling that if I didn't keep a hold on her this time, she'd disappear. Leaning into her so I could absorb her warmth, smell her hair, and hear her breathe, I knew we were safe at last.

We rented a car at the Birmingham Airport and headed for Jim and Paulette's. The reunion was joyous.

That evening, once we settled in, I went into the guest bedroom for privacy, turned on a small table lamp which softly lit the room, and called Karen at her parents' lake house to let her know we had the children. I told her we were all well, and we were safe. I called the kids in briefly so they could both speak with her. Karen cried with elation while still reeling like the rest of us from the ordeal.

Karen told me her father had received a call from Klaus. He had been arrested. Three officers from Orange County Sheriff's Department were waiting outside his apartment door when he got home from work. They supposedly threw him up against the wall, patted him down, handcuffed him, and took him to jail.

I sat in the darkening room on the edge of the bed and wept. How could any of this be real? I mean, I married him, lived with him for ten years, gave birth to his children, and now he was in jail for kidnapping them. My entire body hurt, exhausted mentally, emotionally and physically. I kept asking that insane question "why" to which there was no answer. I felt sick, sad, and sorry for him. But make no mistake, I'd do it again.

The next day, November 23, my attorney received $1,000 earmarked for the Sheriff of Marion County for the extradition of Klaus Manthey. More borrowed money, this time from a friend who had promised help if I needed it. Though I knew the only way California would honor Indiana warrants was an extradition agreement, I hated it. I didn't want to punish Klaus. I just wanted my children.

And I had them. Never had a Thanksgiving filled my heart with so much gratitude. My brother and family gladly took us in and loved on us for days. After clothes shopping for Ty and Megan, there were hours of conversation with good company and good food; we were a family. For at least the moment, everything felt normal. Experiencing that stability would prepare us for the days ahead when normal was a memory. On Monday, November 28, 1977, we said our goodbyes, headed for the airport, and flew home.

FIFTY-ONE

Aftermath

December 1977 to the Present

B ack in Nashville, which the four of us would officially call home, we felt nurtured by its peaceful and laid-back setting, surrounded by the beauty of Brown County.

Was I enjoying this land of enchantment? Not really. I found out Orange County authorities released Klaus on bail within a week. Locking our doors and windows became an obsession. We dealt with one challenge after another, not the least of which involved sleep, or lack thereof. Multiple times each night, I checked on the children, confirming they were in their beds, safe and secure. Admittedly, Haywood's very presence, size, and stature provided some sense of security. The local police and sheriff's offices were also, gratefully, ready and willing to protect my children. We briefed the school principal and teachers on our situation; no one was to pick up either Megan or Ty without our express consent.

And there was the protection afforded through the arrest warrants and extradition. Though Klaus fought extradition, he knew by entering the State of Indiana he risked immediate arrest.

Still, I kept Megan and Ty close and watched over my shoulder at all times. I remember once, when Ty and I were shopping in Indianapolis, I was admiring a blouse when, within a split second, the boy disappeared. I turned, and he wasn't there. "Ty? Ty, where are you? Ty?" I shuddered, whispering, "Oh my God. Oh my God," and frantically searched the area. My voice grew louder as I yelled, "Ty! Ty!"

moving through the store. He crawled out from under a clothing rack, wearing a proud grin. "Hi, Mommy. I'm right here!" Releasing my heart from my throat, temper in check, I wrapped my arms around him as I tried explaining through my tears we needed to save hide-and-seek games for another day.

Life after the kidnapping was a tortuously tender time. We wanted to make life as normal as possible, but high alert rules of protection were a priority. Remaining in a hyper-vigilant state was the cost—a small price to pay—to have them back in our lives.

Though it would take me years to author this story, I knew my memoir would at best be one-sided: authentic though not altogether accurate, told through my eyes, my perceptions, my pain. And how much of the story, how many years of pain, did I want to delve into? Ultimately, I chose to write about the kidnapping and only the kidnapping, rather than include the ensuing years of ongoing drama: a second but thwarted kidnapping, a lawsuit, court scenes, threats, and therapy.

The telling of the kidnapping provided the incremental healing building blocks of forgiveness not just for Klaus, but myself as well. Forgiveness meant I could release the tight fist of hatred. The morass of hate and bitterness served no purpose. Over time, I've learned self-compassion for who I was then, and in so doing, found the path to self-forgiveness.

Do I think Ty and Megan came out of this okay? Without question. They each possess a strength about them and a boatload of resilience, not to mention skills as writers in their own right. Tyger, a systems engineer for a large telecommunications company, has an innate and mind-boggling ability to clearly and creatively explain details—even to his mom. Megan, owner of a successful exhibit and planning design firm, recently changed her name from Megan Elizabeth to her poetry pseudonym of Olive. She chose Olive (and kept Elizabeth), named after Olive Byrne and Elizabeth Marston, the two women who served as the inspiration for her beloved Wonder Woman. My admiration only grows. Both are married, living in Austin, Texas, near me: Olive with a daughter of her own, and Tyger, choosing Great Danes over parenthood. Each has, over the years, offered invaluable help, encouragement, and support. I love them to pieces.

I never kicked my door-locking habit, even after Klaus died in 2001. The story of his death follows as a postscript. Haywood and I closed the door on our marriage after twenty-six years and went our separate ways. I remain indebted to him for his strength and perseverance, and being my knight in shining armor throughout the worst nightmare of my life. Sadly, the very things that served our union well in the beginning proved the undoing of the marriage in the end. We both found partners we were much better suited for, and continue to happily share in the life of our daughter, Abby, her husband, and their two young girls.

FIFTY-TWO

Postscript: He Dies

November 2001, Austin, TX

"**M**om, Klaus is dead."

The wind had picked up and navigating a wet Hill Country road while talking on the phone was not a good idea. I pulled into a parking lot, killed the engine and took a slow deep breath before pressing the cell phone to my ear. "What happened, Ty?"

"I just got a call from Kathy."

My thirty-one-year-old son described the terse conversation he'd had with his stepmother. As the story was told to me, Kathy had come home from work, ten days before, and found Klaus on the kitchen floor, blue and unconscious. After a week's hospitalization, he died without ever coming out of the coma.

"I guess it was the prostate cancer," Ty said, emotionless.

"I'm so sorry, honey." I couldn't find the right comforting words, knowing how his attempts to connect with Klaus over the years had resulted in frustration for both father and son.

"Mom," he said, punctuating each word, "he died last Sunday."

"Sunday? Ty, this is Thursday."

"Yeah. It's obvious she doesn't want us to come to the funeral." His anger was palpable. "Her neighbors called right after she did and confessed they'd forced her to call me. The service is tomorrow."

After offering to check flights, take care of the dogs—whatever they needed—I hung up, wondering how Ty and his sister would get from Austin to their father's funeral in California on such short notice. Klaus's second wife of twenty years had left my children few travel options.

My son and his wife, Kim, barely got to Los Angeles in time for the funeral. They told me the eulogy all but skipped over them and Megan, as if they didn't exist, as if Klaus had gone directly from West Germany to California and married Kathy.

Megan, twenty-seven, elected not to attend the funeral. She had suffered a strained relationship with her father that had degraded over the preceding decade. I remember clearly a phone call from her around the time of her graduation from the University of North Texas. She graduated cum laude with a BA in Communication Design and created her own graduation announcement based on Rosie the Riveter.

"Mom," she said after she'd spoken with Klaus about her clever announcement, "Do you know what that, pardon me, asshole said? I asked if he'd received the announcement and he grunted and said, 'Oh that flimsy little postcard? Yeah, I got it. Couldn't you do any better than that?' Do you believe that?" I heard her choke back tears. "Why does he have to be so hurtful? Every time we try to talk, he's just plain rude and arrogant as hell. God, I hate it."

Her pain—the pain he caused her—cut right through me. I couldn't protect her from his venom, which was nothing more than secondhand hatred. Her crime? She reminded him of me. I had learned to be fearless. She was born fearless.

I sat alone in the car, the sound of rain hitting the windows. "He's dead," I said out loud. A sense of relief washed over me. Thoughts of the past, though, began spinning around in my head like a roulette wheel, until the ball landed on 1977: the year my ten-year marriage to him finally ended, the year of the acrimonious divorce, and the kidnapping.

I had loved Klaus. I married him. I gave him two beautiful children. And I grew to hate what he stood for. Now, he was dead.

Dead. Gone at age sixty-three, probably still filled with hate and anger. Maybe that's what killed him.

My house, quiet when I arrived, offered a welcome invitation. I propped my feet up on an ottoman, sank back into the sofa, and drank a glass of merlot. I poured and sipped a second as I sorted through a barrage of emotions. Then I remembered the briefcase, long ago hidden away.

I had wanted many times to purge my life of Klaus's post-divorce letters, stuffed in a dusty old Bell Telephone zippered briefcase with the diaries, hotel and rental car receipts, aged newspaper articles, documents and notes relative to the kidnapping, all of which felt like hazardous materials. The collection, kept for legal reasons, had remained untouched all these years. Each time I came near it, its negative energy overpowered me.

He was in that briefcase.

I pulled the bulging bag from the depths of my bedroom closet and spread its contents on the living room floor. The dim glow of twilight filtered through the blinds as I began shuffling through the toxic yellowed papers for a particular letter.

There it was—the letter dated July 26, 1977, in his tight, precise handwriting, so different from my own American script. I shuddered as thoughts took me back in time to the night he and the children vanished. Klaus's written words, even after twenty-four years, kindled the old pain. I read the musty pages, reached for my wine and stared into the dusk, transfixed.

"You son of a bitch," I whispered under my breath. "Someday, I'll have the nerve to write the story."

EPILOGUE

June 2015, Austin, TX

My son, over the years, supported my decision to write about the ordeal, though was very reticent to talk about the kidnapping. Ty said it was "my book" and really didn't want to get too involved. In June 2015, when we were all living in Austin, Texas, he agreed, at my bidding, to help me clarify some mysteries surrounding the story. He and his wife, Kim, came over for pizza and wine. Having him sit in my living room, willingly working so hard at dredging up the events of nearly forty years prior, made for a memorable evening.

Later that night, I wrote him an email. I said how much I appreciated the evening's Q&A and made a mother's apology for my part in whatever stress he suffered as a child. I also acknowledged how proud I was of the man he had become.

Ty responded with the following email:

> You are welcome to ask as much as you want. It's always interesting when I remember something I was previously unaware of, or a memory gets clarified with other details.
>
> Also, you shouldn't be sorry for the way I grew up, I'm not. I've told you before, I couldn't imagine doing what you did when I was your age. I think about how stupid I was in my 20s, and you got married, had kids, got divorced and dealt with Klaus. You got past all that and then moved on, all the while providing a loving family for us.
>
> You've always done the best you could, and one of the

things I admire most about you is your continual self-examination and desire for personal growth. Pretty much the opposite of Klaus, although I loved him too, and was formed as much by his perceptions of the world as I was by yours.

All in all, everything turned out pretty good.

Photo credit: Kim Manthey

ACKNOWLEDGMENTS

My forte is writing irreverent (but educational, of course) personal development blogs. Writing the memoir? Painful. Without the help and encouragement of the three thousand people I mention below, I'd have given up long ago.

Three mentors in particular top the list: authors Christina Baldwin, Susan Wittig Albert, and Mary Day Long.

Christina Baldwin (https://peerspirit.com) and I met in 2003 when she facilitated a Texas retreat for fifty women writers sponsored by Story Circle Network (https://storycircle.org)—an organization to which I am deeply indebted—dedicated to helping women share the stories of their lives through memoir, poetry, fiction, nonfiction, and drama. Meeting Christina was the beginning of a deep friendship that changed my life and has endured to this day.

Two years later, as a gift from Robert, my architect/husband, I attended Christina's "Self as the Source of the Story" writing retreat on Whidbey Island, where I wrote the fourteen-page synopsis of what would become *You'll Never Find Us*. I was reluctant to pen the memoir but she convinced me to write the story. "Just get it out. It needs to be told."

Shortly thereafter, based on that encouragement, I packed up my laptop and all kidnapping-related documents (translation: a boatload), and joined my husband on a business trip where I sat in a Houston hotel room for three weeks and dumped all my memories and the documentation onto the page.

Over the years the memoir evolved as a front burner/back burner dance, with a great many dance partners coming from Story Circle Network (SCN). I am very grateful to award-winning author Susan Albert, the founder of SCN. She remains a beloved mentor in both my writing world and my personal life. In addition to Susan, other

SCN members have aided and abetted my work: Amber Starfire, Judy Alter, Susan Tweit, Len Leatherwood, and Jude Walsh. The members of SCN's online Work-in-Progress Roundtable have all shared their wisdom and support. You ladies know who you are and I thank each of you.

As luck would have it, Story Circle Network (Jane Ross, to be specific) led me to author PJ Pierce. I sent PJ ten pages of my memoir and was accepted into her critique group, *the Wednesdivas*. We met every other week on (yes) Wednesday and provided serious critique of each other's works-in-progress. These women changed my novice writer's life: PJ, Marty McAllister, Mary Day Long, and Debbie Winegarten (with a nod of thanks to Maida Barbour, who was part of the group initially). After Debbie left to focus on the publication of her work and create her own indie publishing company, Ellen Humpert participated for a while and then author Laura Cottam-Sajbel joined the group. I owe them all a debt of gratitude.

After the critique group disbanded, Mary Day Long and I became a team of two; she reworked and expanded the memoir's first one hundred pages into a better book. Sometimes, that's what it takes. Mary believed in my story. She would not quit and would not let me quit either. What a superb writer Mary is—and a funny and brilliant force to be reckoned with.

I must give a shout-out to the Writer's League of Texas for their excellent classes (one in particular led by author Donna Johnson) and their impressive annual Agents & Editors Conferences.

And then there's Brooke Warner, author and publisher of She Writes Press (SWP). I remember our first meeting when Story Circle Network invited her as the keynote speaker for its 2018 conference. As a board member and the conference emcee, I introduced her, commenting on how talented—and tall—she was. Both are still true today. There isn't anything I don't like and admire about Brooke. She flat out has my back and the backs of all her authors. Julie Metz nailed the book cover design, Stacey Aaronson's exceptional interior design blew me away, and no matter how needy I've been, the remarkable Shannon Green, my talented SWP manager and high-speed email queen, has gracefully put up with me.

Hats off to Julia Drake, owner, and Bradley Jones, Senior Publicist, at Wildbound PR. They treated me with kindness and respect, and made me feel my book mattered as much to them as it did to me.

Sarah Bird, besides being a well-known, respected Texas author, is a woman of integrity. I met her a few years back; she happily and with great encouragement agreed to read and blurb this debut memoir, cheering me on during the publication process. Thanks, Sarah.

In the summer of 2018, my former critique collaborator and dear friend, Debbie Winegarten, and her wife, poet Cindy Huyser, attended The Writers Hotel (TWH) conference in New York. When they returned, Debbie insisted I submit my memoir draft and apply to attend the 2019 conference. Sadly, an aggressive cancer took Debbie's life in September 2018. Her loss hit hard. I was stunned when informed she had bequeathed me a paid TWH scholarship believing I would be selected. I applied, was accepted, and, with deepest gratitude to Debbie, went to New York—with Cindy, whose talents had garnered her an invitation to return as a TA—where I immersed myself in the intense week-long event.

Thanks to the copyediting skills of TWH Founding Editor Shanna McNair and Consulting Editor Scott Wolven, my book went through a long process of micro-edits and rewrites. Author and poet Richard Hoffman reviewed the first five thousand words and made me rethink my approach and structure. Those who attended his intensive during that week offered their advice and encouragement: particularly Hillary Webb (who helped editorially even after the conference), David Meischen, Robert Spiotta, Seja Rachael, Jennifer Brown, Stephanie Cotsirilos, Stuart Thomas, Kristin Thomas Sancken, and Patrick Murphy.

Friend and talented writer, Amy Praskac, and I met monthly for several years, discussing and encouraging each other's writing over lunch. Friends Jen Slaski-Halligan, Jonathan Halligan, Suzanne Mitchell, Richard Zansitis, and Leilani Rose read and listened to several sections of the manuscript, asked helpful questions, and offered encouragement.

Carolyn Scarborough, author and women's circle colleague, created a small beta writers' group which pushed me over the finish line. The members (including Carolyn)—Jan Meyer, Susan Corbin, Cynthia Treglia, and Julie Anderson—all read the draft and offered suggestions. Julie went the extra mile and spent hours combing through the document, offering excellent observations.

My longstanding LifeArt women's group (Danelle Sasser, Candyce Ossefort-Russell, Joan Harman, Kate Cronkite, Francoise Debacker, Marsha Caven, and Rhonda Caffee) has cheered me on over the years. Danelle has also assisted me by offering her computer and photography skills as I worked my way to completion.

She Writes Press author Stephanie Raffelock fell out of the sky and into my life at a most synchronistic time to help guide me into the unknown territory of the publishing world. What a gift she has been both personally and professionally.

And where would I have been had Stephanie not introduced me to editor Barrett Briske? What a lifesaver and hand-holder she was, taking care of things I had no clue how to handle.

There are many people who lived through the events described in the memoir, who have been of immeasurable assistance. Best friend (forever) Karen Ross helped with edits and accurate portrayals of characters, including her father—which caused her profound sadness and disappointment as she reflected on his actions. Dotti Leffler Wiggins facilitated a long overdue conversation with Rev. John Roof to resolve critical mysteries surrounding the story. Dotti and friend Nora Brown joined me at a lunch with my former attorney, Dennis Wegner, who provided assistance in researching legal information. Haywood Ware, to whom I was married at the time, gladly responded when I asked for help clarifying some details. My brother, Jim Baker, and sister, Joanne Smith, remained supportive and provided missing pieces critical to the story. A special thanks to my son, Tyger, and his wife, Kim, who spent time with me discussing memories of his early days as a six-year-old.

All my children, Megan (who now goes by Olive—see Chapter 51 for details), Tyger, and Abby have loved me through this ridiculously long process and have done their part to help with the book's completion. Thank you for being who you are.

Though I wouldn't recommend my fifteen-year process to others, I'm grateful for the personal growth it provided. Since the book's inception in 2005, my impatiently patient husband learned not to say "Is it done yet?" replacing such comments with "How can I help?" And help he did. My perseverance was in no small measure a result of his undying love, dedication, and cheerleading. Robert worked so I could write. Since his retirement in May 2020, he has provided computer-savvy assistance, handled formatting concerns, and offered advice (and hugs) whenever he saw me wringing my writerly hands.

It's done. I'm toast, but I'm happy, and indebted to all my friends, family, colleagues, and supporters. Thank you.

ABOUT THE AUTHOR

Photo credit: Danelle Sasser

JEANNE BAKER GUY of Jeanne Guy Gatherings is an author, speaker, and journal-writing coach. (Her first name is pronounced *Genie*, though she is without magical powers.) Born and raised in Indiana, she received her bachelor's degree in English lit/drama from Indiana University. After a twenty-five-year career in office management and business development, she found her calling in facilitating personal growth circles. Years of blogs, filled with her irreverent humor, serve as the basis for her classes and her 2015 book *Seeing Me: A Guide for Reframing the Way You See Yourself Through Reflective Writing*, coauthored with photographer David Rackley. Mother of three grown and married children, Jeanne lives in Cedar Park, Texas, with her retired architect/husband Robert and their two spoiled, formerly feral cats. *You'll Never Find Us* is her first memoir.

Learn more about Jeanne at www.jeanneguy.com.